TRANCE JOURNEYS
OF THE
HUNTER-GATHERERS

"Nicholas Brink's *Trance Journeys of the Hunter-Gatherers* suggests ecstatic trance is the most visceral way to be one with Earth. We speak the language of the goddess when we use sacred body postures to embrace our inherent shamanic powers. His hugely important book matures our ecstatic trance work since 1977, the year Felicitas Goodman found the magical key into the hunter-gatherer world. Sacred postures are now spreading all over the world, helping us regain our full spiritual consciousness, the fabled New Dawn. As more and more people use daily ritual to stay directly connected with Earth, the Great Mother nurtures them by offering her knowledge. This book is a must-read for anyone who wants to explore shamanism to help save the Earth."

Barbara Hand Clow,
author of *The Mind Chronicles* and
certified teacher for the Cuyamungue Institute

"We are indeed entering a new era in the eventful history of humankind on the planet. This can only be an era where we recognize our common origins and essential connections to each other, to the Earth, and to the cosmos; for it will either be an era of this 're-cognition' or it will not be an era at all but the end of the human adventure. Nicholas Brink helps us access this deeper reality the ancients called the Akasha and that the new physics knows is the deeper reality of the cosmos. His book is a precious resource and a great contribution to our shared future."

Ervin Laszlo, author of *The Immortal Mind*

"*Trance Journeys of the Hunter-Gatherers* is a masterful call to action with a passionate vision for how we can effectively participate in the time-critical, eco-spiritual awakening that is occurring now in Earth's evolution. . . . Nick Brink has formulated a brilliant new spiritual lexicon to help us access and unlock the deeper meaning expressed in our multidimensional metaphoric journeys. For anyone who has had an experience with the ritual postures, or is considering learning more about them, reading this book is as close an experience that one could have to intrinsically feel the magnificence of what is truly possible in regaining our cosmic spiritual citizenship as evolutionary co-creators with Mother Earth."

Marianne Carroll, astrologer and certified instructor in the Cuyamungue Method of ecstatic ritual trance postures

TRANCE JOURNEYS
OF THE
HUNTER-GATHERERS

Ecstatic Practices to
Reconnect with the Great Mother
and Heal the Earth

Nicholas E. Brink, Ph.D.

Bear & Company
Rochester, Vermont • Toronto, Canada

Bear & Company
One Park Street
Rochester, Vermont 05767
www.BearandCompanyBooks.com

Text stock is SFI certified

Bear & Company is a division of Inner Traditions International

Library of Congress Cataloging-in-Publication Data

Names: Brink, Nicholas E., 1939–
Title: Trance journeys of the hunter-gatherers : ecstatic practices to reconnect with the great mother and heal the earth / Nicholas E. Brink, Ph.D.
Description: Rochester, Vermont : Bear & Company, 2016. | Includes bibliographical references and index.
Identifiers: LCCN 2015034841| ISBN 9781591432371 (pbk.) | ISBN 9781591432388 (e-book)
Subjects: LCSH: Ecstasy. | Trance.
Classification: LCC BL626 .B77 2016 | DDC 204/.2—dc23
LC record available at http://lccn.loc.gov/2015034841

Printed and bound in the United States by Lake Book Manufacturing, Inc.
The text stock is SFI certified. The Sustainable Forestry Initiative® program promotes sustainable forest management.

10 9 8 7 6 5 4 3 2 1

Text design and layout by Priscilla Baker
This book was typeset in Garamond Premier Pro with Bougan, Legacy Sans, and Helvetica Neue used as display typefaces
Artwork by M. J. Ruhe

To send correspondence to the author of this book, mail a first-class letter to the author c/o Inner Traditions • Bear & Company, One Park Street, Rochester, VT 05767, and we will forward the communication, or contact the author directly at **www.imaginalmind.net**.

CONTENTS

Among the many pieces written by essayist and naturalist Gary Gripp that he has shared with me, this prologue well describes a person who believes that the ways we have been living our lives are all wrong. Gary, whose life has been dedicated to the remote regions of Central Oregon, has done his best to live his own life in a manner that is at one with the Earth. "The Meaning of Life" describes how he was led to his current beliefs and offers the groundwork for how we should lead our own lives in order to save the Earth, if it is not already too late. There are those classic naturalists who in our collective past brought alive this enchantment of the Earth: Henry Thoreau, John Muir, and Aldo Leopold, to name a few. But it is rare that any of us have the opportunity to personally know such a person, and I rank Gary among those great figures. Through his childhood experiences in nature, and thanks to the support of his mother, he has been able to maintain his connectedness with the Earth, a connectedness that is so natural for young children. This naturalness of children is generally destroyed by our educational and religious systems as well as through a lack of parental understanding of the importance of our connection with nature. Gary has written many essays that I have found most enlightening, essays that are available on his website, www.wildearthman.com.

PROLOGUE

THE MEANING OF LIFE

By Gary Gripp

Many a human being has pondered the meaning of life, and the results represent a range from no meaning at all (the nihilistic perspective), to some institutional (religious) perspectives, to the highly personal. My own take on the meaning of life is nowhere on this continuum, because I represent a perspective that is not necessarily human-centered, even though I am a human, and the product of a human-centered culture. Within that culture, and the society it informs, I am a near anomaly, and as such, part of an extremely marginalized minority. Amid the controversy about meaning and meaninglessness I hold to a position that I regard as rock-solid . . . well, really, more solid, more dependable, more enduring than any rock ever was or will be. But before I share with you the meaning of Life, I want to briefly explore how I came to the moral stance of giving my first allegiance and loyalty not to my own kind, but to the Whole, to Mother Nature herself.

When I was eight, nine, and ten, I lived on a remote lake in Northern California. It was far enough out in the sticks that I had to walk or be driven three miles on a dirt road to get to the school bus turnaround, which was itself fifteen miles outside of the six-hundred–person town where the school was located. This entire area, even today, is still remote and unsettled enough to have no franchise fast-food outlets whatsoever. But it was not the school or the town that had such a big effect on me; it was the lake.

The lake was on the Pacific Flyway, which then supported six million waterfowl migrating South, then North, then South again with the changing seasons. Our lake was in sight of Mt. Shasta, except at those times when the ducks and geese were on the fly and so filled the sky with their wing beats and raucous cries that they made the mountain disappear. There were lesser and greater Canadian honkers, and it was a delight to see them fold back their wings and stretch out their webbed feet as a squadron of them cruised in for a landing in the lake that was our front yard. The ducks would poke around in the tulles and cattails, feeding on whatever they could find there. Grebes would also fly in with the ducks and geese, and for some reason we called them *hell divers.* There were also black-bodied white-billed coots, which we called *mud hens,* and unlike the ducks and geese that could rise off the water with graceful alacrity, the mud hens had to flap and flap and kind of run along the lake's surface for a good long way before they finally achieved flight. I had the use of the family rowboat then, and had developed a slow, gentle stroke that would take me out among all these birds feeding or squabbling or sunning themselves on the odd protruding log, or just paddling easily along, sometimes in formation and sometimes in broken ranks.

My young mind and sensibility took all this in with an excited delight. The part of me that was trying to be a hunter wanted to exploit all of this bounty with my new .22 rifle—or at least there was a voice in my ear telling me that I *should* be thinking along these lines. But mainly I just enjoyed being out in the middle of so much Life, embodied among so many life forms. The geese would gather in the fields across the lake and feed by the hundreds and thousands. One day when I was watching them feed and take off and land and feed some more, something happened to make all of them take off at once and fill the sky as a mass, and then break off into their own flocks and form their characteristic lopsided *V* shapes as they headed to their next destination. When I looked back to where they had been feeding I noticed some movement. It was a goose trying to fly but unable to get off the ground. I told my mom I was going to go get that goose and bring it home, and she gave her consent. I rowed across the lake as quickly as I could, jumped out of the boat, and ran down that goose, amid much drama and noisy complaints. I stuffed it in a gunny sack, tied it off, and deposited the goose in the stern. By the time I got to our side of the lake it had settled down a bit, and I got it to the house with only a bit of a struggle. When I opened the sack in our living room, Mom looked the goose over and determined that it had been shot in the shoulder and had broken its wing bone. "What should we do with it?" I asked. "What do you want to do with it?" she asked in return. I thought about how it would be good for at least a couple of dinners, and how this would be my first goose, and how much the family would appreciate me for bringing a fresh goose to the table. Sitting in our small living room, so composed, the bird seemed very large, and not just large, but stately, its eyes alert but not alarmed. What would I do with it? Shoot it in the head with my .22? Take an axe to its neck?

Looking at it without the excitement of the chase and finally giving it my full attention, I began to realize that this goose was its own being, just like I was my own being, and I just didn't have it in me to take this being's life. Mom helped me get it back in the bag, and I rowed it back to where I had found it and turned it loose. It occurred to me that a coyote might end up having a goose dinner that night, but that was out of my control. I had gone to a bit of trouble to catch that goose and bring it home and bring it back again, but I now knew something I hadn't known before: in just the same way that all dogs are the same and yet each is an individual, and just as all people are the same and yet each is an individual, so too are geese all the same and yet each has its own essence and will to live and even its own sense of dignity. I saw that in the living room of our house when I was nine years old, when a wild creature brought into an alien enclosure showed me something of itself—its personhood.

As Fall turned into Winter, only a few ducks and geese stayed on at our lake. Then in the Spring they came back again by the tens of thousands, on their way North. Next fall they came back again, and I then began to see that there was a pattern here, a cycle, and that this was part of something much bigger than me or my family, bigger, even, than all humankind. This was Nature, and Nature was the source of all this abundant life around me, as well as my own life and that of my family and of all of humanity. Nature was the source of all Life, and Life was good, and Nature was good because Nature was the source of Life.

The Korean War was going on back then—1950, '51, and '52—and this last little bit of the last frontier was a rarity in the world even then. The experience I had then is now available to almost no one. In the year 1900, the Pacific Flyway supported twelve million migratory waterfowl. In 1950 it was six million. Today it is just about a million. There is a pattern and a trajectory here. In 1950 there were about 150 million people in the good 'ole U.S. of A. Now we have more than doubled that number. There is a pattern and a trajectory here, too.

I got a taste for life in all its abundance when there was still a little abundance left. It was a remnant then, and now only a remnant of a remnant remains. Before my European ancestors arrived on this continent half a millennium ago, North America was the very picture of natural abundance. Life thrived here; ecosystems were intact; there was integrity, stability, and beauty within the biotic community. Nature was whole. From my perspective, this is what it is all about. The meaning of Life is Life fully expressed. It is Life in dynamic balance, in all its complexity, diversity, and abundance. If you were to ask me for my best vision of the future, it would be a continuation of this 3.8 billion years of geo-biological evolution—with or without the human being.

Being still a partisan for my own species, I would prefer a human presence within the Community of Life on a thriving planet. Right now that isn't looking very likely, as we drive to extinction two hundred species a day while devouring the planet in order to feed our addictions and our growing numbers. Something in this equation has got to change. I would like for that change to occur within the single species that is taking the rest of the world down with it, but failing that, my deepest loyalty goes to Life itself, to the Community of Life and to a living planet. If the only way for the great experiment of Life to go forward is for this one species to die out, then I say: the sooner the better, because the meaning of Life is more Life, and not what we are seeing now.

Gary Gripp lives, hikes, and writes in the Cascade Mountains of Western Oregon, where he also served for many years as a Wilderness Ranger—the dream job he worked up to after five years of teaching university English. As it turned out, those three years on the lake shaped the rest of his life, providing him with a nature-centric view of the world and a waking-dream-vision indicating that he would become a writer and share this perspective with others. To that end, he is now working on a book project where he attempts to explain to a future survivor where the people of his own time and culture went wrong, and how things came to be the way they are.

ACKNOWLEDGMENTS

The two persons who have influenced me most in writing this book are Thomas Berry, author of *Dream of the Earth,* and Felicitas Goodman, author of *Where the Spirits Ride the Wind.* Berry so clearly stated that what is needed in the ecology movement to save the Earth is to listen to our dreams and waking visions and to regain our shamanic personality, while Goodman has shown us how to fulfill this need when she unveiled to us the shamanic ways of ecstatic trance. Thank you.

FELICITAS GOODMAN AND THE CUYAMUNGUE INSTITUTE

The Cuyamungue Institute promotes the original research and findings of Felicitas Goodman. Dr. Goodman's work, known as the Cuyamungue Method, focused on the use of ancient sacred practices and postures that, when properly used, provide an experience that creates a doorway to an ecstatic experience of expanded reality. Dr. Goodman captured the essence of her work and findings in the book *Where the Spirits Ride the Wind.* I received formal training in the history and proper usage of the Cuyamungue Method at the Cuyamungue Institute in Santa Fe, New Mexico. To learn more about Dr. Goodman's original work in ecstatic trance and her development and use of the Cuyamungue Method visit the Cuyamungue Institute's website at www.cuyamungueinstitute.com.

INTRODUCTION

TO SAVE THE EARTH IS TO SAVE OURSELVES

We are living in a time of crisis: we see this in the environment, but above all we see this in mankind . . . Man is not in charge today, money is in charge, money rules. God our Father did not give the task of caring for the Earth to money, but to us, to men and women: we have this task! Instead, men and women are sacrificed to the idols of profit and consumption: it is the "culture of waste."

Pope Francis, Standing Up for the Poor and the Environment, Vatican Radio, June 5, 2013

To save the Earth* is to save ourselves. Our capitalistic and technological/industrial way of life considers everything of the Earth as just another commodity from which to create monetary gain, and we ourselves are just one of those commodities, expendable, to be thrown in the landfill when our usefulness has expired. Forests are destroyed, and fertile soil becomes toxic, to be washed away by the rain or blown away by the wind. Wetlands are filled in with developments, and approximately

*Throughout this book the words *Earth,* the four seasons, and the seven directions are capitalized, as are *Sun* and *Moon,* which are kin to the Earth, with the intent of raising our awareness of our interconnectedness.

ten thousand species disappear from the Earth every single year. As we greedily capitalize on the Earth's "resources," her flora, fauna, and elements, we are hastening toward extinction. This includes humankind. In our dualistic view of seeing ourselves as separate from the Earth and from other beings, we are destroying our Great Earth Mother and ourselves.

Where did our thinking, our consciousness go so wrong? Over generations the view that places human beings above all else has become completely engrained. For the last 400 years scientists and philosophers have taught that the only life on Earth with a soul, the only species with consciousness, is *Homo sapiens*. The rest of life is soulless, without sentience. As Brian Swimme, a modern-day philosopher and cosmologist, puts it:

> For Descartes, only human beings had a soul, only humans were conscious and had feelings. Given this attitude and the scientific motivation for control, the way was open for unbridled experimentation, including vivisection. Animals could not feel any pain, said Descartes, because they were no more than biological machines. By extension, plants, rocks, rivers, oceans, and atmospheres certainly could feel no pain, could suffer no dis-ease. Science, and its stepchild, technology, could—did, and does—carry out Francis Bacon's dictum of "putting nature to the rack," excavating and exploiting the environment in the name of research and social progress.[1]

But even before Descartes we humans were in the process of exploiting and destroying the Earth.

FROM HUNTING AND GATHERING TO CULTIVATION AND DOMESTICATION

The cultural myth that we are to have dominion over the Earth is biblically justified as a mandate from God. For those scholars of the

Bible who believe that the Earth was created 6,000 years ago, this biblical mandate must have been written less than 6,000 years ago, yet our domination began approximately 10,000 years ago. It was then that we as humans began to leave our hunting and gathering ways in favor of controlling the Earth through agriculture and the domestication of our fellow animals. According to Jim Mason, an author and attorney who focuses on human/animal concerns, humankind's domination over the Earth "was already there when the Bible, even the oldest parts, were written."[2] Our destruction of the Earth is most apparent now, but it was apparent back then with the gradual progression of agricultural cultivation from East to West between 7500 and 5000 BCE: from the area known as the Fertile Crescent, between the Tigris and Euphrates rivers in what is now Iraq; into Eastern Europe; along the Mediterranean; and then North from Greece into the Balkans and the Danube Valley. As described by British archeologist Barry Cunliffe, this migration of agricultural ways to the West occurred because the agriculturists had to continually leave behind the soil they depleted, soil that would become the deserts of the Near East as they moved to more fertile ground in which to grow their crops.[3]

Thus the hunters and gatherers left or were exiled from their paradise, the Garden of Eden—in Nordic mythology, the Garden of Idunn[4]—when they took up cultivation and domestication of the Earth with their new so-called knowledge of good and evil. Up until that time the hunting-and-gathering peoples were one with the Earth and appreciated the Earth's ability to sustain them with her flora and fauna. Mason recognizes that the biblical story of Adam and Eve, of being thrown out of the Garden of Eden, is the story that metaphorically explains the beginning of our separation from the Earth, the end of our sense of being one with the Earth.[5] American anthropologist and linguist Felicitas Goodman beautifully and succinctly describes this early time. According to Goodman, the hunter-gatherers arrived on the scene no earlier than 200,000 years ago. She explains:

> In a very real way, the hunters and gatherers open the first chapter of our human history. And fittingly, this dawning was as close to paradise as humans have ever been able to achieve. The men did the hunting and scavenging, working for about three hours a week, and the women took care of daily sustenance by gathering vegetal food and small animals. It was such a harmonious existence, such a successful adaptation, that it did not materially alter for many thousands of years. This view is not romanticizing matters. Those hunter-gatherer societies that have survived into the present still pursue the same lifestyle, and we are quite familiar with it from contemporary anthropological observation. Despite the unavoidable privations of human existence, despite occasional hunger, illness and other trials, what makes their life way so enviable is the fact that knowing every nook and cranny of their home territory and all that grows and lives in it, the bands make their regular rounds and take only what they need. By modern calculations, that amounted to only about 10 percent of the yield, easily recoverable under undisturbed conditions. They live a life of total balance, because *they do not aspire to control their habitat; they are a part of it.*[6]

This picture of the hunter-gatherers has been documented by many other authorities, including American anthropologist Marshall Sahlins, in his book *Stone Age Economics.*[7] As well, cosmologist and geologian (he has been called an "ecotheologian") Thomas Berry describes this same period in prehistory:

> In our early tribal period we lived in a world dominated by psychic power symbols, whereby life was guided toward communion with our total human and transhuman environment. We felt ourselves sustained by a cosmic presence that went beyond the surface reality of the surrounding natural world. The human sense of an all-pervasive, numinous, or sacred power gave to life a deep security. It enabled us over a long period of time to establish ourselves

within a realm of consciousness of high spiritual, social and artistic development.[8]

POSTCAPITALISM AND TECHNOLOGY

Something, though, is happening now to change the downward spiral of modern existence. There are many of us who are beginning to wake up and see ourselves as not just another commodity, and the Earth as not just another commodity. We are beginning to realize that we are part of the Earth, one with the Earth, part of the Great Mother who sustains us. The duality between us and everything else, the other, is dissolving. As sociologist Robert Bellah states, "We must have to treat others as part of who we are rather than as a 'them' with whom we are in constant competition."[9]

The old assumption was that we stand separate from and superior to the rest of the experienced world, with the subject being "me" and all the rest the objective "other." This dichotomy is no longer compatible even with modern science. According to Thomas Berry, "A countermovement toward integration and interior subjective processes is taking place within a more comprehensive vision of the entire universe. We see ourselves now not as Olympian observers against an objective world, but as a functional expression of that very world itself."[10] Joanna Macy, an environmental activist, author, and scholar of Buddhism, general systems theory, and deep ecology, says, "From living systems theory and systems cybernetics emerges a process view of the self as inseparable from the web of relationships that sustain it."[11] Swedish writer and Mayanist Carl Calleman states, "The separation from the divine source that the dualist frame of consciousness has caused will disappear as a result of the evolution of consciousness, and it has been said that this separation is the sole cause of human suffering."[12] We are recognizing that all of Earth is interdependent. To paraphrase Joanna Macy, I would not cut off my leg because it is separate from the rest of me, and we cannot cut down a tree in the Amazon because it is also part of us; trees are our external lungs.[13] We are all interdependent. The tree is my source of oxygen, and I depend on oxygen as much as or even more than I depend on my leg. I am not just that which exists inside my skin and thus ready to use up anything that is not "me," anything that is outside of my skin. We are all intertwined; the Earth and everything on, in, and above it are interrelated. If a part of us is separated from the rest, it dies.

For millennia our rational, scientific way of thinking has been to separate each species of flora and fauna and each element of the Earth in an attempt to understand each part rationally and scientifically. We have separated each species and each substance from all others as a way to study and understand nature, and through this study and so-called understanding we in our greed and hubris have sought and found ways to profit from this mistaken thinking. Now we are beginning to realize that this path has led us to the Earth's destruction. As Indian activist and editor Satish Kumar says, "Learning about each species is not learning *from* each species."[14] Everything around us, when we become part of it, has much to teach us. Science tells us that each part of our body has something to cybernetically teach, and learn from, every other part of our body at any given moment. Extending this beyond our own skin, we have much to learn from everything around us, every part of the Earth, below, on her surface, and above her. We realize that our body is composed of unending cybernetic loops of communication through the myriad of hormones, amino acids, and other chemicals that tell each cell and each organ of our body what it needs at any given moment. These communication loops are everywhere, all around us, not just within our own body, but connecting us with everything else that is beyond our individual bodies. Yet science's discovery of this fact of life still misses something that our hunter-gatherer ancestors knew: the sheer spiritual power of being one with the environment, of experiencing the spirits of everything around them and learning from these spirits. This book is about how to do just that—how to make these interconnections spiritually alive for us, and how to become one with the the Earth. As we become one with the Earth, we again experience it as enchanted.

Like Gary Gripp's journey, each of us will have a very personal journey of finding oneness with the Earth. Yet listening to the personal journeys of diverse yet similar others can synergistically add to our own personal experience of discovery. As we begin our journey to find oneness with our Great Mother, we need leaders and teachers to renew within us that which was lost when we became the rational adults we were trained by society to be.

SPIRITUAL ECOLOGY

Something is happening in our world of consciousness. Many of us are insisting on eating organic foods, foods not grown and made toxic with herbicides and pesticides. People are turning to solar and wind energy and driving less. People are recycling and putting less in our overflowing landfills. People are out on the streets demonstrating against the Keystone XL pipeline and against fracking for natural gas. People are demonstrating to protect the whales, wolves, polar bears, and other species from imminent extinction. People are refusing to shop at giant big-box stores and choosing local businesses that support local communities and local farmers. People are lobbying hard for an end to the genetically modified so-called food being shoved down our throats. Much is happening that demonstrates a concern for ecology, for protecting Mother Earth. But this is not enough. A basic change in our consciousness, in the way we look at the Earth, is needed. We must see ourselves as being one with nature, and not superior to and separate from the world, from its flora and fauna, and from all the features and substances of the Earth. We are not the final end of an evolutionary continuum but part of the Earth, where we will continue to evolve only if we evolve with her. According to American author, ecologist, forester, and environmentalist Aldo Leopold, we "are only fellow-voyagers with other creatures in the odyssey of evolution."[15]

So how do we become one with the Earth?

Paying attention to everything around us, stalking the world like a cat,[16] is a beginning. But there are ways to become even more deeply and spiritually part of everything that is around us. Using our imagination to experience what everything in the world is experiencing brings us even closer to being one with the world. Thomas Berry believes that all of creativity is derived "from the visionary power that is experienced most profoundly when we are immersed in the depths of our own being and of the cosmic order itself in the dream world that unfolds within us in our sleep, or in those visionary moments that seize upon us in our waking hours."[17] He believes that we again have to embrace our inherent shamanic abilities to attain those visionary moments, moments that are so natural to children but become lost to rational thinking as we become adults. As we progress in our pursuit of becoming one with the Earth, we will discover that we can readily reconnect with these visionary moments we once experienced in childhood by going into trance, where we can attain through the power of an altered state of consciousness a much deeper integration with the Earth, with the spirits of our Great Mother. Trance allows us to see through the eyes of each species of flora and fauna, of the animate and the supposedly inanimate, of that which is deep within the Earth, on the Earth's surface, and above the Earth, in each corner of the cosmos, in each nook and cranny of everything.

Early humans were one with the Earth. As so aptly stated by cosmologist and philosopher Christian de Quincey,

> There was a time when our ancestors moved with the animals and sang with the wild symphony of the natural world—the swoop of a hawk, the roar of a waterfall, the whisper of evening breezes, the kiss of moonlight. We lived *in* the world, responded to its *felt* and subtle messages, understood its deeper meanings. We not only communed with nature, we were in open communication with all its great variety of sounds and rhythms. In short, we understood and spoke the *language* of nature.[18]

According to Thomas Berry, in earliest times our consciousness was participatory, that is, we participated within the circle of intimacy of all things and with one another. But this participatory consciousness was "perhaps undifferentiated to its distinct sense of self and other, and almost certainly had no sense of what we currently understand as unrepeatable developmental movement over immense expanse of time."[19] This earliest era was identified by German philosopher, linguist, and poet Jean Gebser (1905–1973) as the *archaic era,* in which consciousness is likened to a state of deep sleep, a dreamlike state.[20] This state of trance is not a lot different from, although deeper than, ecstatic trance, which is the shamanic state of trance that we will experience in this book, and which I believe is an important tool in relearning how to become one with the Earth.

When we no longer ran with the animals as our ancestors did and no longer experienced being one of them, we separated ourselves. And as we separated ourselves from the Earth, we created gods and god myths in an attempt to fill the sense of emptiness created by this separation. But the gods and myths were artificial, an inadequate attempt to connect with nature on some level. According to psychologist and historian Bob Curran, at some point in our collective past we created a god known as the Green Man, with his myth and magic, to fill that which we had lost, to re-establish a sense of connectedness with nature.[21] Trance can bring us back to being one with nature. Early humans' consciousness has been likened to dreaming, and trance brings us back to that fluid dreaming state.

James Lawer, a practicing druid and the provost of New York–based Druid College, as well as an instructor of ecstatic trance, talks of being at the edge, referring to the energetic field or aura that extends beyond the physical boundaries of living things. This edge is all around us because the life of the other is all around us. We can feel the edge of the personal space around a tree; we need to learn to stop at that edge and ask permission to move closer.[22] We need to be aware of this edge and show respect for it, and for all such edges that are all around us. This edge is easily experienced in trance. Trance enlivens the auras of all beings, auras that when seen and experienced allow us to communicate with those beings, so that we can learn about the needs and concerns of those beings. Experiencing beings' auras brings us to a state of communion with nature.

As we shall see throughout this book, ritual is a key element in accessing the trance state. Physician, psychologist, and practitioner of integrative medicine and Native American healing Lewis Mehl-Madrona, in *Healing the Mind through the Power of Story;* and writer and shaman Hyemeyohsts Storm, in *Seven Arrows*, identify the use of ritual as central and necessary in gaining oneness with the Earth. As we will see, the ritual developed by Felicitas Goodman that we use to invoke the trance state involves calling the spirits of each direction, thus very directly bringing one into contact with the spirits of the Earth, as these spirits are considered living entities. Goodman's method to induce ecstatic trance is Earth oriented. The New Dawn, Nydagan, is upon us. It will usher in a new world of peace and compassion, and will be characterized by time-free transparency, in which we will be able to shift between the dimensions and access the realm of magic that was so real to our ancient ancestors. This era will move humanity beyond its rational, scientific, but impotent way of experiencing the Earth and return to us the ability to experience an earlier era's oneness consciousness. Let us explore this, now, in the coming pages.

1

BECOMING ONE WITH THE GREAT MOTHER

The mountains, I become part of it . . .
The herbs, the fir tree, I become part of it.
The morning mists, the clouds, the gathering waters,
I become part of it.
The wilderness, the dew drops, the pollen . . .
I become part of it.

NAVAJO CHANT

What does it mean to be one with the Earth and with the cosmos? First, it means to recognize, value, and venerate the interdependence of everything. Consider something as basic to life as walking. Wherever we step, whatever we touch and disturb, is a form of interaction with the Earth and therefore should be done with sacred awareness, the awareness of what effect it has on our interdependence. A simple example we can all relate to are the signs in the national parks and certain other natural areas that ask us to stay on the trail while we hike. We need to cultivate the awareness that the life forms we may step on, the steps we take that compact the Earth may harm the microbes and other microorganisms on which life depends, thus our steps diminish our interdependence.

Yet walking, taking steps, is central to our daily activities. That is why it is important to cultivate a sense of awareness, of respect and reverence for the Earth, even when walking.

What is this "everything" of which we need to be aware? First it includes all the flora and fauna of the Earth, because it is these life forms that provide us with what sustains us, with our nourishment. In considering human evolution, all flora and fauna are our ancestors. Our ancestors also include all other substances and geological features—the valleys, mountains, rivers, lakes, rocks, soil, and all that is within the soil, as well as the weather, with its wind, rain, and the different temperatures, which provide the living conditions for all living things. One thing I recently learned in reading cosmologist Brian Swimme is that our ancestors also include the stars.[1] In the process of the creation of the stars, the elements were formed—the elements that we have studied in chemistry that are part of the periodic table of elements, the elements that compose every substance known to us. In this sense we need to consider ourselves as also being one with the stars and the formation of the universe itself.

This evolution, from the beginning of time, from the Big Bang that formed the gases, the hydrogen and helium, eventually formed the stars and the universe with its many galaxies and innumerable planets. This led to the creation of our Earth, a planet that has provided the conditions that have sustained life for eons. This evolution was purposeful in the sense that the entire universe was formed with a sense of interdependence; the size, nature, and distance of each planet from its sun is determined by and determines the strength of the gravitational fields that hold them in place. And as life evolves in this interdependent dance, the habitat in which each organism lives provides the balanced conditions that sustain it. This is an ongoing process, continually changing, each change requiring other changes to maintain the balance that sustains life and the environment. Again, to be one with the Earth we must be aware of this continuing process of evolution and balance.

THE NEW AWARENESS OF INTERDEPENDENCE

By definition interdependence is mutual need whether for support, survival, help, or something else. It can arise between two or more individuals or between groups. However, interdependence is also understood in a much broader spiritual context as the intrinsic relationship between humanity's consciousness and the reality we perceive around us. In this way, interdependence describes what we call *oneness,* the unity of everything.

Becoming aware of our interdependence with all of life and the cosmos naturally imparts a sense of oneness with the Earth. This awareness is not something new in the thinking of humankind. According to Elinor Gadon in her book *The Once and Future Goddess*:

> The upper Paleolithic (ca. 35,000–9000 BCE) was a "revolutionary" period in human evolution. There was a virtual explosion of symbolic behavior. Ice Age people were fully evolved humans much like ourselves, capable of speaking and comprehending symbolic based language and of established communities with shared norms and values. Like us, they must have speculated about the origin of life and the meaning of death. The earliest human intuition of the sacred was that the earth was the source of all life and ground of being.[2]

The writings of the anthropologist Marija Gimbutas have provided extensive research that shows that the people of that earlier era worshiped the divine feminine. Riane Eisler brought this divine feminine research more to the awareness of the general public in her book *The Chalice and the Blade,* and it has been popularized by the books written by Jean Auel in her Earth's Children series.

About 10,000 years ago humankind began to lose the power of the magic of this earliest hunter-gatherer consciousness when humans began controlling the Earth with the discovery of how they could grow their own food and domesticate animals. With the development of early agriculture, dominion over the Earth became the religion along with the worship of a controlling masculine god. Gadon writes of the invasion of a "warlike people who overran Old European civilization" and how by 1500 BCE "the Goddess would have to share her domain with male gods."[3]

But now as we relearn the importance of our interdependence with all life, we are again moving toward the veneration of our Earth Mother, the Mother Goddess, the awakening of the divine feminine. Gadon notes, "The first signs of the Goddess's return were in the nineteenth-century Romanatic Movement with its renewed appreciation of nature and emphasis on the imagination and emotions."[4] According to David McClelland, "Men represent powerful activity as assertion and aggression, women in contrast portray acts of nurturance as acts of strength."[5] In continuing our control over nature, our destruction of the Earth, we are acting in the same way life has been led over the last 10,000 to 15,000 years—the ways of men, the ways of assertion and aggression—but to move on to the time-free and transparent world of the nurturing Goddess we must reclaim and bring forward the strength and power of the nurturing magic of the much earlier Goddess culture. This awakening is now being led by a long list of women who voice reemergence of the feminine including Joanna Macy, Mary Evelyn Tucker, Elinor Gadon, Vandana Shiva, Barbara Hand Clow, and Carol Gilligan, among others.

The study of interdependence from the perspective of biology, sociology, physiology, botany, and many other academic disciplines is important, but is usually limited to a study of mutually dependent relationships; this approach often misses the big picture. Scientific research is generally experienced as "objective" and may not be personal or at the subjective level of feeling one with the Earth. Classical psychology has similarly operated from a dualistic, "objective" point of view, however, the new field of narrative psychology, as exemplified in the work of Lewis Mehl-Madrona and others, is concerned with how human beings deal with experience by constructing stories and listening to the stories of others. Operating under the assumption that human activity and experience is filled with meaning and stories, rather than logical arguments or lawful formulations, narrative psychology is the study of how human beings construct stories to deal with experiences. As this book progresses we will hear many such personal narratives as recorded by those who have undertaken ecstatic trance journeys. In sharing these ecstatic narratives, we can each relate to them in diverse ways. These narratives can elevate us to a higher level of spiritual consciousness in allowing us to recognize the diversity and similarities of all life on Earth. Stories like these have been told by our ancestors for millennia, in the many myths of Earth's creation and the creation and purpose of the flora and fauna of the Earth. Though scientists and academics might point to the falseness and inaccuracy of such stories, they nevertheless connect people with nature in a very real and sacred sense.[6]

Thomas Berry suggests that the way to reconnect with nature is through our nighttime dreams and waking visions, and by becoming one with the shamanic personality.[7] These dreams and visions are ways of creating our own myths and stories—stories not much different from those of our ancestors and that continue to be so natural for the true children of the Earth. We will examine and learn from these ways of reconnecting in the next chapters, which is the core of this book. We have different ways to reconnect and become one with the Great Mother Earth at our disposal: we can learn how present-day hunting-and-gathering tribes of the Earth, and particularly their shamans, relate to the Earth; and we can also experience this ancient hunting-and-gathering way of life by journeying in ecstatic trance.

Life forms other than we modern *Homo sapiens* live in an interdependent way instinctively. That is what makes us different from the rest of life. Our consciousness and knowledge of these interdependencies, and our free will to live in a way that either supports these interdependencies or interferes with them makes us different. It is this free will and knowledge that has led to our being thrown out of the Garden of

Eden, when we began our 10,000-year-old journey of controlling the Earth through agriculture, domestication of animals, and otherwise exerting dominion over the Earth. This kind of control has led to the destruction of nature and the extinction of species. As Aldo Leopold so aptly states,

> The Lord giveth, and the Lord taketh away, but He is no longer the only one to do so. When some remote ancestor of ours invented the shovel, he became a giver: he could plant a tree. And when the axe was invented, he became the taker: he could chop it down. Whoever owns land has thus assumed, whether he knows it or not, the divine functions of creating and destroying plants.[8]

With our free will and new knowledge we have the opportunity to change, but it will take all of us following the growing number of elders who recognize the need for us to become one with everything of the Earth. Environmentalist of Ojibwe ancestry Winona LaDuke writes:

> In the time of Thunderbeings and Underwater Serpents, the humans, animals, and plants conversed and carried on lives of mischief, wonder, and mundane tasks. The prophets told of times ahead, explained the causes of the deluge of past, and predicted the two paths of the future: one scorched and one green, one of which the Anishinaabe would have to choose.[9]

The Anishinaabe people have the free will to choose. For our salvation we must too choose; we must choose the interdependent green path. Our role in this interdependent world is to take what we need to survive, but our taking must be done with a sense of understanding its effect on all other life forms, and with a sense of sacredness, taking no more than what we need. As with the American Indian* peoples

---

*I explain in chapter 7 why I eschew the term *Native American* in favor of *Indian.*

who, when taking the life of the other, offer a token of appreciation and thanks to the other, for example, a pinch of tobacco or cornmeal, we need to embrace this concept with the understanding that there will come a time when it will be our turn to give ourselves to the other. In the time that I have spent with Indian peoples I have heard them say, "Today is a good day to die!" This expresses an attitude of recognition of their role in this interdependent cycle of life.

BECOMING AN ELDER

We have now begun to recognize our destructive impact on the Earth and the need to change our ways, reestablishing our place among all life forms in becoming one with all that is of the Earth. We are capable of using our knowledge and understanding of interdependence to begin reversing what we have done—that is, if it is not already too late.

In our present age we have a great number of leaders who can show us the way of becoming one with the Earth. We need such elders on this journey of reawakening humanity's potential; we need wise people who can help guide us in this time of the New Dawn. Ecotheologian Matthew Fox speaks to this need for leadership:

> Thomas Berry is a true elder to the young—so important in our time. The young are yearning for elders and there are so few. What can you say of the captains of industry, the Enrons, the Andersons, the Talibans, the World Coms, the Vaticans in this moment of history? They all suffer from the terminal disease called Patriarchal Excess, and from Adultism. They want to use the youth but are not there to awaken the stories of the youth. And Thomas Berry has been inspiring youth for years. The real work of the elder is to pass on stories that motivate the young to be generous and alive and use their god-given gifts to affect history so that history will not be the nightmare . . . but will be closer to that "love of the world" that it can become. Thomas Berry has done this for so many individuals.[10]

Bill Plotkin, a depth psychologist, wilderness guide, and agent of cultural evolution, uses the term *insendence,* first used by Thomas Berry to refer to the descent into our pre-rational, instinctive resources—a descent that is critically important to bring about needed cultural changes. These resources are obtained through dreaming and waking visions, and by cultivating a shamanic perspective:

> The cultivation of authentic adulthood and genuine elderhood goes far beyond any modifications in how we generate energy or conduct business, agriculture, and politics. We need contemporary culture codings that allow our full humanity to once again blossom. We need new, widely adopted practices for parenting children, educating them to become full members of not only a family and culture, but, equally important, of the Earth community as it exists in their particular bioregion. We require new, much more effective ways of supporting teenagers to uncover and embody their most authentic selves and, when ready, to learn the arts of *insendence* so that they might explore the mysteries of nature and psyche and eventually, with good fortune, receive a vision revealing their unique place, role, or niche in the Earth community. By embodying this role, they become authentic adults, deeply imaginative artisans of cultural evolution. . . . We also need in each society a significant number of mature adults who have been called by the spontaneities within them to serve as guides to the initiatory rituals of insendence.[11]

According to traditional peoples, elders are wisdom keepers who have gained authority based on age and experience. Prominent scholars such as Joseph Campbell and Marija Gimbutas suggest that we reexamine an earlier model for living that was based on feminine values of honoring the Earth. During this earlier time period we embraced a more mystical and magical view of life. It was a time when we found more balance in our daily living. This model was based on the circle of interdependence, and it followed universal principles observed in nature. The New Dawn describes the evolution of our consciousness at this pivotal point in time to embrace these earlier values. In reconnecting us with the magical and mystical, it provides a model for the healthy maturation of individuals within cultures and an opportunity for each of us to actualize our full spiritual potential.

2

STRENGTHENING OUR UNITY WITH THE EARTH

Sowing the seed,
my hand is one with the Earth.
Wanting the seed to grow,
my mind is one with the light.
Hoeing the crop,
my hands are one with the rain.
Having cared for the plants,
my mind is one with the air.
Hungry and trusting,
my mind is one with the Earth.
Eating the fruit,
my body is one with the Earth.

WENDELL BERRY

Thomas Berry offers us the means for attaining oneness with the Earth. He suggests that we can find this oneness through dreaming, waking visions, and the sacredness of ancient Earth liturgies. He suggests that a model for such attainment is found among the indigenous shamans of the world.

Dreaming, waking visions, and reconnecting with our intrinsic shamanic potential are all ways we can deeply integrate our experiences of nature. It is one thing to know a thing intellectually; but for it to become one within us, for it to become experiential knowledge in our relationship with the Earth, for it to become instinctual in the way we behave, the same way that all other life forms experience things instinctually, it needs to become incorporated within our *unconscious* mind. This is best accomplished through metaphor, as a way of symbolic abbreviation or shorthand that imprints the consciousness and makes the connection automatic.

Someone who plays a musical instrument knows how learning the fingering of the instrument becomes automatic, that is, it takes no thought; it's the same with typing on a keyboard, where thinking a particular letter automatically takes the finger to the right key on the keyboard, seemingly without any intervening thought. In the broader sense, all knowledge can become automatic through the symbolic abbreviation of when it is registered in metaphoric notation. For example, for 10,000 years the belief that we shall have dominion over the Earth has registered within us in an unconscious way—a belief that now needs to be dismantled. Unlearning this belief requires that we incorporate within us the dreams, visions, and other shamanic ways of connecting with the Earth and everything of the Earth, in a single field of oneness.

Stories for children that give animals human qualities are told to teach values, values that we try to metaphorically instill in the child. The images of these value stories enter the child's consciousness and remain in the unconscious mind because of their imaginal/metaphoric nature. Though these same stories initially teach that animals are equal to humans, that humans are no better than animals, that animals are endowed with human intelligence and emotions, this part of the story later becomes lost as the child matures and is trained through the educational system and society to be a rational thinker. The hunter-gatherer cultures, on the other hand, with their sense of oneness with the animals and their appreciation of the powers of animals, retain this quality of seeing themselves as being on a par with animals all the way into adulthood. In the same way the mythic stories of Earth's creation use metaphorical stories—stories that science has rejected as being "unscientific" and false. Science in this way invalidates our experience of oneness with the Earth, something that has always been taught in traditional cultures.

What we need to relearn at this critical time is available to us intellectually, through what scientists now are only beginning to discover about interdependence. For example, modern physics has taken us beyond the classical-mechanical view of the Earth to time-free dimensions that provide us with new insight and understanding of our role as one small piece of this interdependence. Knowledge about interdependence on the social level is also available through what anthropologists have discovered in their study of contemporary hunting-and-gathering societies. However, shamanic practices are the most powerful and direct methods for allowing us to journey using altered states of consciousness to connect us with the universal mind. In this way we can experience what hunting-and-gathering peoples know. As much as we modern people may think we may know, the shamans of contemporary and ancient hunter-gatherer societies are exceptional models for us in learning how to become truly one with our Great Mother Earth. We have a long way to go to catch up with their depth of knowledge of the consciousness of our interdependence. As we shall soon see, a valuable tool for achieving this state of oneness can be found in using the ecstatic postures and the ecstatic trance journey techniques as taught by Felicitas Goodman in *Where the Spirits Ride the Wind.*

WHAT IS TRANCE?

Trance is often defined as an altered state of consciousness. The various forms of meditation, dreaming while sleeping, hypnosis, and ecstatic trance represent altered states of consciousness; each has their differences and their similarities. One similarity is that each is a way of sidestepping the incessant thoughts of the conscious mind, the thinking that interferes with seeing beyond the rational mind. Rational thinking depends on sensory input from the five ordinary senses: sight, sound, taste, smell, and touch. Trance, on the other hand, takes us into an *extrasensory* world, a world beyond the ordinary senses, connecting us with our unconscious mind and beyond to what is variously called the *collective unconscious,* the *universal mind,* the *akashic field,* the *morphic field,* or the *divine matrix.* Trance logic is different from rational logic. Whereas in rational logic *B* is caused by *A,* or *B* follows *A,* the logic of the trance state, whether in dreaming, hypnosis, or ecstatic trance, can be that *B* may also cause *A,* or *B* may come before *A* or at the same time as *A.* In the trance state, rational causality and order are lost or become time-free and transparent. Being free of rational causality and linear time allows us to access other dimensions of time and reality, dimensions like those that have provided shamans with visions of the past, present, and future and of the Lower, Middle, and Sky Worlds.

Trance allows us to reach into the world as experienced by the bear, the oak tree, the bird that lands in the high branches of the tree, the vole tunneling underground, the flow of water within its stream banks, the wind as it blows through the tree, or the rock that rests under the hot sun in the desert or in the bed of a stream.

What is key in trance is to experience the moment without extraneous interfering thoughts, in the same way that one fundamental goal of Zen meditation is to focus one's mind on the moment, experiencing the breath, simply inhaling and exhaling. In trance, when our awareness is on what I call the *center of harmony*—that place just an inch or two below the umbilicus, the place that tells us when we are breathing correctly, when our diaphragm rises and falls with each breath, the place called the *dan t'ian* in t'ai chi—we can be in a state of deep meditation, of living in the moment, aware of each breath.

Hypnotic trance also brings us into a state where we can experience the moment in this way. In using hypnotherapy for the last thirty-five years in my practice as a psychologist, I induced trance by leading clients to experience the moment. I did this by suggesting that they pay attention to their breathing, noticing their stomachs rising and falling while being aware of their center of harmony. I encouraged them to feel the warmth of hands resting in a lap, to feel the tightness of the fabric of jeans on thighs, to experience the warmth of a back as it rested against a chair. I suggested that the person bring her awareness to those things that she might be experiencing in the moment. This creates a what is known as a *yes set,* by offering clients a series of truisms of what they are experiencing in the moment, experiences that they are not likely aware of until they are brought to their attention. In this way the person is lulled into a mental state of verbally or nonverbally answering "yes," the mental state of being in the moment that can then be used to take the person to other places and times. From there, the person can be led to go deeper into the unconscious mind or back in time, for example: "Let your mind begin to take you back through time . . . watch time go backward, to what happened yesterday, what happened last Summer, what happened last Winter, what happened a year ago, five years ago. As you go back in time, as you watch your life go by, watch for what first made you feel anxious" (or depressed, or any other troublesome feeling that brought the person to therapy). This process of analytic hypnotherapy opens the door to many other possible hypnotic suggestions that can bring the person to an emotionally healthier place in life. Like Zen meditation, it first requires the person to experience the present, but then it can be used to lead the person to experience the world beyond the limits of their usual sensory experiences.

In this same way, a person can be brought to experience the world as seen through the eyes of a bear, or experience the flow of sap through the trunk of a maple tree. The hypnotic suggestion can lead a person to feel what it is like to lumber along on four legs carrying your heavy weight as you flow or swing from side to side. "Feel your body swaying to the left as you lift your right leg, and then as you move forward, you lift your left leg and your body sways to the right. Let your legs carry you ahead. Tell me where they are taking you. What are you now doing? . . . " In this way a person can be led to experience what life is like as a bear. With my years of experience of leading others in hypnotic trance, I can readily go into a trance state and lead myself to experience what other animals and the flora of the Earth experience. In doing so, I have been able to learn from the other outside of my physical body. I have experienced the other *as* the other. This has taught me a lot. In learning from the other in this way I have found that I can no longer experience the other as a commodity, as a thing outside of myself, but rather, as something I cherish because I have experienced it as itself

As I dream at night, if I have carried with me such images as a bear walking through the woods as I fell asleep, with practice the bear will likely become part of my dream. With practice I can also learn to dream lucidly, that is, being aware that I am dreaming while dreaming. And within a lucid dream I can ask questions and give directions to my dream in other ways, for example: "As I lumber through the woods as a bear, what do I come to? I find myself standing before a rotting tree. I stand, and with my claws I pull back the bark, where I find bugs to eat." My observing, rational mind tells me these bugs are termites and ants, but my bear mind finds them tasty and satisfying treats. My observing, rational mind tells me I am a bear, though that thought feels rather distant and I am experiencing only what I am doing in the moment. I then feel myself drop down onto all fours, and I continue to lumber along, swaying from side to side as I walk. This experience of being a bear was not from a sleeping dream or from hypnosis, though it easily could have been from either; rather, it was from one of my first experiences using ecstatic trance, with a posture for metamorphosis called the Olmec Prince posture (see page 50).

As we shall see in progressing through this book, the ecstatic trance state naturally brings us to experiencing oneness with the Earth and all her beings. But an additional dimension of the trance state, the energy of the ritual that brings us into the trance state, will also be examined. Thomas Berry frames these kinds of rituals as sacred liturgies: "Classical culture itself was a kind of energy pulsating in and through sacred liturgies carried out in seasonal life periods, as well as in the personal life cycle from birth to maturity to death."[1] As we will see, the ritual developed by Felicitas Goodman to induce ecstatic trance involves calling the spirits of the seven directions, which are also the spirits of Mother Earth.

ECSTATIC TRANCE

A form of trance, ecstatic trance, is from the ancient era of magic, when people worshipped the Great Mother, the era of hunting and gathering. Ecstatic trance is induced by the neural stimulation caused by the rapid beating of a drum or the shaking of a rattle. This is a trance experience I first learned upon reading *Where the Spirits Ride the Wind,* by Felicitas Goodman, and subsequently *Ecstatic Body Postures,* by Dr. Goodman's student Belinda Gore. Belinda Gore then became my mentor in my training to become a certified instructor of ecstatic trance through the Cuyamungue Institute, near Santa Fe, New Mexico.*

Dr. Goodman, in her many years of anthropological research into ecstatic trance in contemporary and ancient primitive cultures, found that certain body postures have specific effects on the trance experience. She identified what she believed were some of the postures used by shamans both ancient and contemporary, as depicted in the art objects of those periods. She found that when she induced trance

*For more information on the Cuyamungue Institute, I encourage you to visit cuyamungueinstitute.com.

with a rapid shaking of her rattle while her students sat, stood, or lay in any of these postures, each posture had a specific effect on the trance experience. Some postures were for an inward journey, bringing into the body a healing energy, while others were for journeying outside of the body into the Lower World, the Sky World, or the earthly realm. Some postures were used for metamorphosis, for shape-shifting into an animal, plant, or some other substance or earthly feature. Some postures provided a death-rebirth experience, while some were for divination, to answer a question or look into the future. One posture in particular, the Bear Spirit (see page 41), used for healing, asks us to focus on our center of harmony with our hands resting on our abdomen, where we can feel our stomach rising and falling as we breathe.

Dr. Goodman's research that led to the discovery of the ecstatic trance postures is described in detail in her book *Where the Spirits Ride the Wind,* as well as in Belinda Gore's books *Ecstatic Body Postures* and *Ecstatic Experience.* I also discuss this groundbreaking work in my first book on this subject, *The Power of Ecstatic Trance.* Dr. Goodman developed a simple but powerful ritual: cleansing, calling the spirits from the seven directions (the four cardinal points plus Above, Below, and the Center, or unity of all); quieting the mind by bringing one's attention to the center of harmony; and finally, entering a state of ecstatic trance by sitting, standing, or lying in a particular posture while listening to a rapidly beating drum or shaking rattle. This method of inducing ecstatic trance is referred to as the Cuyamungue Method of ecstatic-trance induction, and it is the method that is employed for the trances in this book. It is described in detail in chapter 3, along with the various basic postures.

The works of art that provided Goodman, Gore, and myself with these ecstatic postures were found in the art of various hunting-and-gathering societies, whether ancient or contemporary. They are all societies that practiced and practice shamanism. Though this shamanic magic is very powerful, there are those of the rational, scientific community who hang on to their linear ways of thinking and consider this magic superstitious. Yet there is growing evidence that demonstrates without a doubt the real power of these practices for healing and for becoming one with our Earth Mother. My recent books *Baldr's Magic* and *Beowulf's Ecstatic Trance Magic* both describe the power of this magic for the ancient people of Northern Europe—magic that is still available to us today, the magic of healing, of spirit journeying, of communicating over distances of space and time, and of seeing into the future. American Indian author, theologian, historian, and activist Vine Delora wrote *The World We Used to Live In,* published just before his death in 2005. It details the experiences of American Indian medicine men that indubitably demonstrate this very real power of healing and of communicating and seeing over great distances, beyond our usual sensory abilities.

These same powers can bring us to a state of being one with the Earth. In using a shape-shifting posture to become a bear or some other animal, a plant, or a substance or feature of the Earth, and in so doing learning from this animal, plant, substance, or feature, we come to see the world through their eyes. By using a posture for journeying into the underworld, besides being able to commune with my distant ancestors, I have been able to experience life as a snake or a groundhog, or experience the roots of trees, roots that sustain that part of the tree that rises above the Earth. I have also gone into the sea to experience the fish. In journeying into the upper world, the Sky World, besides experiencing the stars, the Moon, and the Sun, besides seeing Earth from a distance, I have become at times a winged being. I have become an eagle, a hummingbird, and a wood thrush. In using a divination posture in seeking an answer to some question, an animal spirit guide has often brought me answers to my questions or concerns.

The use of these different postures in spirit journeying has brought me into a relationship of oneness with the Earth, oneness with the cosmos; it has brought me to a much deeper, more visceral level of experience than I could ever achieve by using my imagination alone, though my imagination is an important factor in bringing me these ecstatic experiences.

SPIRITS

Ecstatic experiences frequently involve spirit guides who give us direction; these guides are often animals, but they can be other things, plants or features of the Earth such as a river or the wind. The ritual we use to induce ecstatic trance involves calling the spirits of the seven directions. These spirits are alive and real; we listen to these spirits, and in our journeys we continually relate to these many and varied spirits.

Who or what are these spirits? At first in speaking of spirits we may think of something like the spirit of Christmas, or the spirit of each of the seasons in a more abstract sense. But as we experience the spirits through trance, they begin to become real to us as living essences or beings. We not only feel them, we can see and hear them, and we can learn from them. And we begin to realize that we are no better than any of them, but are in fact one with them. For example, as we call on the spirit of the bear, the bear comes to us in a nurturing and healing way; at other times he might come to us as strong and challenging. The bear shows us how it relates to others in a balanced ecological manner. Life other than human life has maintained its primary spiritual relationship with many others, with all of the spirits of Mother Earth. Only we humans have separated ourselves from these spirits and think of ourselves as better than all other life forms. In this mistaken thinking we have become divorced from our Great Mother.

As we learn more about the ways of the hunter-gatherers, we learn more of the power and strength they found and find in these spirits by listening to them. For the native peoples of this country, the stories of creation and life are stories of animals and their relation to everything of the Earth. These stories are not just for children; they are intended to provide an understanding of the world at any age, an understanding that defines their way of life and influences their very survival.

THE SACREDNESS OF LANGUAGE AND POSTURES

The novelist Jean Auel, who authored the Earth's Children series of books set in prehistoric Europe, has described early hominids as living within a dreamlike state of consciousness, and in this she is in agreement with Jean Gebser. Spoken language was rudimentary, and written language was nonexistent. Auel, in her first book, *The Clan of the Cave Bear,* popularized the rudimentary nature of this prehistoric language, a language that is similar in many respects to American Sign Language, with only a few verbal/auditory sounds. According to cosmologist Christian De Quincey,

> Prior to the development of speech, our forebears uttered spontaneous sounds such as gasps, sighs, screams, and cries as they encountered the contingencies of the wild. At the sound of swishing wings of a swooping hawk, for instance, a sudden gasp of breath might have been the human body's instinctive response. The hawk's movement and sounds, immediately meaningful, spoke a language of gesture initiating a dialogue between animal and human. *Bodies in nature spoke to each other* before the development of grammatical speech. Semantics preceded syntax.[2]

The sacred nature of spoken language was evident among Celtic people in the storytelling of the druid bards, and among the Nordic people in the deification of Bragi, the god of storytelling. The druids perfected an oral tradition of storytelling, as did the ancient Nordic bards, that used a form of chanting in the recitation of stories. The magical nature of this form of incantation placed language in a more sacred space than how we think of it today in our vernacular speech. Likewise, the Finns, in *Kalevala,* a nineteenth-century work of epic poetry compiled by philologist Elias Lönnrot, from Karelian and Finnish oral folklore and mythology, refer to their language as singing.[3]

In early times, spoken language was considered somewhat magical and very special. Even more sacred was written language. In the North, the first alphabet was comprised of the runes, transmitted by the god Odin as he hung from the Tree of Life.[4] From the ancient period all the way up to the middle ages, written language was only available to shamans, druids, or priests; their inscriptions on stone were often thought to hold special magical meanings. Not even kings could read and write. Yet, as time went on and written language began to come into common use, it only abetted our separation from nature, by moving our thoughts and knowledge away from direct connection with the Earth and to the surface of a piece of paper.

The hunter-gatherers likely communicated using a rudimentary spoken language that depended on using body signs and postures and facial expressions. We often refer to the ecstatic postures as sacred postures, and they are sacred in the feelings or emotions they express and communicate. Generally written language promotes separation from the sacredness of nature by removing us from the nonverbal, felt experience of nature. By looking at the body postures we use in ecstatic journeying and putting into words the feelings the postures express and communicate, we gain a deeper understanding of the power of the posture and do not separate ourselves from nature. In addition, this understanding of what the postures emotionally express provides a bridge between those of us who value and use the postures intuitively to those more stuck in their rational thought. The rational thinker needs a more concrete understanding why the posture has the effect it does on the trance experience; exploring the emotions the posture expresses can provide this understanding.

In considering other life beyond the hominid, an animals' greater sensitivity in communicating is often attributed to their acute sense of sight and smell, but I suggest that another factor in this sensitivity is their understanding of facial expressions and what has been called *body language.* Humans are often insensitive to the messages communicated through body language, thus bringing it to their attention offers them a deeper understanding of the power of the posture. This subject will be explored in depth in the next chapter.

Our human intelligence has led us down a path of rationality and dualism, but now is the time when we humans must redirect it away from a need to control the Earth and toward a new understanding of the integrity of the cosmos and our place in it. Both the living and nonliving components of the Earth work together as a single system. Through ecstatic trance we too can begin to again become one with her, with all of her components. We can learn from the animals through ecstatic trance by following them as our spirit guides or by shape-shifting to become one of them. We can learn from the spirits of the seven directions, from the four seasons, and from the entire cycle of life. We can directly experience a sense of being interdependent with everything of the Earth, both animate and inanimate. And by experiencing and understanding these interdependent relationships, we progress toward becoming spiritually mature elders, capable of teaching and leading others in the ways of planetary oneness that we so desperately need at this time. By developing a deeper connection with the Earth through ecstatic trance, we become sensitive to and can feel the pain we have inflicted on her—an important step in the healing process. And as the ecstasy of trance becomes part of our life, the ecstatic postures of divination can guide us in discovering what we can do to heal the Earth. In trance, we will reconnect with our childhood experiences of nature, and from these experiences we can discover the daily rituals we can enact to keep this sense of connection always in the forefront of our consciousness.

What follows from my collection of over 2,000 ecstatic trance experiences recorded from the many groups I have led in ecstatic trance journeying are those experiences that I believe will help readers understand and move toward oneness with the Earth and all her beings.

3
THE ECSTATIC POSTURES

I sing to the Mother Gaia
I sing to the Father Sun.
I sing to the living in the garden where
The Mother and the Father are One.

ANONYMOUS

I had been a professional psychologist who extensively used the therapeutic tools of dream work, hypnosis, and guided imagery for thirty years when in 2001 I first read Felicitas Goodman's book, *Where the Spirits Ride the Wind,* a case study in experiential anthropology that proposed that certain body postures may help induce specific trance states. Intrigued, I then read Belinda Gore's first book, *Ecstatic Body Postures.* Belinda, also a psychologist, was a close student of Goodman and became the president of the Cuyamungue Institute after the death of Goodman. Her book offers precise instructions for achieving ecstatic trance and describes in detail thirty-nine of the postures used by the institute. My first experience using the ecstatic postures was in 2007 when I offered a morning ecstatic trance workshop for a group of attendees at the annual conference of the International Association for the Study of Dreams (IASD), in Sonoma, California. This was my very first experience using the ecstatic postures with a group, and each morning for the four days of the conference I followed Dr. Goodman's methods for establishing ecstatic trance precisely as she had outlined them. There were about eighteen people in the group, and over a four-day period we used eight different postures—an experience I will describe in greater detail later on. I was very impressed with how everyone's experiences matched what Goodman had learned to expect, even though the participants at the workshop went into each posture blind as to what was expected of it. With this initial success I returned to my home in Pennsylvania to start an ecstatic trance group that initially met weekly. The group continues to the present, meeting once or twice a month. Currently we have a basic core group of about nine people, and one person in the group is now taking on the role of leading the ritual.

FELITAS GOODMAN AND THE DISCOVERY OF ECSTATIC TRANCE POSTURES

Felicitas Goodman (1914–2005) was born in Hungary and educated in Germany. Following World War II, she came to the United States, and with her proficiency in a number of languages she found work at Ohio State University as a scientific translator. In 1965, at the age of fifty-one, having raised four children who were then grown, she decided to return to college as a student to work toward a master's degree in linguistics. In the process she took a course on religion in native societies, taught by anthropologist Erika Bourguignon, who had been studying the role of religious or ecstatic trance in 486 small societies around the world. It was then that Goodman discovered her passion, and she decided to pursue a doctorate in anthropology.

For her dissertation, Goodman chose to study the form of trance that caused glossolalia, the phenomenon of speaking in tongues, among members of several Mayan and Spanish-speaking Pentecostal churches in Mexico. With her interest in linguistics, she was curious about the effects of the different languages and dialects on the glossolalia of the church members, who believed they were possessed by the Holy Spirit. She found that the person's native language had essentially no effect whatsoever on their glossolalia. What would ultimately be of even greater interest was her discovery that there were four basic elements of the church's religious ritual that were consistently necessary to induce ecstatic trance. There had to be (1) a private physical space; (2) a belief that the trance experience is normal, enjoyable, and pleasurable; (3) some sort of meditative technique to quiet the mind; and (4) aural, rhythmic stimulation to the nervous system.[1] The church sanctuary provided the private physical space; prayer quieted the mind; and the energetic clapping and singing during the church service provided the rhythmic stimulation to the nervous system. Finally, because the participants in the church service believed that speaking in tongues was a sign of being possessed by the Holy Spirit, and this was considered a good thing, this belief was an assurance that trance was normal and even enjoyable and pleasurable.

Following her fieldwork research, Dr. Goodman gained her doctorate in cultural anthropology from Ohio State University and started teaching at Denison University. As a result of her discoveries about trance during her fieldwork, she developed a more indigenous ritual to induce ecstatic trance that duplicated the same four basic elements found in the Pentecostal church ritual. She offered her students at Denison a private physical space where they were cleansed by smudging, after which the spirits of the seven directions were called. This ritual of cleansing and calling the spirits defined the space as sacred. She then explained to her students that the trance experience would be enjoyable and pleasant. She had them focus on their breathing for five minutes to quiet their minds before providing them with rhythmic stimulation by rapidly shaking a rattle or beating a drum at approximately 210 beats per minute.

Dr. Goodman found that her students were able to attain an adequate state of trance by following these four steps, but she still felt something was missing that would deepen the trance state. Then she read a journal article by V. F. Emerson, a Canadian psychologist who had examined the effects of different body postures on the meditative/trance state. The article was titled "Can Belief Systems Influence Behavior? Some Implications of Research on Meditation," and in it the author proposed that during meditation, different postures affected such things as skin moisture, hormone secretion, and blood pressure. This intrigued Dr. Goodman, who then began to search the literature and museum artifacts of the hunter-gatherer peoples of the world, both contemporary and from antiquity, to find what she believed were the postures used by the shamans of those peoples. She identified approximately fifty such postures, and she returned to her research with her students at Denison, where she added a fifth element to her sequence: she had the students sit, stand, or lie in the different ritual body postures while inducing ecstatic trance as she had done before.

Dr. Goodman was impressed with the effects the postures had on the students' trance experiences. Some postures brought a healing energy into the body, while others were for divination, for finding answers to questions and for looking into the future. Some postures led the students on journeys into the underworld, while others were for journeying in the Middle World, and some were for journeying into the Sky World. Some postures provided initiation, or death-rebirth experiences, and some provided shape-shifting, or metamorphosis, experiences.

Accordingly, the ritual she now used to induce ecstatic trance included the following five steps:

1. A sacred space was defined by smudging a room with smoke and calling the spirits of each direction to come to the sacred space.
2. The participants were then prepared by hearing a description of the posture that they would use, and given an opportunity to practice that posture and ask questions before the start of the trance session, thus putting them at ease.
3. Participants' inner dialogue was quieted by having them find a comfortable position in which to follow their breathing during a five-minute period of quietness.

4. Their nervous system was then stimulated while they assumed the position of the posture. This part of the ritual would last fifteen minutes, during which time Dr. Goodman rapidly beat her drum or shook her rattle at approximately 210 beats per minute.
5. Finally, the participants were asked to record their experience in a journal before each person was given an opportunity to describe their experience to the rest of the group. By first recording and then describing their experiences, each person had the opportunity to gain greater personal understanding and validation of the experience's importance.

HOW DO THE POSTURES WORK?

Ecstatic postures are often referred to as sacred postures. They are sacred, or magical, in how they give direction to the ecstatic trance experience. But because it is who I am to ask questions, I have asked, "Why or how do they work?" Some instructors in the method don't ask this question, feeling that it diminishes the sacredness and ineffability of the experience. I feel otherwise. I believe that understanding why and how the postures accomplish what they do gives us a deeper power of understanding. In my defense I offer the thinking of Jean Gebser.

In his seminal work *The Ever-Present Origin,* Gebser examined the stages of development of human consciousness over the past 200,000 years. He provided the thesis that we are currently leaving the era of rational consciousness that has existed for over 2,000 years and are now moving into the era of what he called *time-free transparency.* Before the present era of rational consciousness from which we are transitioning, and going backward in time, was the era of mythical consciousness, and before that, the era of magical consciousness. These two eras followed the first era of consciousness, the archaic era, which is essentially zero-dimensional consciousness, when the consciousness of humankind was likened to "a dimly lit mist devoid of shadows." The archaic man "had no notion of anything beyond his own existence—no lofty thoughts of a higher power or any noble ideals. His self was inextricably part of his total life-world. In himself he united as it were heaven and Earth, inside and outside. He lived from moment to moment, without strategies or plans, borne by the inherent wisdom of the unconscious."[2]

The second era, that of magical consciousness, was the era of the hunter-gatherers who, for example, drew the cave paintings of hunting depicting such images as the auroch with a spear stuck in its flank—a magical image that improved the success of the hunt. Following this era came the mythical era, the era of stories that explained creation and the nature of life—an era that became possible because written language became available.

The people of both the archaic era and the magical era showed a deep connection with and were one with Mother Earth. This changed, as I mentioned earlier, with the introduction of written language. Then, during the fourth era, that of rational consciousness, the magic and myths of the previous eras were suppressed and labeled superstitious and false in light of science and empiricism.

Now that we are moving into the era of time-free transparency, we are asking questions with a deeper sense of the breadth and depth of consciousness. This era is characterized by the relativity of time and the power of the magic and myths of the previous eras as they become transparent to us; we have developed a new relationship to time and space (as indicated in science by new developments in physics, which confirm our interdependence). According to Gebser, "The moment we are successful in wrestling with past 'time' that is latently present . . . then the importance we accord to the earlier times and their diverse structures of consciousness will become apparent in the development" of consciousness in the new era.[3] We bring to this new era the knowledge gained over the past 2,000 years, knowledge that challenges us to explain rationally how the magical feats of shamanic healing, shape-shifting, and journeying to other worlds of the early eras could be possible.

This is what leads me to question why and how ecstatic trance works.

As a psychologist I have valued the ability to read the nonverbal signs that clients offer in therapy, signs that tell of deeper feelings than those expressed verbally. For example, sagging shoulders and looking at the floor suggest depression, while a change in breathing rate to heavy breathing can suggest anxiety. Similarly, it is the nonverbal messages that are expressed by the sacred postures that lend understanding as to how and why they give direction to the ecstatic trance experience. That is why exploring what the posture communicates gives the person who comes to ecstatic trance work with strongly rational thinking a greater understanding and deeper faith in why and how the postures work. The postures presented in this chapter provide examples of how we answer the question, "What does the posture express?" Therefore, let us now consider what these postures communicate or express nonverbally.

NINE BASIC POSTURES

In this chapter I will cover nine postures that I most frequently use, postures derived from each category. An additional twenty-four postures from the various categories, which are discussed in later chapters in this book, are illustrated in the appendix.

Healing Postures

One posture that has been found in almost every hunter-gatherer culture, past and present, is what we call the Bear Spirit posture. I have in my personal collection of artifacts from the hunter-gatherer cultures two carved figures standing in this posture from the Kuna people of the San Blas islands of Panama.

With your hands resting on your lower abdomen a couple of inches below your umbilicus, at your dan t'ian, or place of harmony as I have called it, you can feel your abdomen rising and falling when you breathe correctly, from your diaphragm. This sensation of rising and falling makes it clear that something, a healing or strengthening energy, is flowing into your body. In using hypnosis I might say, "As you inhale,

Bear Spirit Posture

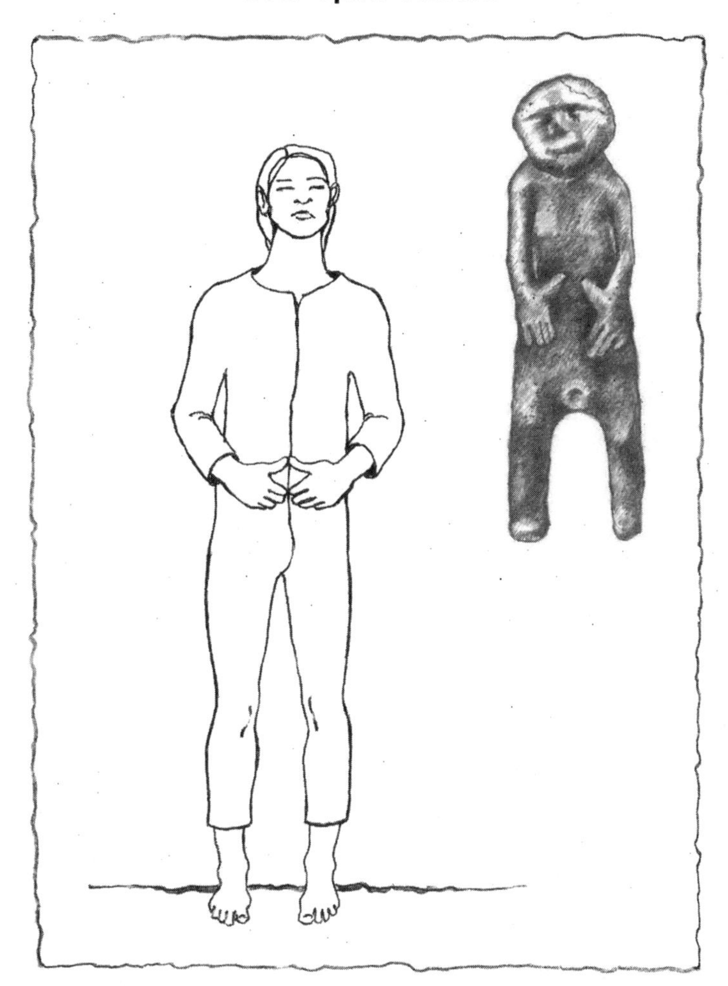

Stand with your feet parallel, about six inches apart, with toes forward and knees not locked but slightly bent. Your hands are resting relaxed on your abdomen, with your thumbs touching and fingers spread apart, flat or together and bent under, such that the first knuckles of your index fingers are above your navel, forming a triangle. Your elbows rest easily at your sides. Your eyes are closed and your head is gently tipped back as though you're looking at a point where the wall meets the ceiling.

feel the healing energy entering your body, and as you exhale, let the relaxation of your breath go deeper inside of you and flow throughout your body," but this instruction is unnecessary and not used with ecstatic trance because the power of the energy flowing in is felt through your hands. In addition to this posture being a healing posture containing the flow of healing energy, I also consider it an confidence-strengthening posture, allowing new strength to flow within you.

Divination Postures

Among the many divination postures are several in which you hold your left hand up in front of your face but not touching your face, as in the Mayan Oracle and the Jama-Coaque Diviner. I found the figurine of the Jama-Coaque Diviner in the Quai Branly Museum in Paris, and it appears on the cover of my book *The Power of Ecstatic Trance*. It was originally found on the northern coast of Ecuador, at Jama, which was a market center for the ancient Jama-Coaque culture. This figurine has a number of decorative features similar to the Jama-Coaque Metamorphosis posture.

When I have asked groups what this posture reminds them of, the answer invariably is Rodin's iconic figure "The Thinker." But I would point out that in this figure the fist does not rest against the chin as in Rodin's sculpture, but is instead more open, giving the answer more room to come from outside before entering your thinking mind. If I were seeking an answer, sitting and waiting for the answer in this posture is likely the pose I would take.

Spirit Journey Postures

Consider the spirit-journey postures, postures for journeying into the Lower World, the Middle World, and the Sky World. In each of the underworld postures you are lying supine, so that you place yourself as close as possible to the underworld. Two of the Lower-World postures are the Sami (see appendix, figure A.15) and the Jivaro (see appendix, figure A.8).

Jama-Coaque Diviner Posture

Sit on the floor with your knees pulled up in front of you such that your feet are flat on the floor or ground and when you lean forward with a straight back, hinging from the hips, you can comfortably rest your right forearm across your raised knees. The elbow of your right arm is on your right knee and the hand of your right arm is resting on your left knee. Your knees and feet should be about ten inches apart. The elbow of your left arm rests on the back of your right hand. Your left hand is raised, palm toward your face, with the fingers together in a loose fist. Your head is tilted slightly upward and facing forward.

Another lower-world posture, one that I identified, is the Tanum Lower World posture, found among the petroglyphs on the northwest coast of Sweden. Across the parking lot of the museum at Tanum, Sweden, is a large battle scene of petroglyphs dated from 1800 to 500 BCE. Among the figures in this battle scene, off to the left of the main part of the battle, is a warrior embracing his consort. Behind this warrior stands another warrior with an axe raised above the in-love warrior's head. Below this portion of the battle scene and below a figure of a sentry with long outstretched arms is a warrior lying supine, with his woman kneeling above his head as if grieving. Attached to the warrior's right foot is a ship that can be assumed to be taking him to the underworld, to Hel's domain, where those who do not die a hero in

Tanum Lower World Posture

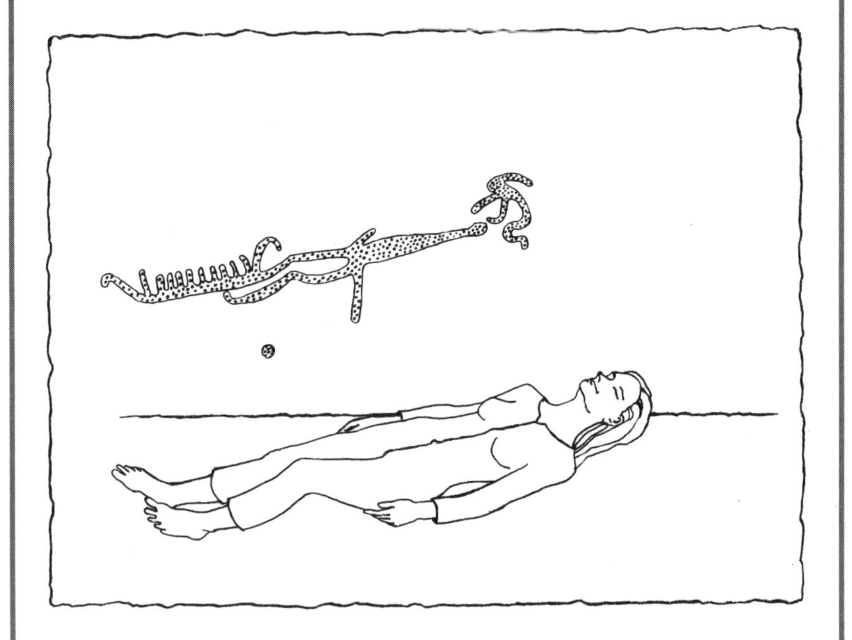

Lie on your back with your arms at your sides close to your body. Your legs are essentially parallel, though your left knee may be slightly raised.

battle are taken according to Norse mythology. Since he was killed as a result of being distracted because of his love for this woman, he did not die a hero, whereas those who die as heroes in battle are taken to Valhalla, in the Sky World.*

In this underworld posture, you may experience the feeling of your right leg being pulled by the ship.

For journeying into the Sky World we find several other figures among the Tanum petroglyphs depicting heroic warriors journeying upward, to Valhalla. Among these Bronze Age petroglyphs I have found at least five figures that are seen rising upward above their ship, at approximately a 37-degree angle, similar to the Lascaux Cave posture, found among the petroglyphs at the French archaeology site famous for its Paleolithic cave paintings, and also similar to an Egyptian Osiris petroglyph. The Tanum warriors are carrying swords; their arms rest either at their sides, or one (the right) or both arms are raised above their heads. In one case the man has wings. These petroglyphic figures are obviously men because they show a penis. A king or chieftain often had twelve berserkers among his retainers who fought for him. A story that I heard many years ago said that when a berserker worked himself up into a fighting frenzy, the sign that he was in a sufficient frenzy for fighting was that his penis became erect. This suggests that the warriors seen in these petroglyphs are berserkers.

These figures are tenuously connected to the Earth, as suggested by the 37-degree angle. Their feet are neither planted firmly on the Earth nor are they lying supine on the Earth. This angled position suggests that in this posture you are floating or rising above the Earth. Again, this posture nonverbally makes considerable sense as an upper-world posture.

For greater convenience for journeying into the Sky World I have often used the Venus of Galgenberg, an upper-world posture, because it

*Pictures of this battle scene can be found on my website, www.imaginalmind.net.

Tanum Sky World Posture*

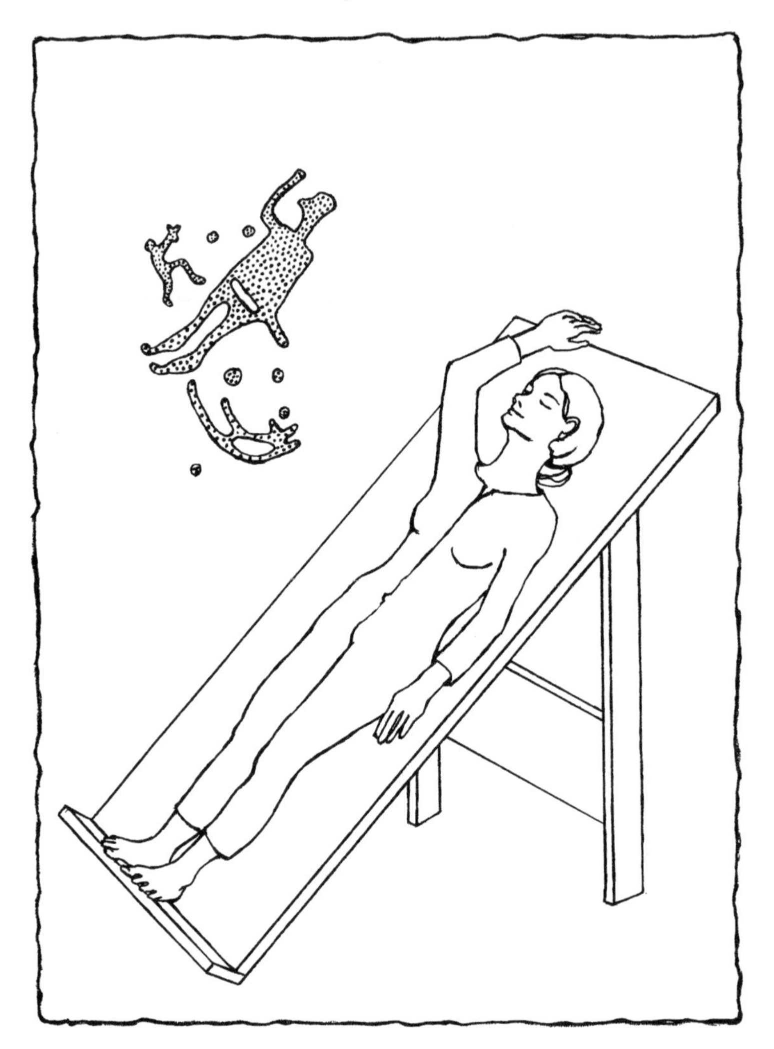

Lie on a launching pad† at a 37-degree angle. Your legs and feet are together. Your arms resting at your side, or one, your right, or both may be raised above your head.

---

*This posture is also known as the Lascaux Cave Sky World posture.
†The launching pad is a platform slanted at 37 degrees, strong enough to support a reclining person.

Venus of Galgenberg Sky World Posture

Stand with your left leg straight and your left foot pointing forward. Bend your right knee slightly, with your right foot slightly turned out, away from your body. The fingers of your right hand are together and point toward the ground, possibly holding a stick that rests along your right leg. Your left arm is raised at a 37-degree angle from the vertical line extending above your head, and that hand is cupped, with the palm of that hand turned toward that vertical line above your head. Your head is raised and turned toward the left, as though your eyes gaze at your raised hand, though your eyes remain closed.

does not require dealing with the cumbersome angled launching pad. The Venus is the oldest of the figures we use for ecstatic trance. She is 32,000 years old, is only 2.75 inches tall, and stands with her left arm raised at 37 degrees, pointing to the heavens. She was found along the Danube River in Austria.

The Venus communicates the idea of rising into the Sky World as directed by the position of her left hand, and with her right foot turned out she does not suggest the feeling of being planted on the Earth, as does the next posture, the Priestess of Malta.

For journeying in the Middle World my favorite posture is the Priestess of Malta. This figure dates from around 5,000 years ago and was found in the Hypogeum, an underground labyrinth on the island of Malta. The Hypogeum is thought to have been a center for the training of priestesses of the island. Felicitas Goodman, Belinda Gore, and others determined that this posture takes you on a journey to the Middle World.

Notice the sense of how the priestess is planted on the Earth, especially because of her heaviness, with her right hand pointing toward the Earth, toward where she seeks to travel. I find that this traveling in the Middle World may be in the present or it might be going back in time or even to the future, but in each case your spirit journey in this posture will take you to places in this Middle World. When I ask what her posture communicates, the answer that comes to me is, "I feel planted on the Earth."

Metamorphosis or Shape-shifting Postures

The metamorphosis or shape-shifting postures also communicate your intent in becoming some animal. For this purpose my favorite and most powerful figure is the Olmec Prince, the one most frequently used in this book for attaining oneness with the Earth (see page 50). The Olmec people of pre-Columbian Mexico date from around 1500 BCE to about 400 BCE, preceding the Mayan and Aztec civilizations. This figurine was found near Tabasco, Mexico. The Olmec Prince was the

Priestess of Malta Middle World Posture

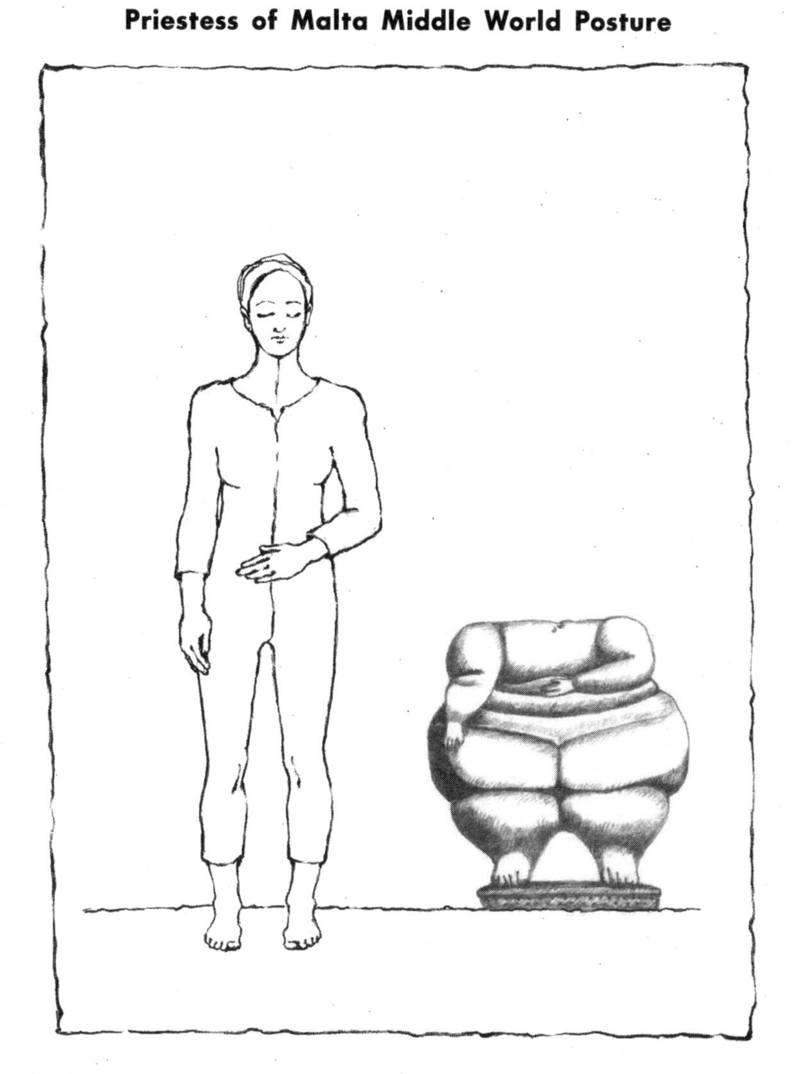

Stand straight with your feet parallel and slightly apart, toes pointed straight ahead and knees slightly bent. Your right arm is held firmly beside your body, locked at the elbow, with fingers hanging down. The palm of your left hand, with fingers and thumb together, rests against your waist with fingers over your navel. The elbow of your left arm is bent at 90 degrees and held close to your body. Face is forward, with eyes closed.

Olmec Prince Posture

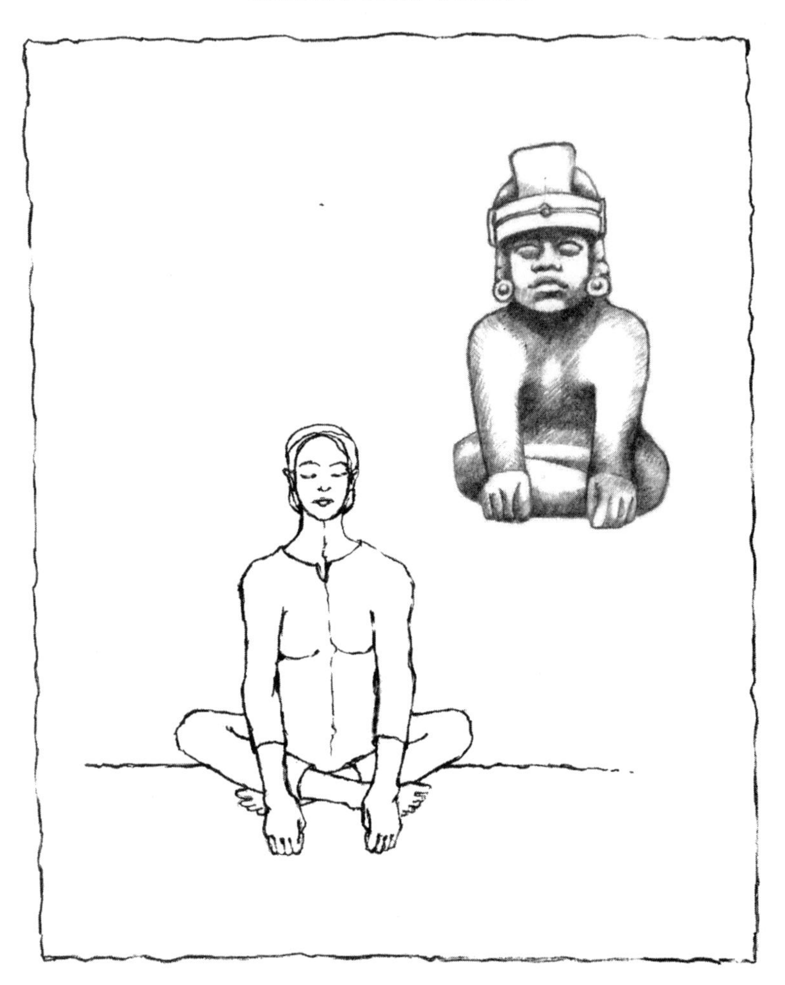

Sit on the floor with your right leg crossed in front of your left leg. Stretch your arms, with elbows locked, straight in front of you, with your fingers curled inward, toward your body, such that only the middle segment of each finger rests on the floor. Your shoulders, elbows, wrists, and knuckles are held rigid. To maintain this position you will need to lean slightly forward with your back straight, hinging from the hips. Lift your head with your closed eyes looking forward. Let your tongue protrude slightly from between your lips.

very first posture I ever used. The evening before my first workshop at the International Association for the Study of Dreams conference we had a drumming circle, and I sat at the back of the circle against the wall sitting in this posture. I found myself quickly becoming a high-stepping parade horse. It just so happened that the drummer nearest me was drumming with a parade cadence, and when I asked him about it he reported that he had been a drummer in his college marching band.

The Olmec Prince communicates the intention of becoming an animal. Your knuckles rest on the ground as if they are forelegs, yet this posture does not always indicate a four-legged animal, as sometimes I can become a bird or a snake using this posture.

Initiation or Death-Rebirth Postures

Of all the initiation postures, the most powerful one for me is the Feathered Serpent (see page 52). The other name for this Toltec deity is Quetzalcoatl, a deity who takes us through the cycle of death and rebirth. This figurine is from the period between 600 BCE and 900 CE and was found in Zacatecas, Mexico.

When in our group we have discussed what this posture is trying to express, the conclusion is that with your hands resting on your hips you are communicating a sense of determination, suggesting a strength that you are ready to let die some part of you that needs to die. Before you were ready to let go of that part of yourself, you would likely feel some fear or hesitancy in releasing that part of yourself, but now that you are ready, your posture expresses your fearlessness.

Realm of the Dead Postures

A posture that has been most powerful for me in going back in time to visit my ancient ancestors is the Hallstatt Warrior (see page 53). This figure, dated from around the fifth century BCE, was found in Hirschlanden, Germany.

Feathered Serpent Posture*

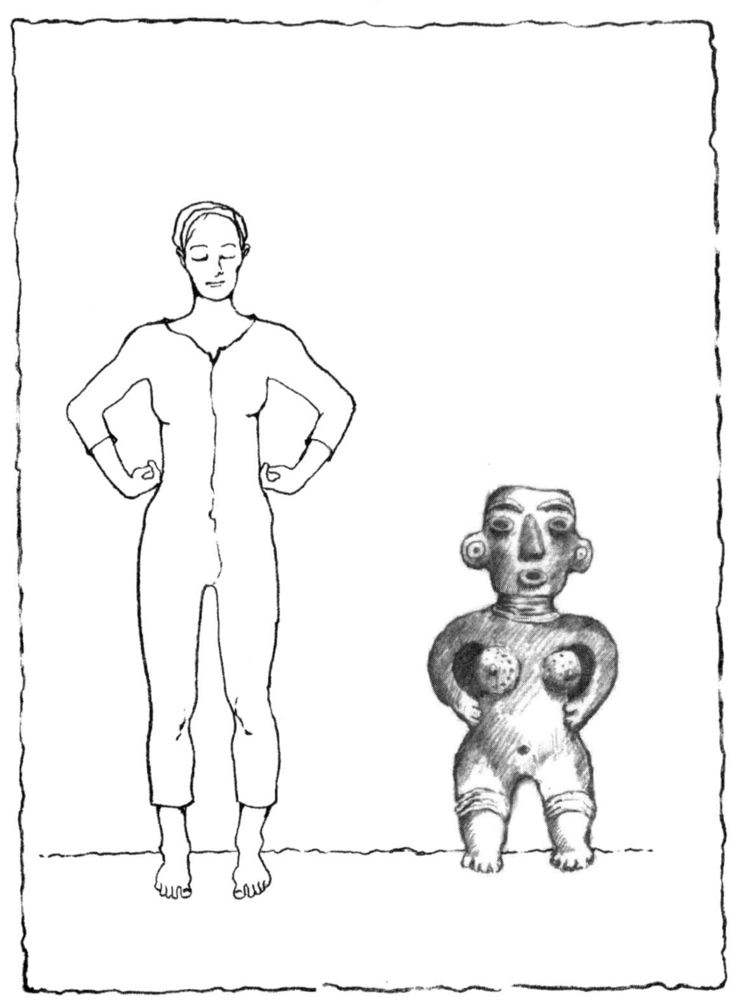

Stand with your feet parallel, about six inches apart, knees lightly bent with toes pointing straight forward. Cup your hands and place them at your side at waist level, with fingers curling upward and your arms rounded outward with bent elbows pointing to either side. Your face looks straight ahead, and your eyes are closed and your mouth slightly open.

*This posture is also known as the Nyborg Man posture.

Hallstatt Warrior Posture*

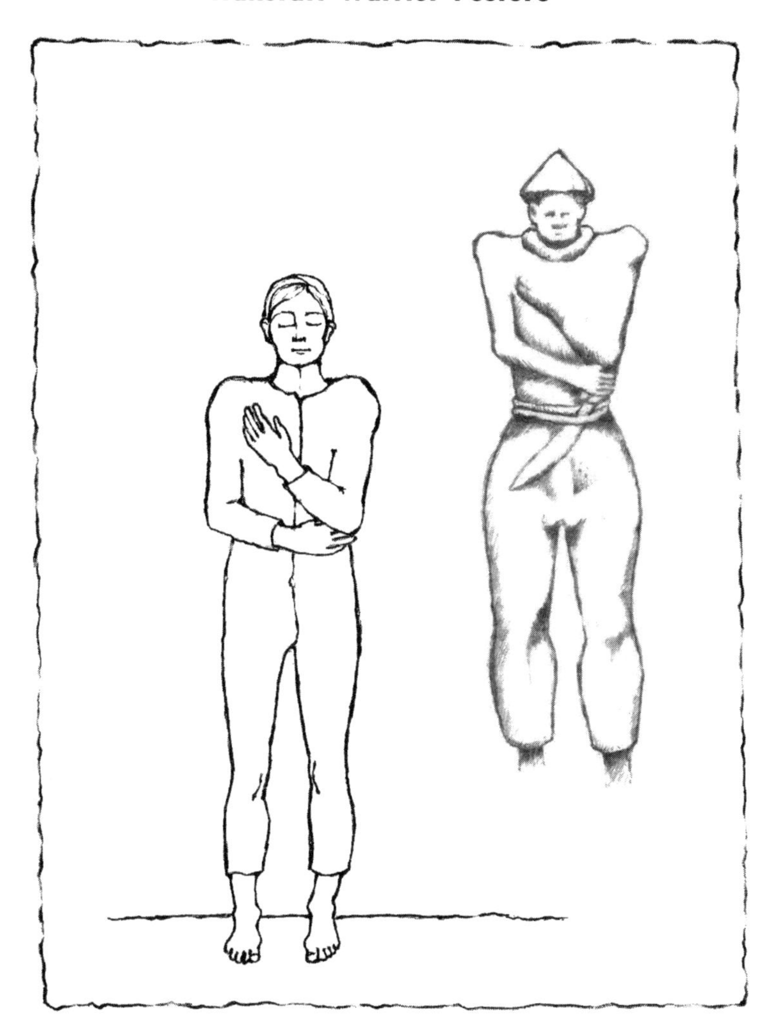

Stand with your feet about five inches apart and toes pointed forward. Keep your knees locked. Place your right arm along your waist, with the base of your palm covering your navel. Your left arm rests along the side of your torso, with the left hand resting on the right breast, fingers pointing toward the right shoulder. Face forward with eyes closed.

*Also known as the Danish Realm of the Dead posture

This warrior is standing with his arms wrapped around his chest, as if cold or apprehensive. It is as if he is about to enter a cold place such as the Realm of the Dead. If I were to go into the Realm of the Dead, this is likely the posture I would use, and indeed I used it quite a lot in going back in time to visit my ancient Nordic ancestors, experiences I describe in my book *Baldr's Magic.*

There are many postures other than those mentioned here, but these are the basic postures for the various types of journeys available through ecstatic trance. The other postures discussed later in this book are illustrated in the appendix. I find that with each posture, by asking what it expresses, a deeper understanding of the nature of the posture will emerge. I expect that for each person, specific postures will rise above others in becoming important and powerful; that has certainly been true for me. For example, besides the Hallstatt Warrior, my other two favorite postures are the Olmec Prince, for shape-shifting, and the Feathered Serpent, for initiation or death and rebirth.

4

SPIRIT GUIDES

The beauty of the trees,
The softness of the air,
the fragrance of the grass,
speaks to me.

The summit of the mountain,
the thunder of the sky,
the rhythm of the sea,
speaks to me.

The faintness of the stars,
the freshness of the morning,
the dewdrop on the flower,
speaks to me.

The strength of fire,
the taste of salmon,
the trail of the sun,
and the life that never goes away,
they speak to me
And my heart soars.

CHIEF DAN GEORGE

When you start experimenting with the ecstatic postures, one of the first things to do is to find a spirit guide that in some way leads you to some new discovery about yourself. This makes sense in that the hunters and gatherers, both ancient and contemporary, see the world as being full of spirits—the spirits of specific animals, plants, or other substances of the Earth. In tribal societies, a clan name is generally that of an animal who is considered an ancestor of the members of the clan. This animal is protected by the clan and is considered a spirit guide in life. The clan members are sometimes extended family members, but people are also assigned to a clan by various other methods, for example, as the result of a vision quest, by some specific rite of passage in the person's life, or by the person's role in the community. As well, a person may have more than one spirit guide. Spirit guides are central in the rituals, celebrations, and dances of the tribe, and honoring them is a way of showing them respect. The costumes and masks worn by tribe members during these rituals are generally of their spirit guides and are worn to call these spirits to join them in the rituals.

Spirit guides have specific personalities that have something to teach a person. Take the coyote: a commonly accepted personality trait of this animal is that of the playful trickster. The personality of the bear is that of nurturer and healer. Trees are often experienced as the axis of life, and rivers are a guide to our flow of life. Paths across the Earth can also be spirit guides. In this chapter we will examine some of the many spirit guides as they appear in the trance experiences of different journeyers—our brethren living on the Earth and in the air and water, as well as other earthly kin such as trees and rivers.

OUR FOUR-LEGGED SPIRIT GUIDES

Many native cultures believe that if we put our ear to the ground, we can hear Mother Earth's heartbeat. Earth animals are keenly aware of this heartbeat. They are aware too of our human heartbeat and know what we need from them at any given moment, knowledge that allows them to guide us. The messages they carry to us are very individual and personal. We need to wait with patience, holding the experience before us, for understanding of the message to eventually become clear. Each animal may have characteristics that can be considered universal, but more important is our individual experience with the animal. Sometimes our experiences may differ from the universal, and holding to the universal characteristic may lead us astray in gaining understanding of a personal experience.

The bear is a frequently appearing spirit guide in my own trance experiences. Symbol of healing in many cultures, as well as a consummate mother and child protector, caring for her young with fierce devotion, the bear is a massive animal who forages peacefully in the woods but can be potentially explosive when provoked, displaying independence, courage, and aggression. In Scandinavian myths the bear was the invincible warrior, the spirit guide of the berserker who was known to wear bearskins to enhance his ferocity in battle. In the ecstatic trance experience the bear may appear to be the nurturing and protective mother bear to one person, the strong, ferocious male bear to another, and something totally different someone else, depending upon the needs of the person at the time. I have received different messages from the bear at different times in my life, depending on the message I needed at that time.

While using the Bear Spirit posture (see page 41), Marsha, a member of an ecstatic trance group I led at the Cuyamungue Institute, had the following experience:

> **7-27-13:** *Fox greets me and then greets bear. I greet Bear and see him walking into the field outside the student house. He stands on his hind legs and I now see through his eyes. We are then in a high green meadow and I find myself focusing on my heart chakra, feeling energy flowing in and out of it. Bear tells me to send energy from my heart outward to others and to the Earth, and I soar into the starry universe. I feel surprised, and Bear says I am connected to the stars through my heart. Bear says healing comes*

from the heart's connection to the Earth, to other people, and to creation. I learn that my healing, my calling, is to be in my heart and to send and receive energy through my heart. At some point Bear laughs and says that Bears are from the stars. Peace. I am now sweating in the posture. Bear says it is a cleansing and says that I should avoid meat these days. That might be hard. My feet become Bear's feet planted on the Earth.

In this journey, the Bear Spirit offers teachings about healing to Marsha, an experienced healer in her own right. The message is clear: healing comes from the heart's connection to the Earth and the stars. The stars are our ancestors. In the process of Creation, after its beginning with the Big Bang, in the birth of the stars was the original formation of the chemical elements that are listed in the periodic table of elements—the same elements from which we are made.[1] For Marsha, the Bear Spirit is the healer who shows her the heart's connection to and her interdependence with all things of the Earth as well as of the entire universe—which is the source of healing.

From my own personal experience with the Medicine Wheel and the directions, both the bear and the coyote are animals of the West, of the middle, productive years of life, and of experiencing life with deep emotions, though I acknowledge that the Medicine Wheel is personal and other people may have other interpretations of the animals and the directions.

Coyote is the clown of the natural world, and many American Indian tribes view the medicine of coyote as that of trickster, shapeshifter, and transformer. Coyote loves to poke fun at our egos, so whatever message coyote brings you, you can be sure it will come in a way that pops the bubble of self-importance. In this way coyote teaches you to have a sense of humor. Coyote tells us to be mindful of our actions, to be wary of playing tricks on ourselves or others, and so coyote sometimes comes with a message about learning from our mistakes. The coyote does not always take this more universal role, but in my experience below some of the traits hold true.

One of my very first experiences with the coyote was while using the Jivaro, an underworld posture (see appendix, figure A.8). I was in the kiva at the Cuyamungue Institute outside of Santa Fe, New Mexico, with eight others in the group:

> ***8-28-10:*** *I slide out of the top of my head and along the ground outside of the kiva. As I glide along the ground on my back, a coyote paws at me with its front right paw. To get away from its paw I float up onto a tree branch. There I see I am in a native village with thatched huts in somewhat of a circle. I float down to lie on the ground with the native dancers dancing around me. I am not the only one. We, all nine of us, are there lying with our feet toward the center of the circle, where a fire is smoking. Between us here and there are geysers of smoke rising from the ground, and several coyotes are jumping around from geyser to geyser, pawing at them as if to try to stop them. There are two or three geysers that I consider mine. When my coyote leaves my geysers of smoke I am able to breathe the smoke in. The smoke feels cool, like a cool breeze, but it smells like smoke. Then I find myself back in my body with the cool breeze and feel myself back in the kiva.*

In this ecstatic experience the coyote was being very coyotelike in his clowning around, but in this way he was also bringing my attention to certain things: first, to an awareness of the native village, and then later, to the geysers of smoke, but most of all, to an awareness of him. Over the next couple of years the coyote became an important spirit guide for me, always making fun of me, and each time he visits me I know I have something valuable to learn from the experience. In this experience he was being quite playful, pawing at me as if I were a toy and pawing at the geysers. The geysers were full of smoke, like the cleansing smoke we use in the smudging part of the ecstatic trance ritual—smoke that I could smell in the kiva. In the coyote's playful way he was telling me to pay attention to being smudged, to feeling the cleansing of my aura. Since then I have learned to value more this sense of cleansing as an important part of the ritual.

OUR WINGED BRETHREN

There are many different species of birds, and each have their own characteristics. To understand the meaning of an ecstatic experience that contains a bird, it is sometimes useful to consider the species. For instance, the raptors can see mice, a likely meal, from very high up—indicative of their exceptional vision and vigilance—while the scavengers may clean up a mess—indicative of their interdependence, both receving from our Mother Earth and giving to her by cleansing the Earth of what others might consider disgusting. Many are colorful and joyful in their singing, exuding vigor for life. Again such universal characteristic are important to consider, but the meaning of the person's experience is very personal and unique. The following three experiences show some variations on how they are experienced.

In the following trance experience, Abby noted that she "felt like a bird," an experience that is more commonly attributed to shape-shifting, the subject of the next chapter. However, in recording her experience later she expressed some uncertainty and also indicated that she may have only seen the bird: "I saw or felt like a bird beating its wings . . ." Either way, the bird was Abby's spirit guide on this occasion when she used the Olmec Prince (see page 50).

> ***1-9-11:*** *I see or feel like a bird beating its wings over and over rhythmically in time with the rattle, fighting to move up, up, up, up, to move up through a bright white vertical tunnel. Also there seems to be another person wearing wings, moving or dancing around me in a circle. I have a busy mind today, so that interferes, but the feeling or sensation of strong beating wings comes to me more than once. When I quiet my thoughts, I feel as though I am fighting to rise and to shed heaviness, to get into the light, to beat something off or away from me.*

Abby added during the discussion period after our session that over the past year she had been trying to shed something heavy from her past.

She had a shape-shifting experience that reflected her need to shake off this heaviness. The flight of a bird is an experience of lightness, and fighting to gain height in flight does strongly suggest a struggle to shed heaviness.

I personally have had many experiences with birds. The eagle was an especially powerful spirit guide for me in dealing with my prostate cancer some years back, as described in my book *The Power of Ecstatic Trance.* He gave me the important message of "go with the flow" as he rose in a thermal current, literally rising above it all. The wood thrush and the hummingbird were also important spirit guides for me during that time, and birds continue to offer me guidance.

More recently I used the Olmec Prince posture (see page 50) while sitting on our sauna deck, which overlooks a small pond. This is one of my sacred outdoor spaces. It was fifty-two degrees outside and I felt a need to seek comfort. The Olmec Prince, a metamorphosis posture, is that for me. After cleansing and calling the spirits, while sitting for the five minutes of silence I heard the sounds of many birds in the grove of trees to the left of the pond. Still breathing deeply, I opened my eyes to watch the birds flitting from branch to branch and down to the left, to the ground, and back up again to the trees. On this day I used a recording of drumming and rattling, and as I started playing the recording I had the following experience:

> ***10-17-13:*** *The birds' chirping and trilling seems to become louder and louder. I can hear them above the rattling. Then I hear a woodpecker cawing in the same rhythm as the rattling. This very auditory experience lifts me above the frustration of my increasing deafness. I can see birds scratching in our compost pile to my left, next to the grove of trees, just out of my line of vision from where I am sitting. There they find plentiful seeds and insects. Their scratching and what they leave behind in the pile adds nutrients to the pile. Above the compost pile is a winterberry tree, and on the lawn below the compost pile are three dogwood trees full of their fall berries. What a paradise for birds! They seem very cheerful and happy this morning, letting their presence be known to me and to one*

another. When the rattling ends, I open my eyes and sit there for some time watching the birds. They are quiet for a brief time after the end of the drumming before resuming their chatter. I notice that what seems of greatest interest to them is the three dogwoods, and also a dogwood bush next to the winterberry, where they seem most busy as they periodically leave the grove of hemlock and white pines.

Small, joyful birds such as finches are often guides to signal happy times, or to remind us about the simple joys of life, of being in the present moment, and their bright colors and cheerful songs point us toward creativity and expressiveness—especially if they are lacking in our life. The knock of the woodpecker is an attention-getter; their loud knocking on trees can remind you of the old adage, "When opportunity comes knocking . . ."

In this experience the bird spirits made me realize how our gardening practices have been so beneficial to them and to our ecology.

OUR FINNED BRETHREN

Water can be a powerful symbol of cleansing, freedom, and mobility. Most significantly, it also can be a symbol of expressing something of the unconscious; therefore, water animal spirit guides can help us reveal and identify our hidden thoughts or actions. Going under the water can be an experience of going into the unconscious, something I have done frequently over the past thirty years. Though unconscious conflict is often expressed as something frightening or as an emotionally negative experience, I have lost my fear of facing my unconscious and often experience pleasant feelings when I journey "under the waters."

While using the Sami (see appendix, figure A.15), a lower-world posture, Sarah had the following underwater experience:

6-5-11: *All is dark. I call on the spirits of the underworld to accompany me on a journey and to show me something meaningful. We go into deep* *water, where I can breathe, but all is dark except for some electric eels that swim with us and light up once in a while. I can see a huge form emerging from the depths, and as we swim toward it, there is a neon glow coming from behind it. When we get closer I see that it is a huge turtle rearing up on its hind legs. The view behind the turtle is phosphorescent, all lit up with beautiful sparkly colors, with beautiful fish and human-looking forms. We start to swim around the turtle, but the turtle turns into a snapping turtle with pincers on the ends of each finlike leg and starts chopping the electric eels into little pieces and eats them. Then I notice what looks like a button in the center of the pattern on the turtle's undershell, and I push it. The shell opens, and I walk into a void but eventually end up in the phosphorescent light. It is wonderful! Bubbles are sparkling, and there are moving lights everywhere. There is a large woman with octopus arms who is grabbing the men, wrapping them up in her tentacles and turning them into women. There is a jellyfish who is oozing over the women and turning them into men. The men and women pair off and a huge fish sucks them all in. I follow and see that inside of the fish is the house in which I grew up . . .*

Underworld postures often take you underwater, where you find you can breathe—a very exhilarating experience. The presence of so much beauty in Sarah's experience suggests that what she was experiencing unconsciously was beautiful and positive. There was a hint of threat from both the electric eels and the snapping turtle, but apparently the turtle protected her from the eels and it became the doorway to the message from her unconscious as we will see in her reflection below.

I generally follow up on group members' experiences by returning it to them by e-mail a few days afterward. Understanding the meaning of an ecstatic experience generally does not come immediately or all at once. Recording the experience and then reading it again several days later can facilitate deeper understanding. The experiences are personally meaningful and it is important for individuals to find their own meaning, because it offers them greater self understanding. Though I had returned this experience to Sarah several days after our group session, offering her another chance to examine its meaning, I contacted her about it again two-and-a-half years later while writing this book. Rereading an experience several months or years later provides new perspectives, opens even more doors to meaning, and provides useful information, as you will see in many such examples throughout this book. Two-and-a-half years later, Sarah was able to elucidate what this underwater experience meant to her:

I remember thinking that the turning of women into men and men into women was how I see the sexes becoming less defined now. The sexes today are more combined and overlapped. I was raised with very strict definitions and separation of the sexes, much to my frustration. I was always told I could not do many of the things I wanted to do because I was a girl. I think bringing these more evolved beings into my childhood home is a way of expressing hope and letting go of those negative feelings.

It is my belief that as we go into the New Dawn, an age of ecological spirituality, that we are moving from the patriarchal world into a world of balance between the masculine gods and the feminine goddesses, a world where men are open to and can become one with their anima, and women with their animus. Sarah's experience well describes this shift.

One of my own fish experiences occurred while using the Lady of Thessaly (see appendix, figure A.10), an initiation posture. So often a posture takes me to where the artifact of the posture was found, as in this case:

10-7-10: *I am sitting on a rock somewhere along the coast of Greece, watching the water. I roll and lurch forward, stretching out my arms to dive into the water. With my arms forward I glide, swimming with the fish. I can breathe underwater. As I watch the fish around me I feel their freedom* *in turning, diving, and rising in the water, such freedom of motion. I see a shipwreck and glide through a window or hole in the wreckage and along the deck. I go beyond and head toward a cave and go in. Light is flowing into the cave from a hole in its ceiling. I continue on to a beach in the cave and glide up to the beach. I climb a ladder out of the cave and find myself in the bright sun. I lie there.*

I believe the conflict that I was dealing with at the time was that I was about to receive the results of my PSA test that would indicate if there were cancer cells present. The shipwreck, representing some personal conflict, was my unconscious fear that the test would find cancer, but in the trance experience it was something I simply swam through and not at all frightening. My fish guide showed a lack of fear, suggesting that I do likewise, that I would find some positive resolution regardless of the test results. Fish was telling me I could just breathe and go with the flow.

OUR KINSHIP WITH THE REPTILE WORLD

Reptiles and amphibians are highly adaptive due to their cold-blooded nature. Very often, spirit guides provide wisdom that helps us adapt to difficult situations, while still maintaining integrity. Snake is a particularly frequent visitor in dreams and altered states of reality. In many cultures snake is a harbinger of change. In Celtic mythology, snake brings the message of transformation as a result of the shedding of its skin. This shedding of the old self and emerging anew can represent the snake as a guide for healing, rebirth, and renewal. Understanding traditional symbolism of the snake can often help a person find meaning in their experience, but it is important to acknowledge one's own intuition and unique situation as standard symbolic interpretations can sometimes interfere, inhibit, or distract a person from finding the true meaning of an experience.

Violet used the Singing Shaman posture (see appendix, figure A.18) and had what seemed to be several separate experiences or scenes:

> ***6-30-08:*** *I stand and feel my face twitch, first around my left eye, which continues, then the right, which is distracting. After a bit I'm aware of a snake slithering out of my mouth. I am for a short while a male snake charmer of sorts from the Middle Ages, dressed in tunic and tights, with a snake in a basket. The snake and I walk along a European country road heading toward a village, where the snake will entertain. Then a new scene: I watch as the snake goes up a tree, and there it becomes my father's clarinet, and then a saxophone, that is, I observe the snake taking the shape and role of these instruments, but I have the sense of music being played rather than hearing it. Then the snake is an elephant's trunk. New scene: The snake wraps itself around a tree again and goes up into the sky. I climb up its now-extended body into the night sky. New scene: The snake is inside me. It somehow fits into my head. It crawls along my acoustic nerve from the brain and then to the ear and eats the tumor that resides there. Sometimes it seems to eat, and then it stops to blow what it eats out of my head in a gentle puff.*

Five and a half years later I e-mailed this experience back to Violet, asking her if she could elaborate on its meaning. She answered:

> *I'd completely forgotten this experience. I like the images! Snakes are really interesting creatures for me. I do not have the strong Christian history around snakes, that is, tempting Eve to eat the apple, or the fear that many people experience. I am more likely to think of snakes as having the amazing ability to move in a way that appears to be effortless and is in the process very sensual. When I was in an improvisational dance group, I loved the experience of moving across the floor laterally and vertically like a snake. At the same time, I'm aware that some snakes are dangerous, but that is rare here in central Pennsylvania, so mostly I love to see them.*
>
> *In the first scene, the snake becomes both snake and snake charmer.*

As I wrote in my notes, my father was a professional musician (clarinet and saxophone) and charming in that role, slender like a snake and able to entertain others. At home, though, his charm was mostly missing. I don't recall thinking about how the musician plays the clarinet, holding it like an elephant's trunk, which gives it so much more power. I think in a way this image let me step into the power of the musician that my father was, which I always envied but did not pursue myself.

Regarding the image of the snake going up a tree and then eating the acoustic neuroma: again, I do not recall those thoughts either, unfortunately, but now this image is like the physicians' caduceus (snake wrapped around the stick), and it is healing for me. It occurs to me that bringing these images back into my consciousness is as healing now as they were five years ago when I first experienced them. I have a strong sense that the snake eating and expelling the tumor would be good to return to, and as with the snake images, I find this one especially healing now.

The snake spirit guide is a healer for Violet.

I too have had many experiences with snakes. One of them involved using the Mayan Oracle (see appendix, figure A.12), a divination posture:

8-14-11: *Right away I thought of all my spirit animals, none specifically, wondering which one would come to me, but the snake was there from the beginning. I see three snakes: to the right in the green environment of home I see a water snake, copper in color, slithering through the grass. To the left I see a much larger snake in a desert landscape, slithering over the sand and rocks. In the middle I see the snake from an earlier experience who led me down into a temple/room below a tree in a park. I asked what the snake has to teach me, and what I sense is how the snake can feel all the vibrations of the Earth because of the way its body connects with the Earth. To become one with the Earth I need to focus on and feel deeply the vibrations of the Earth. Seeing the vibration of an aura that surrounds each life form has brought me closer to feeling the Earth's vibrations.*

OUR KINSHIP WITH THE INSECTS

Insect animal spirit guides point to a few key characteristics of insects. Seemingly unaware of their surroundings, some like the bee and ant go about their business, yet at the same time they have a strong sense of community. Some insects are individualistic and do not live in a community. Insects are highly adaptive to the environment and never let little things like natural disasters get in their way. Insects may be considered insignificant or even annoying to some people, but they are much more numerous than human beings and true survivors on this planet. These characteristics can be considered in seeking the meaning of our ecstatic experiences, but do not let these characteristics get in the way of your own personal connection to a particular insect and what it means to you.

One of my insect spirit guides, the bee, came into my experience while using the Calling the Spirits posture (see appendix, figure A.2):

> ***10-6-10:*** *A bee is caught in the in-and-out flow of air of my breath. It asks me to hold my breath for a moment so that it can escape and bring me the spirit I'm calling. I do, and it leaves only to soon return, followed by a bear, one of my power animals. The bear asks me to feed it by gathering some honey. This places me in a dilemma as a beekeeper who has successfully kept bears from my hives by using an electric fence. An electric fence does not stop a bear that is protected by its heavy coat of fur, but hanging bacon over the electrified wires does stop him. My coyote guide is standing to one side, laughing at my dilemma. Though the bear is not laughing, inside he is too. He puts me on the spot and I feel it. Though the bear is nurturing and strong, I still give him electric shocks instead of honey. He wants me to appreciate him.*

Even though I was protecting the honeybee from the bear, the message I got from the bee was that keeping the bear away from my beehives was putting myself above the network of the interdependence of nature. This network of interdependence always has its victims; that is part of the balance of nature. I protect the bee because I take its honey. The bee, bear, and coyote were laughing at my superiority complex, putting myself above being a victim.

THE GUIDING TREE

Trees metaphorically represent the axis of a person's life. The tree's health, strength, and rootedness may reflect the health, strength, spiritual height, and rootedness of the person. The Tree of Life represents the interconnectedness of all life on our Great Mother. Many cultures have a tree at the center of their community around which they dance and hold various celebrations—the Tree of Life, Tree of Knowledge, the World Tree, or the World's axis around which all life flows.

While using Tlazolteotl (see appendix, figure A.22), a cleansing and healing posture, Violet had the following experience:

> ***6-16-08:*** *I walk into the woods following the song of a wood thrush. The woods become more tropical the farther I walk, more dense with large leaves and very tall trees. The path narrows and widens alternately. At some point I climb up a tree to the top and look out. I am above the tree, higher than the other trees. I step out into the air with enormous strides and walk until I stop, where I climb down another tree. I find myself in another place; it's Hawai'i, where I lived in the late 1960s, and I'm on the beach. I wander around a few of my old haunts, especially where I lived the last year I was there. Then I am up in the top of another tree I've climbed, and again I step out into the air and walk until I stop. This time I'm in Japan. I do this for three more places, Bangkok, Kabul, and Paris. From there I wind up at my parents' house. I climb down the tree that was in the middle of the backyard. In each place, there is a sense of eased anxiety, of possible healing. I return to hearing the wood thrush.*

In response to my e-mail to Violet five-and-a-half years later, she elaborated on what this trance experience meant to her:

I do remember this one—the climbing up into the trees following the wood thrush song (my favorite bird call). Stepping off the tree in Hawai'i on my journey East to Japan, Bangkok, Kabul, Paris, and on to my parents' house is actually the reverse of what I did when I was twenty-one. I left my parents and went to Europe, where I lived in Paris. After a few months, I took off with a new friend to Japan via Kabul and Bangkok, among other places, but Kabul and Bangkok were two of the most memorable stops. I wound up in Hawai'i, where I lived for four years. I have a strong sense of the trees in the dream as being powerful friends, perhaps guides, leading me "home." Trees are important energies for me—I do relate to and even talk to them, mostly those I live with, and I have done this for years. I tend to see them as guardians, incredibly strong and powerful.

Though the following ecstatic experience was important in connecting me with the sacred directions, which I discuss in chapter 6, it was also important in helping me recognize the tree as both a spirit guide and the axis of life. My experience while using the Jivaro underworld posture (see appendix, figure A.8) follows:

3-27-11: *I slide into the opening at the base of a tree and the four men I have been with before are sitting on two roots that form a circle in the tree cave. We sit silently in the circle, then one stands and starts climbing up the root, while we follow. We are all wearing bearskins, and as we emerge in the Middle World we become bears and walk in a circle around the tree. I can feel myself swaying as I walk, like a bear. Then the leader climbs the tree and we all follow him into the Sky World, where we sit in a circle around the tree on branches. Then we come down again as men, and the four men walk away in the four directions, leaving me at the tree, my center of life. This is a ritual celebrating the three levels of the universe. The men are my spirit guides from the four directions, guides with the strength of a bear.*

In this defining experience I realized for the first time that the four men I have frequently visited are my spirit guides for the four cardinal directions, but also that the tree was the guide leading me to this discovery as we climbed it to each level—the underworld, the Middle World, and the Sky World, completing a tour of the seven directions—the axis of my life.

THE FLOWING RIVER

The river as a spirit guide reveals something about the flow of life, and as water, much of the same metaphoric or symbolic meanings apply. Many experiences of the river involve boats of various forms—again, spirit guides related to the flow of life. An early experience I had in following the river, or in this case a waterfall, occurred while using the Bahia (see appendix, figure A.1), a metamorphosis posture:

> ***6-16-08:*** *With my tongue hanging out in this posture I feel myself drooling. My tongue is a waterfall coming out of my mouth. I am inside of my mouth, straddling the river flowing out of the cave, which is my mouth. I can't stay straddled over the river, and so eventually I give up and go over the waterfall. On the way down I grab a hanging vine and swing over to the crotch of a tree in the jungle. I look back at the cave with the tongue hanging out, smooth with a crease in the center. I become curious about what's inside the cave so I swing back to it such that I fly far into it, the cave. The water is coming up from below, shooting up and out the mouth. I slide down the up-flowing water into a pool of water at the bottom, a quiet pool that is open to the outside behind the bottom of the waterfall. I swim out into the beautiful pool from behind the waterfall and climb up on a rock with my left knee. I lay there feeling younger and looking at all the rainbows in the mist of the waterfall.*

In examining this experience, what jumps out is that I did not want to go with the flow of the river and struggled against it before giving in. But then I swung out of it and watched it from a distance. From this distance I gained a new perspective and became curious about it, was ready to face it, so I swung back to its source in the cave. From there I was able to swim out from behind the waterfall to find a beautiful pool. By facing the flow with a sense of curiosity, I really had nothing to fear and could find beauty in this flow of life. I see this experience as reflecting the remnants of my early feelings of having little self-confidence. The river taught me that I have nothing to fear in ecstatic trance, in facing what arises from my unconscious. This belief frees me from my anxieties and lack of self-confidence.

THE GUIDING PATH OR ROAD

While the river is a guide that carries you along while you are not under your own control, taking you places you might not expect or even want to go, places that are likely related to unconscious beliefs and memories with their many emotions, the path, on the other hand, allows you to have the choice of whether to follow it. The next ecstatic experience uses both a path and a water slide. The water slide functions as a river. Gerry had this experience while using the Jama-Coaque Diviner posture (see page 43); the experience first took her up a mountain path, which then became a water slide:

> ***12-6-09:*** *I ask Jama-Coaque what he has to show me. He beckons me up a mountain path with many small cave openings along the path that are lit from inside. I ask him repeatedly what he has to show me. The sky is dark. The path turns into a water slide. Jama-Coaque and I have bright blue lights coming from our heads and feet. I ask what is in the caves. I can see people and activity. Jama-Coaque says not to pay attention to them but to follow him. We land in a beautiful clear turquoise pool of water at the end of the water slide. I'd been there before. Whales are swimming and singing. They want me to carry a message for them to a town meeting. I ask Jama-Coaque what he has to tell me. He answers, "Speak loudly with*

a soft voice." We leave the town meeting to go to skateboard ramps, where I became Woody the Woodpecker, laughing wildly and loudly.

Four-plus years later, I e-mailed Gerry to ask her if she had any deeper understanding of the meaning of this experience:

As Jama-Coaque beckons me up a mountain path with many small lit caves along the side, I repeatedly ask him what he has to show me. The darkness does not allow me to see clearly, both outside and within myself, and I wonder what opportunities for knowledge and experience I am missing. Jama-Coaque tells me to pay no attention, and I wonder if he is the trickster who is tricking me. Blue light emanating from our hands and feet indicate spiritual strength or possibly a razzle-dazzle distraction, but this show of enlightenment makes me want to follow him. I believe he wants the best for me, and that I do not need to visit the lit caves. Believing this, the water slide takes us to the beautiful turquoise pool and the singing whales. The power, size, and extensive journeys of the whales across the seas and their tenderness toward one another continually amaze me. Their songs awe me, uplift me, and take me to another dimension. I've seen whales in both the Atlantic and Pacific, and these experiences make me laugh and cry with joy.

Yet, as the path turns into a water slide and skateboard, I feel that I am not on firm footing, and I relate this to my discomfort in public speaking at town meetings, loud speech and uncontrolled loud laughter, behaviors that are atypical for me in my daily life. Yet when I become Woody the Woodpecker, laughing wildly and loudly, it seems that I revert to a state of nature without my normal restraint, and I am happy. I have a fondness for woodpeckers. One of the most beautiful depictions of a woodpecker I've ever seen was an ancient Mexican ceremonial cape of red, white, and black. I enjoy watching them at our suet and sunflower feeders outside the kitchen window. Yet I have not resonated or related to Woody until now.

Most of my life I have been the happiest in nature, in my garden and in the woods, and at the beach and the ocean. I have a strong commitment to support environmental causes, and I wish I had a "louder voice" in service of the environment and wild creatures. This ecstatic experience seems to be saying that I must be willing to be uncomfortable, to try new things, and to trust in order to connect with the rich spiritual worlds symbolized by the whales in the clear and beautiful pool.

It should be noted that besides the path and the water slide, Jama-Coaque was also a spirit guide in this journey, as the figures who provide us with the postures often become our spirit guides too. It was her decision to follow Jama-Coaque up the mountain path, and she was in control although she did not know where the waterslide would take her. But where she landed was beautiful.

While using the Tennessee Man (see appendix, figure A.21), a divination posture, a path became my guide, leading me from the winds of a tornado to a beautiful, quiet spiritual place:

6-9-08: *First, the sound of the drumming places me in a tornado, flying around in a circle, a circle that moves through plowed farm fields. The wind is carrying nothing else but me, and the ride is actually quite comfortable. The wind deposits me on a rock on top of a mound. Two deer come up to me, one behind me and one to my right, and nudge me with their noses. They lead me forward to my left. The direction they nudge me on is onto a pathway. The path leads me across fields, to a rock and into a box canyon. There is a narrow crack in the left wall of the canyon. We go through the crack, and on the other side there is a stream with lush green bushes and cottonwoods along it. It is beautiful and very peaceful. I walk along the stream and come to a small, attractive one-room cabin, where I sit on the porch in a comfortable chair, watching the stream. The deer were leading me to this spiritual place.*

This experience was full of spirit guides. The path led from a noisy and chaotic world—my world, in which I live with a relative degree of comfort. The deer and path showed me the way through a crack into a spiritual world of quietness and peace. On this journey, besides the path serving as a guide, the two deer and the wind were also spirit guides, making three guides of Mother Earth who encouraged me to move in a particular direction. From these guides I learned that even though I function adequately in a world of noise and chaos, it is important for me to learn to relish the spiritual world of quietness and peace.

THE POSTURE ITSELF AND THE WIND AS GUIDES

The wind as a guide is somewhat like the river in that it takes you somewhere not under your own control. When moving fast, the wind suggests something fast moving in your life such as your mind racing. A quiet breeze suggests something refreshing and slow moving. A hurricane might suggest something chaotic is going on.

While using the Jama-Coaque Metamorphosis posture (see appendix, figure A.7), Sarah first called on Jama-Coaque to come to her through the ages:

> ***12-6-09:*** *I feel a wind in my face. It is cold and grows stronger. My hair is blowing straight back. I realize I am standing on a subway platform. A train stops with the door right in front of me, and when it opens this tiny dwarf of a man walks out and I ask, "Are you Jama-Coaque?" He does not answer but takes my hand like a child would and we go up the stairs and we're in NYC. I ask him if he can heal my toe that was distracting me, and he says, "Forget your toe, it doesn't need healing." I ask him why I had called for him, and he says, "Joni needs us." I then feel the cold, strong wind blowing in my face again, and we are in the back of a pickup truck on the Long Island Expressway, on our way to Joni's in Mastic Beach. When we get there, Jama-Coaque disappears inside of me, up through my hand that he was holding, into my arm and into the trunk of my body. I come into Joni's house through the walls and hear her crying in her bedroom. The door is closed. I open it and go in. The room is all dried up, wrinkled and shrunken, and there are no colors. Joni looks at me and I say, "I brought*

someone to help with your grief." Then Jama-Coaque oozes out of my hand in the form of a half man, half peacock, all glittery and colorful, with a huge tail. He goes to Joni and puts his arms around her, and squeezes his colors into her.

The wind as a spirit guide led Sarah to New York, to then hear the message from Jama-Coaque that a good friend was in need. The wind again blows through her hair as she was taken along the expressway in the back of a truck. The wind and Jama-Coaque, as Sarah's spirit guides, knew the way.

MY SPIRIT GUIDE, THE MOUSE

My experiences with the mouse as a spirit guide have been many. And while many of the experiences I am about to relate could be included in other chapters of this book that deal with shape-shifting and the sacred directions, I decided to include this sequence of mouse experiences here, at the conclusion of this chapter, to illustrate not only the power of this small but mighty spirit guide, but in general how spirit guides often persistently return, again and again, to lead you to some new discovery about yourself. Notably, mice love to burrow. Our ancient ancestors observed their affinity for burrowing in the ground and likened this to mice being one with Mother Earth. This ground-loving behavior was also seen as a connection to the underworlds, which makes the mouse a kind of mediator between the worlds.

In *The Power of Ecstatic Trace,* I told part of the story of my journey with my mouse spirit guide. Here this story continues, though it is likely still not complete. Only a few years ago did I make the connection between when this story began and a very vivid yet bizarre nighttime dream. Though I don't remember the exact year I had the dream, I believe that it was sometime in the 1960s. It started, "I was walking down a dirt road that ran along a culvert or drainage ditch. I noticed a hole in the opposite wall of this culvert, and from somewhere I grabbed a high-pressure fire hose and began shooting water into the hole . . ."

The vividness of that dream and the way it remained with me for these fifty-some years told me that it was important, though for many years I could make no sense of its meaning. Then in June 1990 I had a series of experiences that again began with a dream that woke me one morning with a feeling of anxiousness. This part of the story is told in greater detail in the appendix of *The Power of Ecstatic Trance;* the gist of it is that it was then that I realized that since childhood I have felt inadequate to my peers, whether because of my dyslexia or because of being repeatedly chosen last for the kickball team in elementary school. I struggled hard, and in junior high school, when I first heard about the sequence of college degrees, of earning first a bachelor's degree, then a master's, and finally a doctor's degree, I set my sights on getting my doctorate. Yet in attaining my goal of a doctorate in psychology, I felt I had to work much harder than others to get there. Only in 1990, twenty years after receiving my doctorate, upon waking that one morning from that anxious dream, did I realize that I had succeeded, and that I had created a successful private practice in psychology. It was time for me to let go of my feelings of inadequacy. For the next ten days I repeatedly told myself, "I am successful and as good as anyone else," even though I knew that you cannot change by willpower alone. For change to occur, it has to register in the unconscious.

As those ten days came to an end, I was on my way to a conference of the American Association for the Study of Mental Imagery, in Washington, D.C. At this conference I was to present a paper on dealing with power struggles, but the day before I presented my paper I went to an experiential workshop led by Florida internal medicine physician and pastor at Christian Healing Ministries Rene Pelleya-Kouri. Rene had us imagine an animal coming out of each of our chakras. These experiences were powerful to me and led me to internalizing unconsciously that I am okay and as good as anyone. From my first chakra emerged a buffalo, on which I was riding comfortably, nestling in the fur of its back. Though I forget which chakra, my next experience was of sitting in an alleyway against the wall of a brick building with a trash can across from me. Between me and the trash can was a mouse asking my permission to rummage in the trash. Then the next experience was of me standing at the edge of a meadow, where a deer was contently eating the grass. I finally found myself in the driveway of a suburban house, washing a car. A squirrel was on a tree in the parkway next to the driveway, beckoning me to climb the tree with it. It just so happened that Rene came to my workshop the next day, and at the end we discussed these images, but they made little sense to me with regard to the meaning of each chakra.

The next day while driving home to Pennsylvania, I experienced a flash of insight. Over the years I have enjoyed reading American Indian literature, and some of my favorites are of the Medicine Wheel. When I examined these four experiences from my understanding of the Medicine Wheel, they made great sense. Though each of the four directions has different meanings for different tribes, my favorite is from the book *Seven Arrows*. The buffalo and deer are animals of the North, the spiritual direction of wisdom and knowledge, the direction of our elders. In the North I find contentment and am satisfied with my spirituality. The mouse and the squirrel are animals of the South, the direction of childhood, growth, and playfulness. The mouse is that inadequate part of me who wants to rummage in the garbage, while the squirrel is that part of me who seeks to climb the Tree of Life, to rise to a higher level, above those feelings of inadequacy. It was as a result of these four experiences that I found great relief from my anxiety and long-held feelings of inadequacy. I had a friend illustrate these experiences with paintings on two rawhide circular shields, my North and South medicine shields.

But the story does not end here. Since 2010 I have gone each year to summer workshops on ecstatic trance at the Cuyamungue Institute in New Mexico. In my experiences at these workshops in 2010 and 2011, the mouse returned with great, unforgettable energy. First, Ki Salmen, a certified instructor of ecstatic trance from Germany, offered a workshop at the institute on soul retrieval. While using the Olmec Prince (see page 50), I found myself at both my power spots, across from the dormitory at Cuyamungue and near the road leading down into an arroyo on the institute's property:

> ***8-28-10:*** *I am a mouse looking up at me. I can feel my nose twitching as I am squeaking, "Don't ignore me, don't ignore me," over and over. "Don't ignore me as you did for so many years." Then I/we notice a coyote to our right. He first puts his face right against mine, then turns his back to me, repeating this sequence of gestures over and over. I understand this as the coyote making fun of me and again telling me, "Don't take yourself so seriously."*

The following January while at home, I had a related shape-shifting experience using the Olmec Prince posture:

> ***1-9-11:*** *I'm a mouse out next to our garden, and I run across the snow to a hole under the mulch. As I go through the tunnel in the mulch, horse manure, and hay, I come to a den with a mother mouse and babies. I am running back and forth, bringing seeds and other bits of food from the compost pile. Under the mulch there is grain in the manure and seeds from the hay. It is a very warm and cozy place, with more than enough to eat. Then I become the rat of my South medicine shield, rummaging in the garbage can in the alley. Again the food and warmth is plentiful, with food scraps coming from a nearby restaurant. I feel good, experiencing the more positive side of the rat than the disgust I felt years ago. I let go of the inadequate side of myself. The rat and mouse, or as I sometimes call it, "the mousey rat," has a side that is responsible, reliable, and curious, in search of sustainability—traits that I value. These conventional traits tell me again that I need to value this mousey rat.*

In Summer of 2011, again at the institute, I was participating in a mask trance dance workshop with my mentor, Belinda Gore, and the mouse would not leave me alone. In this workshop we were first to identify a spirit guide power animal for which we were to make a costume. The series of trance experiences of the group over the next three days came together the final morning, with the experiences providing us with the choreography for a dance in which each of us wore our costume. My spirit guide was again the bear, a powerful guide that has led me from my earliest experiences with ecstatic trance. The first part of the costume involved making a papier-mâché bear mask, which I left on an outside table for the night to dry. The next morning at breakfast, one of the other guys in the group told me to go look at my mask. A mouse had chewed off its left ear, which I proceeded to repair. Then later that day while in the kiva, we used a healing posture, Tlazolteotl (see appendix, figure A.22), and as before when I used this posture I found myself in a small adobe chapel:

> ***7-21-11:*** *I enter a small adobe chapel with a low rectangular altar, and behind the altar on a cushion or low stool sits a priestess of Tlazolteotl. Each previous time as I entered the chapel I had a gift for her. This time as I stand before her I become incredibly hot and melt like wax into a puddle on the floor. Behind her to her left is a low door that on previous occasions I entered, where I met spirits dancing around me with various messages. This time the spirits come out of the South and become mice running all over me playfully, sitting on my shoulders and scampering up and down my melted body. I become the bear who now embraces or gives freedom to the mice to run over him/me. I/the bear honors them.*

The bear from the West opens himself to valuing the playful, childlike spirits of the South. It brings unity to the West and South. With this experience I decided to paint mice all over my bear costume. The next morning we used the Tennessee Man (see appendix, figure A.21), and I found myself walking slowly uphill to the South, and the mice were again scampering over me:

7-22-11: *One at a time I took a mouse in my right hand and honored it by offering it to the seven directions, and then let it go as I offered it to Mother Earth.*

At the end of this experience, while I sat in the North in the kiva, we each told our experience to the group. The circular wall of the kiva is covered with masks from previous mask trance dances, and above my head among other masks was a bear mask. While I was telling my experience to the group, a person across from me let out a gasp and pointed to the bear mask above my head: a mouse popped out from behind the mask and then scampered across the kiva and out the door!

I am not sure when it was, but some time during these past few years I had an insight about my dream of shooting high-pressured water into the hole on the side of the culvert. The hole belonged to a mouse, and at that time I was not ready to face the mouse, so instead I tormented it with the high-pressured spray of water.

The mouse is not only the inadequate side of me; it is also the humble side that is playful and does not take life as seriously as I have been taking it in my drive to prove that I can overcome my dyslexia by writing. The mouse has also led me to give up my superiority to dominate the Earth so that I can find oneness with it.

While again in the kiva at Cuyamungue, sitting in the North, I used an initiation posture, Shawabty (see appendix, figure A.17), and had the following mouse experience:

9-7-11: *I move to the center facing South, and at first mice come and crawl over me, then they become children, pulling my hair, biting and pinching me, twisting my arms—but it does not hurt. I am strong and let the mice or children do it to me, though I wonder if I shouldn't stop them so as to teach them that it is not right to hurt anyone. Then I turn to face the West and watch a lot of people fighting with one another. I feel somewhat removed from the fight, but I have the thought that they are fighting over whether* *or not global warming is real or not, a political fight in Washington now that has been a concern to me. Then they become wolves and big cats tearing at one another. I am drumming for this journey, and as I turn the drum the sound changes. It becomes deeper, and I feel very tall and strong and now more distant from those who are fighting. I then recall what I was reading that afternoon, Frank Waters'* Masked Gods, *reading about the Pueblos' sense of freedom, their noncompetitiveness, and their simplicity in life while living communally, with no concern about poverty.*

These experiences with the mouse have evolved to the point that I now feel somewhat parental to them in my concern for them. I see my concern for the health of the Earth as another dimension of caring for the mice, for which the wolves and big cats show no concern. The message I get from this is that it is important for me to distance myself from the fight going on in Washington, over which I have no control, and instead to value the communal sharing we experience in our valley as a living example of how things can be different.

5
SHAPE-SHIFTING

Sometimes, when a bird cries out,
Or the wind sweeps through a tree,
Or a dog howls in a far-off farm,
I hold still and listen a long time.

My world turns and goes back to the place
Where, a thousand forgotten years ago,
The bird and the blowing wind
Were like me, and were my brothers.

My soul turns into a tree,
And an animal, and a cloud bank.
Then changed and odd it comes home
And asks me questions. What should I reply?

Hermann Hesse

The idea of shape-shifting is part of the mythology and folklore of many cultures and is a key feature of shamanism. In my book *Baldr's Magic,* the gods and goddesses of the North used shape-shifting quite often for seeking answers to their questions and problems among other uses. The goddess Freyja became a falcon, and the trickster god Loki shifted to become many different beings, including a salmon, a falcon, a fly, a horse, an old lady, and a seal. Shape shifting may have many purposes—for Freyja, to rescue or to protect someone, for the trickster Loki, to trick others or to protect himself from the rage that his tricks produce.

In ecstatic trance journeying, we gain access to the intuitive and sensory abilities of an animal or a living feature of the Earth, such as a river, mud, or a tree, by using any of the shape-shifting postures. We see through the eyes of the animal; we become the river, the wind, the tree. As in trance journeys with spirit guides, when we go on a shape-shifting journey we gain teachings. For me personally there is a slight difference between learning from spirit guides and learning from shape-shifting, in that with shape-shifting I see through the eyes of the being, I take on the characteristics of what I shift into, and I learn through direct sensory and experiential input, whereas my spirit guides tend to take on human traits and serve as guides through whom there is a lesson for me to learn so that I can discover something about myself that I might not have known.

Naturally, I am often asked by those who don't know about ecstatic trance if in these shape-shifting experiences I actually physically shift forms and take on the form of another being, as described in a lot of shamanic literature. In my ecstatic trance experience the shift in shape generally *feels* very real to me, but if you were to observe me while I was in trance you would not see an actual physical change of my form. But then again, who knows what could happen as my shape-shifting experiences deepen and time-free transparency becomes the norm? Certainly many indigenous cultures relate how shamans actually shift their forms into those of animals and other beings. Yet even if my form does not change outwardly, my shape-shifting experiences are no less important to me in leading me to see through the eyes of the other and in this way, becoming a part of Mother Earth's multitudinous form.

BECOMING FOUR LEGGED

A particular animal is neither good nor bad but part of nature, part of us. Animals often symbolize our shadow sides, that is, the part of ourselves we are unaware of due to our mental tendencies of suppressing some personal trait we do not want to face. As a result, we often are unaware of our deeper levels of feeling and perception, pushing those out of the light of awareness, into the shadows of our deep unconscious. Frequently the value of shape-shifting in ecstatic trance is that we gain a perspective on ourselves that we otherwise are lacking; very often this perspective—as we shall see in the following examples—sheds light on our intrinsic connection with the Earth and all life forms.

Sarah was in my original ecstatic trance group that met weekly; she was especially adept at shape-shifting. On this occasion she used the Olmec Prince, a metamorphosis posture (see page 50):

> ***2-11-08:*** *I feel I have four legs and am very large. I get extremely hot and want water. I start walking on all fours and feel wonderful muscles I have never felt before. I also feel my huge tail behind me. I am walking through tall yellow grass and come to a river. Moving feels so good, and when I lean over the water to drink I see two huge yellow eyes and big teeth. I am a lioness! I look down at my feet and I see huge paws. As I am drinking, a crocodile surfaces and snaps at one of my paws, and I roar at it. Then it lunges at me and hangs on to my shoulder. I claw the crocodile's underbelly with my claws and bite deep into its neck. It lets loose and I back off. I start to notice all the things I can smell—the blood, the mud, the water, the insects, zebras, snakes, humans, human food, rain. It starts to get cool and dark and the stars come out. I lay down and am perfectly contented lying all alone in the grass with a cool wind moving over me, bringing with it all sorts of odors to contemplate.*

The lioness, the queen of the jungle, generally feels no threat from other animals. She can even brush off a crocodile. Sarah felt this power, and with it could relax and be perfectly content with the protection of all her senses. She feared nothing. The lioness within her comes alive and she no longer lets others like her father define who she is. She stands up for who she is in her own right.

During this same group session in which we used the Olmec Prince metamorphosis posture, I became a different kind of powerful animal:

> ***2-11-08:*** *I feel myself moving forward and swaying from side to side as I walk. This swaying feeling was as I had felt before as a bear, and at first I think I am a bear, but then I realize I am upright as I sway. I'm a gorilla. I am walking on two legs through the jungle, brushing aside the flora with my arms. I come to a clearing where I see a chimp jumping up and down screaming at me, but I ignore him. I am looking for something or maybe just looking at everything. Then I come to another gorilla. We sit together and preen each other. I hear a noise, and we both swing up into a tree where we are safe and just sit there eating some sort of fruit from the tree.*

In Sarah's experience as a lioness she felt safe and contented, even sitting alone. I, as a gorilla, found this same kind of contentment in being with another gorilla in what felt like a safer place, up in a tree. I had a greater need to react to things in a more protective manner. The gorilla who is able to protect himself teaches me a new sense of self-confidence as he comes alive within me.

BECOMING WINGED

Again, different species of birds exhibit different aspects, qualities, and personalities. For example, American Indians view the crow as intelligent, curious, and mischievous. Some ancient beliefs held that crows were the tricksters who shape-shifted in order to cause trouble. The eagle's sharp vision gives him (or her) the ability to see great distances. Though for the Celts, the raven could be a symbol of vision, power, and healing, since challenging events often clear the way for new life and new opportunities. In ancient Egyptian, Celtic, and Hindu cultures the symbolic meaning of the owl revolved around guardianship of the underworlds and a protection of the dead. Owl is sometimes considered a seer and ruler of the night. Different cultures and individuals have their own history and thoughts about what the birds mean to them and it is this personal meaning that is most significant.

Sarah recorded another one of her shape-shifting experiences as follows:

> ***1-9-11:*** *I see a stage with a heavy curtain slightly swaying to the beat of the rattle. Next, a huge white owl appears in front of the curtain. She has emerald green faceted eyes. I am drawn into looking closely into them and notice that within each facet is a house with a hearth and a fire in the hearth. All the houses in the different facets are different, and I am trying to decide which one to enter. Some are log cabins. Some are Victorian houses. When the owl abruptly turns and runs behind the curtain, the curtain becomes translucent, and I can see the owl behind it. Then the owl comes through the curtain and the curtain dissolves into the owl. She wraps her wings around me and squeezes me into her body, and now I become the owl. I am flying. It is night, and everything looks strangely orange. I land near the top of a tree, a very tall pine, where I see there is a nest, and I step into that nest. The wind starts blowing, and my shoulders start growing and puffing up. I feel my feathers being blown in the wind. I feel safe, warm, and secure. I realize the freedom of existing without the influence of time. The snow owl may have been Nicole Kidman—stately, beautiful, classy, white, and elegant.*

Three years later I contacted Sarah by e-mail to ask for her thoughts about this experience. She reported that for her

> *. . . the story was about the owl appearing stately, beautiful, classy, white, and elegant. The owl's eyes reflected all manner of habitats, and when*

I became the owl it was all about the safety, warmth, and security of its nest. So to me the experience of becoming the owl was saying that it is rewarding and important to be safe, warm, and secure in life, and not as important to be stately, beautiful, classy, white, and elegant, which was at first what impressed me about this experience.

While using the Jama-Coaque Metamorphosis posture (see appendix, figure A.7), I experienced taking the forms of two different birds:

4-3-13: *I wander through our yard/garden as I did earlier this morning and notice how everything is budding, the cottonwood and the currants. I go out to the blueberries, then back to the currants, which are leafed out and with mature berries. I sit on the ground under the plants with a big bowl, picking the currants that are hanging above me, and I eat some. My hands are dark purple from the currants. I then become an eagle and fly with purpose toward my nest across the canyon. I then am back under the currant bushes, this time as a smaller berry-eating bird, eating, flitting around, and then up into the trees next to the garden, where I perch and rest. I let myself identify with the bird with intent. I have a sense of being more mindless and less directed than the eagle, just flitting with instinct. Life is simple with the large supply of berries and seeds. I just* am, *not worrying about the future. There is a rebirth in the Spring and into the Summer, but what is that rebirth to me? It's just letting go, and just being without worry.*

This trance journey involved experiencing the consciousness of these two very different birds, one flying with a sense of purpose and direction, the other mindlessly flitting around, living in the moment, eating berries. In my own human consciousness, if I find something curious it stays with me, I hold it in my mind with intent focus. The bird gets its sense of direction from instinct. The human being's consciousness is much more complex in the sense that it involves choice and decision making, and it is this higher level of consciousness that allows us to think that has led us in the direction of destroying the Earth. I think the message of this experience is to let go of so much thinking and just experience the interconnectedness of the world around me instinctively, being in the moment.

BECOMING A FINNED BEING

In some myths and legends the fish was recognized as having a connection to the earliest forms of life that emerged from the primordial sea. The power of gargantuan fish monsters also added mystery and power to fish symbolism, as found in the iconic novel by Herman Melville, *Moby-Dick,* or in the biblical tale of Jonah, who was swallowed by a fish, or the fish that survived the Great Flood. In Christian iconography, the fish came to represent a follower of Christ, a symbol derived from the early Christians who used it to recognize one another to avoid the oppressive actions of the Romans.

The fish is a common animal motif in our trance journey group's experiences and each individuals experience with the fish is different. When we used the Mayan Fish Woman (see appendix, figure A.11), a metamorphosis posture, Violet had this experience:

> **7-17-09:** *I settle into the pose and almost immediately my mouth is a fountain, with water shooting out of it. Somehow the water from the fountain takes me with it as it arcs high and then falls into a pool. I experience myself as being both in the water and in the original pose. I swim as a fish into an underwater cave with some light coming into it. Periodically I am back in my land body, and then I go out again in the arching stream of water. I go swirling underwater in the pool, sometimes in human form and part of a chain of people. At some point I am diving back into my mouth/fountain, and then it varies—sometimes I am the waterspout and other times I am diving back into my mouth/fountain whether as me and/or as the fish. Later in the underwater cave, I find*

other fish. I have no sense of gender as I swim with them, but I'm aware that I find other women fish who return with me to the land, so that eventually there are five or six of us lined up in that posture. Now I am both a fish/woman and a heron/bird of some sort, with a long beak. The beak goes down my mouth, all the way to my stomach. The bird pulls out negative things from my guts with its beak. I feel cleansed. I then return to the water as in the fish/woman experience. I'm aware of no thoughts, but I am aware I'm feeling hot in my upper body. It pulsates lightly, perhaps to my heartbeat, which persists until the drumming ends.

Five years after she had this experience, in response to an e-mail I sent her asking her to elaborate, she wrote this:

The Mayan Fish Woman was one of my favorite postures for many reasons, one of which is I love to swim like a dolphin in the water, diving slowly into the deep, my hands at my sides as a fish might do rather than outstretched in front of me. I then surface and dive again, over and over. As I recall, I had the sense of the fish-as-me experience as showing me how to flow smoothly through emotional periods, with water representing my emotions. The heron, as a symbol of the air, is my mind helping me remove negative emotions. Of course, this was before I was aware of how the mind generates negative emotions. But now I know the mind can also help with negativity. The underwater cave, as I recall, felt like my deep inner recesses, like the parts of me that I keep very safe and/or a place of hidden emotions. I do not remember the sense of no gender. Thank you for this—I loved it then, and I love it now!

Violet is quite experienced in working with her dreams, and those who have such a skill are almost always very adept at interpreting and understanding their ecstatic experiences.

BECOMING ONE WITH THE REPTILES

Reptiles, particularly snakes, are among the most ancient and widespread symbols of the unconscious. The serpent is often associated with the Tree of Life such as in the Genesis story. Similarly, in Nordic mythology the serpent gnaws on the roots of the Tree of Life. In India the snake, kundalini, is the basis of a whole philosophical system. Snakes can be revered or feared; an individual's personal history with snakes can effect the meaning of the snake in a person's ecstatic experience.

While using the Jivaro, an underworld posture (see appendix, figure A.8), Sarah became a tree lizard:

> ***5-27-08:*** *I feel my fingers growing long, rubbery, flat at the end, and sticky. I am in the jungle, swinging around in the trees with my sticky fingers. I eat leaves and they are truly amazingly tasty, like several types of herbs mixed together. I encounter a three-toed sloth. She is white, and I stick to her with my fingers. She is larger than me, and I start working my sticky fingers through her thick hair, finding insects and eating them with an amazingly long, catlike sticky tongue. Every time the cicadas trill, a tiny creature in a bubble appears and hovers in front of my face. I am pretty sure they are space aliens and I shouldn't eat them, but I always shoot out my tongue, grab, and swallow them. I am enjoying the smells of the sloth and the breeze, and the noises from the frogs and insects. Sometimes they sound like human voices whispering and singing.*

I e-mailed Sarah six years later to ask her if she had any more insights about this experience. She replied that it was just a wonderful out-of-body experience, which is often the chief value of shape-shifting—that is, being able to escape the bonds of human form to have a pure experience of the other. She felt her senses change: "In being the tree lizard, I was most astounded by just reacting and not worrying about eating space aliens. If it moved a certain way, I was going to swallow it, and that was that." Her experience of the nature of the consciousness of the tree frog is similar to my aforementioned 4-3-13 experience of being a flitting bird in that both experiences examine the nature of the consciousness of these animals as being different from human consciousness.

I had a series of related snake experiences. Using Chalchihuitlique (see appendix, figure A.4), a metamorphosis posture, I became a snake in a place where I would often see one as a child, while climbing on large boulders in the mountains of California. I title this experience "Slowness":

> ***8-29-11:*** *I am lying on a large boulder where I saw snakes as a child, and where I often sat or just lay in the Sun. I can feel the warmth of the rock against my belly and I feel myself warming up in the Sun. I feel life coming into me from the Sun. Then I go back a short time to where I am lying in a den, a crevasse between the rocks, with four or five young snakes. I am the adult/mother. I move very slowly in the cool morning and crawl toward the warmth. I am then back again, soaking up the warmth coming from the Sun and coming alive. The scene then changes. I am in Pennsylvania in our blueberry patch. I am moving with energy among our blueberries toward the hole of a chipmunk, and I crawl into the hole. I find trapped at the end of the tunnel a chipmunk. I open my mouth and take it in whole. I then start to back out but feel very sleepy. I feel the drumstick slipping out of my hand, as I am the drummer for this session. It is a very slow-moving experience. I feel myself moving very slowly to the warmth of the Sun and then into the chipmunk hole.*

In this journey, as with the next one, I experienced one reptilian trait: that of moving slowly in the cold and more quickly when it is warm, with appreciation for the warmth. This brought me to an awareness of my appreciation of the Sun and the energy it gives me. I feel a real connection to the Sun, with the importance it had in my life as a snake and as a the boy I was all those many years ago. It is this early awareness that I believe put me on the track to appreciating in such a basic way our interdependence with nature.

A couple of months later, while using an initiation posture, Sekhmet (see appendix, figure A.16), I experienced a renewal or rebirth with the shedding of my skin:

> ***10-9-11:*** *I am again the mother snake on the same boulder as before, feeling the warmth of the Sun. I have the thought of my young ones in the rock crevasse and my need to get them something to eat, but my vision is foggy and I realize my skin is lifting from around my head and eyes. I need something to help me peel my skin back. There is a branch from a tree, a California live oak, that stands next to the rock, with a branch resting on the rock. I feel my way to it, find it, and gently rub my head against it to pull the skin back. I fear pushing too fast because I could injure myself. I get the skin pulled back. I can see again and can now move faster against the branch, pulling off the rest of my skin. I can see how shiny my new black skin/scales are. I then go to a chipmunk hole and get another chipmunk, swallow it partially, and take it back to my little ones where I can regurgitate it so they can eat.*

The rock—or maybe I should call it a boulder—was a place where I spent a lot of time as a child during the summers at our family's cabin in the San Bernardino Mountains of Southern California. I would go to these boulders early in the morning, when it was cool and damp, to catch a lizard that I would keep in a box until it would eventually get out and run off. I sometimes saw snakes, generally garter snakes, in and among these boulders on which I would climb. I learned a lot about the reptiles and often found snakeskins hanging on the branches of the shrubby California live oaks, especially those that grew among these boulders. I am not sure when I first became aware of how their vision would become impaired when shedding their skin; maybe my dad told me, or maybe I learned this at school. But I do recall seeing a snake with milky white eyes, wondering, and then learning that as the skin pulled away from their eyes just before shedding their eyes appeared milky white. I realized that they were easier to catch when shedding, but also more ornery.

Both these journeys provided me with the experience of being a snake, experiences that did not or were not to teach me something about myself, but reminded me of who I was even at a young age and deepened my sense of interdependence with nature.

BECOMING AN INSECT

American Indians believe that nature talks to us, that Great Spirit sends messages to us through natural things like rainbows, hurricanes, and, of course, animals. In the latter category are bugs. Ladybugs, dragonflies, bees, butterflies—these are considered "friendly" by we humans, whereas scorpions, cockroaches, and other insects inspire fear and loathing, although they too, like the more friendly insects, carry important information about ourselves if we are willing to be open to recognizing their message.

I have read or have heard somewhere that if we humans succeed in destroying the Earth, what will most likely survive on what remnants of the Earth we leave behind will be the insects, especially *la cucaracha,* the cockroach, the survivor of the Mexican wars. Insects generally are not greatly appreciated, though many are very beneficial in gardens and as food in some cultures (in Mexico grasshoppers are a valued source of protein and a delicacy). Insects are truly something worthy of becoming one with. The following are a couple of experiences of shape-shifting to become different insects.

While using the Olmec Prince (see page 50), Sarah became a honeybee:

> ***4-7-08:*** *I am surrounded by the color pink and a wonderful fragrance. I soon realize I am in a huge peony. Then I am having fun going from the underside of a petal out to the sunny surface. I figure I am a honeybee. I want to take flight and land on things. It is like I have magnets on my feet and hands. Whatever I want to land on feels like metal. I land on all sorts of things and realize I am in my own backyard. I have an impulse to*

go back to the peony, yet I am inebriated by the experience of climbing through the petals and the perfume of the flowers. When I come to the center of the flower and rub pollen all over myself, it is as if I have been gilded. Suddenly I have an urge to dance, so I fly back to the hive and start to wiggle my butt and everyone watches with interest. Then we all take off together and fly back to my backyard and dive into the peonies and pack our legs with pollen.

What I noted about Sarah's experience was the seeming impulsiveness of her actions as a bee, acting instinctually, without a sense of conscious awareness, yet her consciousness is very alive with regard to the overall sensuality of the experience—the Sun on the surface of the flower, being inebriated by the perfume, being "gilded" by the pollen—as well as her awareness of the other bees watching. Though we generally do not attribute such consciousness to life outside of human life, I believe there is a sense of consciousness throughout existence, though not in the same way we humans experience consciousness, by putting thoughts into words. Possibly the bee's sense of consciousness exists in terms of feelings and sensations of the warmth of the sun and the smell of the perfume of the flowers. According to De Quincey, our distant ancestors who ran with the animals, "lived *in* the world, responded to its *felt* and subtle messages, and understood its deeper meanings. We not only communed with nature, we were in open communication with all its great variety of sounds and rhythms. In short, we understood and spoke the *language* of nature."[1] Our consciousness was felt, not put into words. What a pleasant and beautiful experience of being a honeybee.

Six years after Sarah's experience shifting into the form of a honeybee I asked her to recall this journey from a greater perspective to see if she had additional insights. It just so happens this bee experience took place about two months before her aforementioned tree-frog experience. For these two experiences she reported that they were "mostly just wonderful out-of-body experiences. I was just having a great time experiencing an alternate reality, so different from my everyday life. I actually felt my senses change with this and the tree frog experience. It is like taking mind-altering drugs." The idea of the sheer pleasure in simply becoming the other is often expressed by shape-shifters. This experience became especially meaningful to Sarah because of her love of flowers, and because gardening is her art as seen in both her garden and in her paintings.

BECOMING A TREE

Becoming one with the very wide range of flora and experiencing the role of each in the interdependence of all that is of the Earth is important, but of all the flora the tree seems to be what we relate to the most in our shape-shifting journeys in ecstatic trance. The Tree of Life, as I noted in the previous chapter, alludes to the interconnection of all life on our planet as well as being a metaphor for human spiritual evolution in all the various esoteric traditions. To shape-shift into a magnificent tree, experiencing its roots, trunk, and foliage, is a truly magnificent experience of interconnection that informs our human potential.

Maria used the Olmec Prince (see page 50) and became a tree:

> ***9-17-07:*** *I begin feeling like my hips and legs are a massive tree trunk. I travel up myself as a tree and at the very top are fernlike leaves dancing in the breeze. I leave the tree and continue upward. When I look down I see a man with a bow and arrow, ready to shoot, but not at me. I continue up high, into a very clear, very blue sky, really high up, looking down on green treetops, all gently dancing. Then I see a clearing and a woman dancing gently in time with the treetops and the breeze. I watch awhile and focus on the drumming. The trees begin to chant in time with each beat of the drum, "What-will-you-do?" Over and over and over. . . . Then high up there in the sky, an enormous word appears in front of me, the word* SHIFT, *but vertically with the S at the top. I then feel lines from me connecting to Earth multiply rapidly, and eventually they draw me back down. I end up sitting in the grass with a handful of warm dirt in my cupped hands.*

Sometime later, Maria recalled "slowly gliding up the tree, very rooted, like a snake." "What will you do?" followed by the gigantic word *SHIFT* was obvious to her as a prediction of her move to North Carolina, which led to a significant change in her life: finding the one she was to marry. The World Tree and the serpent represent the connection between the spiritual and earthly worlds, a connection that provides us with the wisdom of the spiritual word, wisdom that is transmitted through the serpent. The wisdom gained by Maria was the precognitive knowledge that she was about to experience a gigantic shift.

On a number of occasions I too have become a tree. One of my first such experiences occurred while using the Hallstatt Warrior posture (see page 53):

> ***3-6-09:*** *I go to the spot on the hill behind our house where I have gone before. There I stand and see the activity of the chipmunks under the log in front of me. This time I feel a bear standing behind me to my left and a deer behind me to my right. I stand there feeling cold and the breeze/wind is blowing from the Southwest. I am a tree, or I am inside a tree. I become the tree barren of leaves and listen to the other trees around me, a low, deep sound, not distinct, but still joyful, the sound of trees swaying. As they sway, the movement causes the sap, the sweet sap that nurtured the tree, to flow, and the flowing of the sap feels warming and brings me slowly back to life from my winter dormancy.*

This experience occurred after Faye, another participant on our weekly group who you will hear more about in chapter 9, told me about how she listens to and can hear what trees have to say. I took her comment as something of a challenge, because I wanted to hear the trees too. In this experience I felt the flow of sap in the tree as it swayed, a feeling of being one with the tree, showing me how to listen to the trees and the importance of doing so.

BECOMING ONE WITH THE ELEMENTS OF THE EARTH

In our ecstatic trance experiences we may find ourselves shape-shifting into any number of water features of the Earth. Water is a common and potent metaphor in ecstatic trance journeying as well as other forms of trance. Of the four primary elements, it is the only flowing element, symbolizing among other things purity, healing, cleansing, life, and rebirth. It is a very feminine, life-giving element without which nothing would live. The flowing nature of water can also represent the emotions, particularly happiness as the element of pure and simple fulfillment of one of our most basic needs.

Maria used a healing posture, the Chiltan Spirits (see appendix, figure A.5), and had the following experience:

> ***7-1-10:*** *First thing I notice is how deeply I am breathing. My breath is so deep and rhythmic that it begins to resemble ocean waves. I become water, the waves. I just sit with that awhile, then I become a heronlike bird that shoots out of the ocean so very abruptly. I fly and fly over water. I then fly over a wetland with tall reeds. I become a woman with very long hair walking through the reeds. In all forms, as the water, the bird, and the woman, there is nothing else around me. It is lonely. As the woman, I come to a muddy bank, and I am presented a choice. I can stay a woman or let the mud take me and return me to Earth. I choose to stay a woman, and I set out to find more people. The path snakes and zigzags and becomes dryer and dryer. The drumming then ends.*

Three and a half years later, I e-mailed Maria to ask her what she remembered of this experience. She replied, "It was very interesting to reread this three years later. I have a vague memory of the experience and remember that there was no fear attached to it. The choice and the prospect of returning to Earth as mud was comforting, not scary." The rhythmic breathing as the ebb and flow of waves on the shore was a healing experience of breathing in healing energy for Maria. The healing likely had something to do with loneliness, but "with the new energy of a bird flying, as I am entering a new relationship, renewing or completing my role as a woman, with its ups and downs as a zig-zagging experience." She continued:

> *I wonder now if choosing to remain the woman had something to do with reincarnation. Another interpretation could be that I chose to continue in the human path of challenges and lessons in order to evolve and grow. It does not appear, in hindsight, to have been the easiest or most comforting choice. I seem to be looking for company, to fill a lonely feeling. I was at a point in my life where I was absolutely on a quest to fill my loneliness. I had just moved in with someone and had dramatically changed my personal life for the better. That change could be represented by the heron taking flight abruptly.*

Rivers, ocean waves, waterfalls—all are symbols of flowing water, metaphors of surrender and yielding. The metaphor of the path or the road, as noted in the previous chapter, is a symbol that gives us direction. We might also shape-shift into a mountain, valley, a rock, and, as we saw above in Maria's experience, mud. As I watched the fire burning in our woodstove this morning, watching it spread through the wood with an energy of seeking to live, it occurred to me that I have never experienced becoming the element of fire, however, I have collected a number of experiences from others who have experienced being consumed by fire, and in this way, becoming one with this sacred element. Burning in fire is generally recognized as the beginning of a death-rebirth experience.

A DREAMER'S ECSTATIC EXPERIENCES

In chapter 3, I recounted my first experience leading others in ecstatic trance, when in 2007 I led a group of attendees at the International

Association for the Study of Dreams (IASD) conference in a morning session of ecstatic trance journeying. A tradition of IASD is the "Morning Dream Groups," where participants can share and explore the meaning of their nighttime dreams. In 2007 we added an ecstatic trance session.

Nighttime dreams are generally spontaneous, while hypnotic and ecstatic trance sessions are induced by a ritual, yet all three altered-states of consciousness experiences are similar in the metaphoric nature of the content and its connection to a person's unconscious mind and the collective or universal consciousness. When a person discovers the power of their dream experience through recording and working with their dreams, they recognize the same power that comes from the hypnotic and ecstatic trance experience. Thus in this first group experience I had with ecstatic trance, the people in the group were already very open to the power of ecstatic trance because of their experiences working with dreams. Linda Mastrangelo, who is now on the board of IASD, was part of this very first group using ecstatic trance, and her experiences, which follow here, demonstrate a connection with the intent of each of the postures we used.

In that initial 2007 session at the IASD conference we used two different postures for each of the three mornings of the conference for a total of six postures. On the first morning we began with a metamorphosis or shape-shifting posture, the Olmec Prince (see page 50) What is important to note here is that none of the participants were told the intent of this or any other posture prior to using it. The following is an extract from Linda's account of her experience, in which she first shape-shifted into a buffalo, then a dog:

> ***7-1-07:*** *I immediately like this position. It feels familiarly ancient, like I am looking into the world. I see purple and feel very grounded as the sacred buffalo. I see a clearing with large stones. I then feel like I'm guarding something, like the dogs of the ancient Greek myth, guarding the entrance that goes deep into the Earth . . .*

Linda's reference to the dogs of Greek mythology is likely the three-headed dog Cerberus, who guards the river Styx that must be crossed to enter the underworld. Being the guard dog, Linda was guarding others from entering the underworld, that is, the unconscious mind. I do not know if Linda was facing some personal issue while going into this ecstatic trance, but the journey did start out by taking her to the entrance to the underworld before she, as a guard dog, blocked herself from going further. This could be interpreted psychologically as her showing some resistance to exploring her unconscious mind in search of an answer to something.

Some years later, in 2013, Linda presented a paper at the IASD conference, which that year was held in Virginia Beach, Virginia. The paper was titled "Animal Dreams: A Wakeup Call from Forgotten Eden," and was written with very much the same goal as this book—to express the urgent need to become one with the Earth. In this case, Linda's paper focused on nighttime dreams rather than ecstatic posture experiences, but what she said in her paper is equally applicable to the ecstatic posture experience, and reflects her deep concern for our loss of connection to the Earth:

> *As I wander into the folds of night, wading through the tide pools of the imagination and across the border into dreamtime, I encounter something extraordinary, perhaps a strange humming vibrating in the water; or a dark shadow behind the narrow legs of a tree; or maybe even a bright green flash dancing in the clouds above me. These visions are the animals of my dreams, not of waking time. But why do they visit me? Is it an initiation into remembering the forgotten wisdom of some ancient time? Are they my ancestors dressed in fur, gills, or feathers, to offer me medicine and show me my soul purpose? Or perhaps they are harbingers here to warn humanity of a planet in danger, crying to be honored and taken seriously?*[2]

Linda believes that the animals visit us in our "willingness to face our fears, be astounded by Nature, and more importantly be humbled by her in terms of understanding ourselves and our place in the universe."[3] She then offers her thoughts on what her earlier ecstatic trance journey as a buffalo meant to her: we have lost our "reverence for the Earth and therefore a crucial part of ourselves. This is so brutally encapsulated in the slaughter of the buffalo a hundred years ago by the white man."[4] For those of us who seek to become one with the Earth, the buffalo is sacred animal and a vivid example of where we went wrong in our history.

Back to the first morning of ecstatic trance experiences with the group at the dream conference July 1, 2007:

Following the first posture, the Olmec Prince, the next posture we used was the Tennessee Man (see appendix, figure A.21) a divination posture, though again, neither Linda nor anyone else knew the intent of this posture. Her divination experience was quite simply recorded: "I experienced the Sun. It was big."

The purpose of a divination posture is to provide an answer to a question or to learn about the future. A divination experience is generally metaphoric, and often its meaning is not well-understood at first. For this reason I generally suggest that the person keep the experience in mind and explore the associations that connect them with the experience, and in so doing, its meaning will eventually become clear. Associations I might make with the Sun are *warmth, energy, brightness,* and *enlightenment.* Brian Swimme points out that the stars, of which our Sun is one, are also our ancestors in that the same elements that resulted from the formation of stars compose our human bodies.[5] He says, "Rituals ground us and our experiences so we can create new holistic models to solve issues like global warming, disease and wiping out hunger."[6] We use a valuable ritual taught by Felicitas Goodman to initiate ecstatic trance—the ritual of calling the spirits from each of the seven directions, directions that lead us through life, from birth to death, through the seasons, from Spring through Winter, and through the cycle of each day, from sunrise to the sunset, and then through the darkness of night. It is just this ritual, which we will explore in greater detail in the next chapter, that also brings us to a sense of oneness with the Earth.

The next day, the third posture we used in the dream group was the Bear Spirit (see page 41). Linda's experience follows:

> ***7-2-07:*** *I find myself struggling with keeping the posture, holding it becomes a distraction for me. It is challenging to be in the moment, but then I finally let go and allow my body to move naturally. The word/feeling* wind *comes to mind, like I am a tree moving in the wind, and so my body begins to move in the rhythm of the drum even with my feet firmly planted. This feels good and natural, and I am more relaxed and in the present. The experience is very spiritual, like I am in a forest. I want to keep going. I experience lots of side-to-side hip and torso movement.*

In the Bear Spirit posture a person typically experiences a healing energy flowing into their body, in Linda's case the energy of the wind, which caused her body to move. Then, true to her embracing the concept of waking up to the forgotten Eden, she then experienced herself shape-shifting into a tree, with her roots deeply embedded in the Earth and her canopy swaying in wind. Though we often experience healing postures personally in terms of our emotions or some physical condition, it is equally true that we can experience a healing of the Earth, as in Linda's experience.

Next we used another healing posture, the Chiltan Spirits (see appendix, figure A.5), again with the participants blind as to its intent. Linda's experience was right on target in recognizing the intent of this posture:

> ***7-2-07:*** *I felt tremendous heat in my stomach, like a small Sun in my belly, radiating outward and inward. I see images of seeds, impressions of fertility, growth energy, or warmth moving upward.*

Again, in following the energy of this sequence of six postures, it becomes apparent in this fourth posture that healing is of the Earth, though that does not exclude other possibilities, for these experiences may be felt at many different levels.

The fifth posture, used on the third morning was the underworld posture Jivaro (see appendix, figure A.8), and once again Linda was right on target with the posture's intent:

> ***7-3-07:*** *I have images and impressions of traveling by water, images of rivers, death, and of going to the underworld. This experience leads to a transformation from feminine youth to the crone while traveling the rivers in the underworld . . .*

This was not only an underworld experience, it was also a death-rebirth transformational experience in which Linda became the wise crone.

The last posture we used during the conference, one of my favorites, was the Hallstatt Warrior (see page 53). A realm-of-the-dead posture, it often leads a person to a rebirth experience. Linda's commentary reflects her sense of curling like a snail or a snake:

> ***7-3-07:*** *My body stretches upward. My hand feels like I am being pulled back, and then my whole body wants to follow. It is as though it wants to bend backward but I have to stop myself because I could keep going all the way back if I let it. My experience of curling suggests that perhaps I should lie down in this position. I am not sure if my curling is a snail or a snake coiling . . .*

In Linda's "Animal Dreams" paper she says the snake is one of her important spirit guides, a guide to the sacred feminine. This experience is related to her previous experience of becoming the crone. In "Animal Dreams" she offers a related nighttime dream:

> *I am with two women and we're all in a circle wearing hats. My sister comes in with an open turquoise and yellow Easter basket that contains a*

bright yellow snake with emerald green eyes that she bought at a grocery store. I ask her why would she buy such a thing, and she says, "It was the thing to do." The snake is poisonous and locks eyes with me. I am terrified of this snake but know that there is healing power in this and so try to face my fear.[7]

In breaking free of our culture's long-promulgated notion that the snake is a symbol of evil, as described in the Book of Genesis, we can open ourselves up to rediscovering the sacred meaning of the snake: that its essence is that of sacred healing and becoming whole. Linda identifies with the snake as a spirit guide because it is

ancient and wise, with its power held closely to the Great Mother. The serpent's steady gaze reminds me of being fully in the present moment and grounded in the earth: It is a symbol of consciousness and mindfulness of the Now . . . of creative power and the Sacred Feminine. . . . In rediscovering her in all her essence we may begin to heal and become whole again.[8]

As discussed in chapter 8, now more than ever we need elders and teachers like Linda who will help bring others to oneness with the Earth. Linda's transformation into the wise crone that she is signifies that she is just such a needed person.

I e-mailed Linda in March 2014 to show her what I had written about her experiences for this book. She told me,

One of the more interesting trajectories in my life was my going back to school to earn my Marriage Family Therapy license. One of the internships was working at hospice as a grief counselor. During this time I sat with people who have shared many "visitation dreams" of their loved ones who had passed, and they shared profound stories. This time period was also very intense in terms of my dream journeying, where I frequently "traveled" to different dimensions, including the underworld, with medicine elders who gave me many teachings. Many of these journeys brought me new knowledge, including ancestral knowledge. I also continued to have many profound snake dreams that have been very powerful and connected to these new understandings for both the seen/unseen worlds.

Shape-shifting, whether into an animal, a plant, or some other feature or element of the Earth, can bring great personal insights and direction for the individual, particularly when the experience is examined in light of the metaphorical content that is expressed in the transformation. As well, just experiencing shifting shapes to become the other is a tremendous teaching in time-free transparency. But one of the greatest values of this kind of journeying is the unprecedented ability to merge and become one with our Great Mother, the Earth, and thereby dramatically shift our culturally engrained me-focused human perspective.

6
THE SEVEN DIRECTIONS

O our Father, the Sky, hear us
and make us strong.
O our Mother the Earth, hear us
and give us support.
O Spirit of the East,
send us your Wisdom.
O Spirit of the South,
may we tread your path of life.
O Spirit of the West,
may we always be ready for the long journey.
O Spirit of the North, purify us
with your cleansing winds.

SIOUX PRAYER

As described in chapter 3, Felicitas Goodman developed a five-part ritual for entering into a state of ecstatic trance. An important element of inducing trance is calling the spirits of each of the sacred directions: East, South, West, and North, as well as Above and Below—the heavens and the Earth—and from the Center, or unity, of these directions. Calling the spirits of the directions is part of defining the sacred space in which the ritual will be enacted. I have found this calling of the spirits to be a very powerful moment. In calling the spirits we recognize that they are living entities that bring us their wisdom as we invite them to join us.

But what is this wisdom? This wisdom is of the Earth; it is Earth-centered. In calling the spirits we recognize the cycle of life, not just our own personal life cycle from birth to death, but also the daily life cycle of all beings and the Earth herself, from sunrise to sunrise, from season to season. East is the sunrise, the birth of a new day, the birth of Spring, and the birth of new life of the Earth's flora and fauna. Spring is the time we plant our gardens and the time that animals bring forth new life. South is the midday, the warmth of Summer, and the growth of our children, the animals, and our gardens. West is the sunset, the autumn, the time of harvest, the time of maturity of our gardens and the time of the productive years of our life. North is nighttime, Winter, the time of our elder years, the time of dormancy and hibernation in preparation for the new birth of Spring. It is the nighttime in preparation for the new day.

The spirits that come to us from these directions are Earth spirits, and we cannot leave out the heavens, with the Sun that provides us with light and warmth, the four seasons, the cycle of night and day, he Moon that gives balance and stability to the movements of the Earth and the ocean tides, and the stars that provide us with the elements of periodic table of which we are composed. Neither can we leave out Mother Earth, who sustains us and everything on, within, and above her. Everything of the Earth is interrelated and interdependent, and it is this interdependence that brings us to the seventh direction, the Center, or unity of all. It is the recognition of this framework of life that is found in many of our ecstatic experiences.*

*The concept of the seven sacred directions comes from the Medicine Wheel. Historically, the Medicine Wheel has been associated with North American Indians, as a sacred site—whether physical or metaphorical. Because of its universality, other cultures, including nonindigenous people, have used it, sometimes as a tool for personal development, and sometimes as a sacred concept around which we can arouse our feelings of interdependence. This latter purpose expresses our intent in using the Medicine Wheel concepts of the sacred directions.

I recently returned from a trip to Peru where twice a day I used the ritual of calling the spirits to induce ecstatic trance. I quickly realized that in the Southern Hemisphere the spirits need to be called in the reverse direction, counter-clockwise. There the warmth of Summer is in the North toward the equator, and the cold of winter is in the South toward the Antarctic.

THE CIRCLE: FOUR CARDINAL DIRECTIONS

The meaning of the circle defined by the four cardinal directions is so profound and far-reaching that I can only touch on a few of its metaphors. As a human being looking out into the sky you see circles: the Sun, the Moon, the pinpoint dots in the sky that are other planets and stars. The grandeur of the cosmos is spoken in the language of the circle—of the repeated cycle of the four seasons; of the four directions; of the cycle of the sunrise, the middle of day, the sunset, and night. The circle communicates the concept of all-inclusive cosmic unity.

Lisa's experience while using the Jama-Coaque Diviner posture (see page 43) brought her to a shaman wearing an eagle headdress, who then took her to the four cardinal directions:

> **10-13-11:** *I am seated at a Council Fire under a big sky. I am aware of the community around me and some people are packing up. I am particularly aware of tents being folded. Everyone is getting into a line. A very tall male with an eagle head on top of his head comes over and picks me up. He sets me down in each of the four directions. He first points me West, then North, then East, and finally South. Now he lays me on the ground and gives me a spin like the needle on a game board. I spin round and round first very fast but eventually slowing until I stop in the position between North and East. The aligned community begins to file off in the direction, with the line becoming longer and straight and even straighter as I observe. When the journey was over and I recorded this, I wondered what it would*

mean to travel North-East. I heard an answer: between an ending and a new beginning, between death and rebirth.

I e-mailed Lisa about eighteen months later, asking her what this experience meant to her, and she responded: "Thanks Nick. After rereading my experiences, the only thing I might say about it is that since that time I do feel that my life has gotten into 'greater alignment.' I have opened a nonprofit center, the Center for Mindful Living, in Chattanooga, and have moved my practice over to it. Everything is more cohesive." This experience predicted her expanded role in community service, which has brought about a rebirth.

The next two experiences that I had are connected. They brought me to the four cardinal directions. These experiences began with the Sami Warrior, a Lower World posture (see appendix, figure A.15):

6-5-11: *I go into a cave with a lot of cave paintings of animals. The petroglyphs are of my spirit animals. The bear, eagle, mouse, squirrel, coyote, buffalo, wood thrush, and deer are all on the walls. I sit in the middle of the cave room and light a fire. The animals on the walls begin to vibrate, and then they come off the walls and sit in a circle with me, sitting around the fire. One by one they motion with their heads for me to leave. As I get up and move toward the exit, I find a snake lying across the path who tells me, "You can do it." I leave and start walking South, across the desert, just walking and walking.*

The message I received from that snake was that I have the personal knowledge and ability to continue on this journey of becoming one with the world on my own, that I now know the path to walk. Walking South indicates the direction of my youth, the time of growth.

My next journey, a continuation of the experience just described, occurred while using the Nupe Mallam, a divination posture (see appendix, figure A.13):

6-12-11: *I am walking in the desert—just walking. I ask the diviner, "Where am I going?" I am walking South along a dry riverbed. I come to a ravine to the left, the East, and start up the ravine. At the top is Heart Rock, a rock formation above the Cuyamungue Institute. I stop there and meditate on the rock before I continue over the top to the ravine that takes me down to the kiva at the institute. I go into the kiva and stand in the middle of the room. I start calling the spirits of the four directions. I see babies or infants in the East. Then I call the spirits of the South and see a group of young children playing, dancing in a circle. I think I am one of the babies and then one of the children. Then I call the spirits of the West and see a group of adults, including myself and my wife and many friends, including three others of our monthly ecstatic postures group. When I call the spirits of the North, I am by myself as an elder. I see in the West my five children, and in the South my ten grandchildren playing. I feel I need to do something for my grandchildren, but I am not sure what. I walk across the kiva to the South and sit there among them.*

Finding myself in the North indicates that I am an elder and need to do something with or for my grandchildren, something related to helping them become one with the Earth. As I sit among them I realize that I need to tell them stories about the Earth, which I have done on several occasions since then.

Another one of my Medicine Wheel experiences occurred while using a metamorphosis posture, the Cernunnos (see appendix, figure A.3):

6-2-13: *I am in a grove of oak trees with Cernnunos sitting in front of me. My four spirit guides are again with me. Each is wearing a truck stop T-shirt, one with an eagle printed on it, another with a squirrel, one with a bear, and the other with an antlered deer. They are dancing in a circle around me, then the eagle leads us off to the East, where we become eagles and soar into the heavens. Returning, the dance continues, with the squirrel leading us off to the South, and we climb the Tree of Life. Again* *returning to the dance, the bear leads us off to the West, where we go into a dark cave in the underworld. Returning to the dance I then follow the deer and become Cernnunos. I proclaim that something is missing to complete this dance and ask the spirit guides to return and continue the dance for the second animal of each direction. First, in the East, is the wood thrush, who teaches me to hear. Then, in the South, is the mouse, in its timidity and innocence. In the West is the coyote, who continues to challenge me. And to the North is the buffalo in all its contentment. After I follow each guide in his direction and become this animal I feel a totality and unity as I return to sit as the Cernnunos in the North, feeling that I have completed what I need to complete, and that I am prepared to die.*

We will next explore experiences that focus on one or more of the directions, to delve into the messages offered by each direction.

EAST: THE SUNRISE, SPRING, AND THE BEGINNING OF LIFE

East is the direction of birth or rebirth. We enter the sacred circle in the East, the direction of renewal and the place of birth, rebirth, and the New Dawn. The East is the place of all new beginnings, the place of infancy. A person returns to the East many times in the course of her life's journey. Each time there will be things to learn at a new level. East is the direction of illumination, of the rising sun. It is the direction where light comes into the world. It is the ability to see clearly through complex situations. In the East we learn to be totally in the here and now, the infant's consciousness. This is one of the most important gifts of the East.

While using the Tennessee Man, a divination posture (see appendix, figure A.21), Violet had the following experience:

6-9-08: *I stand on a small star/asteroid in the cosmos and do a backflip, and then another and another, bouncing from star to star in an infinite* *blackness lighted by points of light. I somehow approach the East while using the posture and enter into the ground/dirt, where I become a snake. I undulate through the Earth. At one point I am on the Richmond Bridge that goes from San Raphael, in Marin County, California, to Richmond, in the East Bay. I follow the undulations of that bridge. There are no cars. Then I surface up through the ground into bright sunlight in a meadow. That is the last thing I remember, though there was more.*

Though we do not know specifically what kind of rebirth Violet needs, the Tennessee Man seems to be predicting her rebirth, a rebirth in the East, where as a snake she rises from the ground, from the Earth into a sunlit meadow. As we saw from one of Violet's earlier experiences, the snake represents healing and brought her to a greater understanding of her father. She also expressed appreciation for the snake in the effortless manner in which it moved.

I e-mailed Violet about this experience almost six years later and she responded with the following thoughts on this Tennessee Man divination experience:

Based on the emotions of the experience, I recall loving doing backflips from star to star. I remember the fearless joy and exuberance of it all. There was no sense of risk (about not landing on solid ground), and I reveled (or at least that's my memory) in the sensuousness of the snake in the earth. I think my thoughts of undulating bridges related to my experience with bridges in the Bay Area of California. When I moved to California in the late 1990s, and then continued to visit frequently until about 2009 or 2010, I had a low level but always present anxiety about an earthquake happening whenever I was on a bridge, and I was frequently on one, either the Bay Bridge from San Francisco to Oakland, the Golden Gate from San Francisco to Marin County, or the Richmond Bridge from Marin County to Berkeley/the East Bay. My anxiety was largely a continuing reaction to images of cars hanging off the Bay Bridge after the 1989 earthquake. I had a friend on sabbatical in California at the time, and I went to see her soon after that earthquake, so the earthquake possibility was very real in my head. To quell my anxiety, for each bridge I created a relationship with it that would distract me. The story also offered protection, i.e., my special relationship with the bridge (even if it was a fantasy one) would protect me if an earthquake would happen or the bridge would simply not experience the earthquake. The story/fantasy with the lower level of the Richmond Bridge was particularly powerful and emerged from my response to the bridge structure. This is hard to describe, but it is a two-lane bridge not far above the water beneath it. The lower level seems to rise and descend in undulating waves, and it descended enough that you could not see the end of the bridge (where it met the land) in either direction for maybe a quarter of a mile. Because of the visual sense (a false one) that the bridge was narrowing at the end, for me it took on the persona of a snake, of which I was a part, or perhaps I was in its belly as it was carrying me across the water. I loved this feeling, though the few friends I told it to thought it ridiculous. But I loved being on that bridge with/in a snake. I followed the same process with the other two bridges, but neither of them had the same sensuous power and connection for me. I still smile from all the memories—the Tennessee Man experience and my bridge memories.

For Violet, the snake was her protector. Doing back-flips from star to star carried her to the East, the direction of birth or rebirth where she is reborn as the snake, reborn without her fear of driving over the undulating bridge.

While using the Olmec Prince (see page 50), I had my own shape-shifting experience of the East:

12-29-08: *I quickly feel myself swaying back and forth, again, as a bear. Walking slowly I come to a tree and follow a line of ants up the tree, licking and eating them as I climb. I get to the hole from which the ants are crawling and sit there and relax awhile before I climb down. I come to a pool of water to take a drink. I then wander on slowly toward the East, going nowhere in particular. I feel relaxed, and as a bear, in no great hurry.*

The bear is a spirit guide and a nurturer and healer, and wandering East is toward birth and the beginning of new life. The year 2008 was early in my experiences with ecstatic trance, and I think this experience suggests the birth of a new level of comfort with and understanding of the postures. For a person like me who is often in a hurry to accomplish things, the comfort of being in no great hurry is a healing experience.

While using the Olmec Prince metamorphosis posture (see page 50), Jeremy had an experience of the East:

> ***12-2-10:*** *While doing the opening prayer and looking to the East, a dark bird figure appears almost like a vulture or something of that sort. Upon sitting down and going into the meditation, purple spiral lights repeatedly appear. I begin to feel myself sway. After the purple lights leave I see myself as a lively little tiger cub, smiling, playing, and wrestling with other cubs as many others look on. While I am in my cheerful youth of loving and laughing, I notice the dark bird figure flying way above, blocking the light of the Sun. As I grow older the bird falls out of the sky, and I become king of the jungle.*

Initially, Jeremy had related becoming king of the jungle to his recent promotion while working as a civilian for the Department of Defense. Then five years later, in response to my e-mail query to him to elucidate his experience, Jeremy told me he felt that this journey was very directly related to his life: "Growing up I was the All-American Boy, and when I got to college I went on a wild journey of drugs, dealing, and crime. I ended up in federal prison. Time in prison was a time of self-examination. Since getting out in 2005 I secured a job with the government, but I also started a multidimensional nonprofit company to do community building, mentor kids, raise money for kids with cancer, and start different programs in schools."*

---

*A result of Jeremy's personal journey to mentor and help children can be found on his website, Planet Lovejoy (www.planetlovejoy.net).

East represents the beginning of life, or for Jeremy, the beginning of a new day. East is also the farsighted side of the person as represented by the birds. His looking East well describes Jeremy's time of introspection and far-sighted self-examination while in prison, a time that brought him to the new day in his life once he was released. The bird, a vulture, the eater of carrion and the scavenger that cleans up the mess, was there to clean up the mess in his life. When the mess was cleaned up, the vulture fell from the skin to leave the reborn Jeremy as the king of the jungle, with the strength to create a beautiful new social program for the community. The vulture and the king of the jungle well represent the Lakota version of the Medicine Wheel, with the tiger being an animal of the West, the time of maturity and the harvest.

While using the Shawabty (see appendix, figure A.17), a posture for initiation or death and rebirth, I had the following experience:

> ***4-28-13:*** *I am in the Egyptian desert near what I think is Luxor, where the tall figures carved in stone overlook the Nile. I am sitting in front of those figures looking East over the river. I see a barge going upstream carrying a wrapped figure of someone who has died. My spirit leaves me through the top of my head and goes down to the barge, where it sits on the wrapped figure. The barge eventually enters a cave and I get off. I lie on a clay beach along the water as the barge continues to go deeper into the cave. I roll around on the clay, which clings to me, giving me form. Anubis, the dog-headed god, licks my face and gives me life. I am in my form but am different—a spirit being. I wonder what this means.*

Eight months after this experience I was still wondering about its meaning. My thoughts were that by becoming a spirit being along with the other spirits of the Earth, I found greater knowledge of being one with the Earth. East, being the direction of birth/rebirth, is where I found my new birth as a spirit being.

SOUTH: MIDDAY, THE SUMMER, TIME OF GROWTH OF YOUTH AND GARDENS

The South is youth, strength, vigor, a time of growing, and preparations for the fall and winter. The South is physicality. This can encompass diet, exercise, and the senses. In the Summer, the season of the South, we are outside, experiencing nature, spending time with family and friends, taking advantage of longer days, experiencing the heat of the summer sun—fire is the element that rules the South.

Using the Calling the Spirits posture (see appendix, figure A.2), an Olmec figure from Mexico, I had the following experience that took me South:

> ***12-22-11:*** *I am in a South American jungle clearing at night near a fire and the spirits come floating out of the jungle from the four directions, approach me, and then float off to the South, back and forth, beckoning me to follow. I follow them to the South and they form two parallel lines that I walk between. I come to a Mayan Pyramid and there the path between the spirits ends. I am at or next to the bottom step and don't know what I am supposed to do. Then I remember that this is the beginning of the last year of the Mayan calendar and that I have a whole year to climb it.*

After this Calling the Spirits experience and my curiosity about where this experience was going to take me, I decided to return to it on the following day. During the period of quieting my mind I saw myself standing on the North side of the pyramid facing it by looking to the South. I could feel power coming from the pyramid and raised my left hand toward the top of the pyramid; thus I chose to stand in the Venus of Galgenberg posture (see page 47) for journeying into the Sky World. I had the following experience:

> ***12-23-11:*** *I am pulled from the South to the top of the pyramid, feeling great warmth coming from it. Then as I stand on top of the pyramid energy from the heavens continues to pull me upward. I feel myself pulled as if by a magnet toward the Moon, which is on the Southern horizon. As I reach the Moon and turn to look back toward the Earth I continue to feel a great pull of energy between the two—the pull of the Moon, which causes the tides of the ocean to rise and fall, and also the pull of the Earth with its gravity—so the two are in a constant state of equilibrium, steadying each other in their movement. I then picture the image of Ix Chel, the Mayan Goddess, holding the Moon steadily in her outstretched arm.*

With my aim of becoming one with the Earth, I have been thinking of that which is of the Earth, but this experience helped me realize that what is beyond the Earth is also part of the interdependency of everything, of Gaia and of the Cosmos. The pull of the Moon on the Earth is important in this interdependency of maintaining the Earth and life upon it. This journey of first using the Calling the Spirits posture then the Venus of Galgenberg posture brought this understanding of interdependency to my heart. This experience originated in the South, the place and time of growth and learning through experience, of learning more of the interdependence of everything

WEST: AUTUMN, THE SUNSET, THE HARVEST, AND PRODUCTIVE YEARS

The West is the middle age of life, our productive years. West is Autumn, the time of the harvest. It is the place where we learn to accept ourselves by listening to and learning from our emotions. We go within in the West and learn to use our intuition and pay attention to inner guidance and knowing. According to Hyemeyohsts Storm, author of several books including *Seven Arrows* and *Song of the Heyoehkah,* the bear, an omniverous animal, is an animal of the West.

She can be gentle but fierce when situations demand it of her. She goes into the den to become still. At the same time she is nurturing and the healer.

While using the Chiltan Spirit (see appendix, figure A.5), a healing posture, Violet had the following experience of the West:

> ***6-9-08:*** *A long time passes with no images. Then I see a young woman for whom we have expressed concern because of her diagnosis of lupus. She is riding a white bear, which is ambling thru a meadow. The Sun is shining and it is playful. At one point she and the bear are lying on the ground and the bear cuddles her. Later I observe them flying. It is as if they have come a long distance, as if from the West to the Southeast—Florida. They are headed for the beach. The image is of a coastal city in Florida, white, pastel, with a few tall buildings, a lot of pastel buildings, a white, sandy beach, and then the blue water. In my mind they are headed for play and Disney World. The image of them is reminiscent of people traveling in a hot air balloon, that is, they seem to float toward their destination, the beach, which I see—also Disney World, which I don't see. It is very light out and it all seems very upbeat, playful.*

Violet's experience began in the West, the direction of adulthood, with all of its responsibility, and it included the bear, the healer, an animal totem of the West, symbolizing strength and nurturance. This young woman with lupus was just entering the adult time of her life. Violet's experience suggested that the young woman needed to not be in such a great hurry to become an adult, but instead to return to the South and the East, where she could be playful and receive nurturance from the Great Mother and the bear spirit. Listening to the spirits of the directions provides what needs to be known for healing, especially for an illness like lupus, a systemic autoimmune disease in which the body's immune system mistakenly attacks healthy tissue.

Upon my e-mail query about this experience six years later, Violet sent me the following response:

Upon reflection, for me the white bear is/was a form of medicine healing. The bear is white, as in doctors' and nurses' uniforms, at least in the old days. White bears living in cold and bleak polar regions suggest that she can find nurturing even in the barrenness of disease. Also this big fuzzy creature engaged her through a loving, playful care form of healing, encouraging her to take her diagnosis seriously while also being able to be light, as in the white and pastel buildings. Eventually she will arrive at the warmth (emotional and physical) of Southeast Florida and Disney World.

While using the Tlazolteotl (see appendix, figure A.22) for cleansing and healing, Ron had the following experience of the West:

2-3-09: *I am running across the prairie in South Dakota, just South of where my great-grandparents homesteaded. I'm running really fast, and I'm in the midst of a huge herd of buffalo. I just keep running with the buffalo, who seem very friendly. They don't crowd me at all and I'm able to touch them and feel their power. I seem to get my power from them and I don't feel tired at all. We are running West, toward the sunset.*

At the time of his journey Ron had cancer, and he died a few months later. I believe that his running toward the sunset, feeling powerful and not tired, suggested that Ron had accepted and did not fear his coming death, especially in running with the buffalo, an antlered animal of the North that represents our elder years and the time for death in preparation for a new birth at Spring. In venerating the four or six directions, tribes differ in which animals they attribute to each direction. Hyemeyohsts Storm identifies the antlered animals as the animals of the North. Because of my own Scandinavian heritage, I personally relate to this in thinking of the antlered reindeer, caribou, and moose as the majestic and spiritual animals of the North.

About five years later, I e-mailed Ron's wife, who responded: "I imagine that Ron would be pleased if you used this story. I remember that he frequently talked of this experience. He wasn't afraid of death and welcomed it. His last words were, 'This isn't bad.'"

I had my own experience of the West while using the Calling the Spirits posture (see appendix, figure A.2):

> ***7-28-13:*** *I am facing West and I think of the spirits of the West. Suddenly a bear materializes, walks toward me, and at first sniffs at my feet. He then turns, and together we walk West, with my right hand on his shoulder. I am walking on his left side. We go into the woods and walk together for a long time. I keep thinking we should be doing more than just walking. We come to a tree, and the bear climbs up the straight trunk by grabbing the tree with his forepaws, then pulling his hindquarters up, and then pushing off to move his forelegs higher. I can't do that, so I transform into a bear and follow him. We get fairly high up and sit together on a branch awhile. Then we climb down the same way, but in reverse, hindquarters leading the way downward. We walk on farther into the woods and come to an area of brush where we sit comfortably, hidden in the brush. I feel very contented. Walking with the bear is a pleasant experience. I have been with the bear spirit many times with more energy to do or have something done to me. This time I am content to just sit. I growl in contentment, with the bear as my companion.*

This experience just reaffirms the special relationship I have with the bear as a spirit guide of the West. I feel very close to the bear who offers both the qualities of healing nurturance and strength, qualities of value in my work with the ecstatic postures.

NORTH: OUR ELDER YEARS, NIGHTTIME, WINTER, SLEEP

The north is the place of Winter, of elders and ancestors who have much to teach us about how to live in peace with and reverence of all that is of the Earth. It is a place of rest and remembrance, of detachment, of freeing oneself from resentments, jealousy, desire, anger, fear, and other attachments. It means letting go of all things, even those we love best, therefore it is also the place of wisdom. North is the final direction we reach in the circle of life, the place of completion and fulfillment, the place of completing the goals that started with the vision that began in the East. As Becky Reardon sings, in her album *Winter Solstice Round,* "Deep down in the belly of the night, dream deep winter dreams, and lie safe in your grandmother's arms, still as a seed, still as a seed . . ."

Art had an experience of the North using the Feathered Serpent (see page 52), an initiation posture. He titled it "Wisdom from My Mom":

> ***10-23-11:*** *From the spirits of the North I realize that my mom is my ancestor. I should receive her and respect her as such. In the experience I realize I need to let die my expectation of how she would/could contact me. Instead, I have to be ready to receive what she is prepared to offer—and I am not entirely ready. In previous dreams she had smiled silently at me. In real life there were few smiles. Now she stretches out her right arm toward me, gives me a real hug, unlike "real" life. And unlike "real" life, she kisses me on the cheek. Then she takes my hand and we walk off into the forest. Still no words are spoken. I'm probably still not ready for them. I am so surprised when she hugs and kisses me that I don't respond to her—it was so atypical and uncharacteristic of her when she was alive. I need to let my mom be who she is, and I need to keep letting go of expectations.*

From the North, where the spirits of our elders reside, comes Art's deceased mother. In this experience she showed him affection that she did not show him when she was alive, an experience that will take Art some time and contemplation to appreciate. Whether from dreams, ecstatic trance, or hypnotic trance, I have found that this experience of receiving affection from a deceased person who did not show affection before death is quite common and a powerful statement to the person in the altered state of trance.

While using the Singing Shaman posture (see appendix, figure A.18), I had the following experience of the North:

> ***10-8-10:*** *I see the drones of many bagpipes, then the pipes or spires of Shiprock [a rock formation in northern New Mexico]. I am walking from the North toward Shiprock to the South. I see spirits flying/floating around and in between the pipes/spires/masts of the rock. I approach the scree of the rock and start to climb. At the top of the scree, a medicine man is facing East, calling the spirits of the East. As I approach him he turns to me, welcomes me, smudges me, and beckons me to join him in calling the spirits. As we do this I feel exhilarated, and when we finish, we climb off the scree together. At the bottom he motions for me to return to the North and he turns to his place at the base of Shiprock. I walk slowly to the North.*

Again, as with numerous previous experiences, I am repeatedly being told that I am to be or that I am an elder of the North, a role that I feel I am resisting. In calling the spirits from the East, the medicine man is calling for my rebirth as a person of the North, though the mouse within me tells me that I am not ready. Yet, in the North, the place of completion, I am reminded to accept and complete my commitment to following the power of ecstatic trance.

I frequently use the deck of my sauna as a sacred space, which is where I was when I had the following experience of the North while using the Calling the Spirits posture (see appendix, figure A.2). The fifteen minutes it took to go on this journey went by so fast; I knew I was in a trance, but the trance, as frequently happens, did not feel very dreamlike. I felt very present, very "in the moment." Many, if not most Earth celebrations are performed in groves of trees or in the open spaces of nature, and not hidden indoors or even in a kiva. Initially my thought was that the feeling I had of being in the moment was not what I wanted; it was not the deep sense of trance I expected, but as I went into the experience I began to accept that it was exactly what it was supposed to be while out in nature.

I stood on the deck facing North, into a grove of two large white pines and maybe a dozen hemlocks, with the sauna behind me.

> ***10-12-13:*** *I first travel North, beyond the grove, across the farm fields, and beyond the village of Aaronsburg, through Northern Pennsylvania and across New York into Ontario, and then into Northern Canada, the Northwest Territory. I see herds of caribou, bears, and packs of wolves. I call on the spirits and I feel them caressing me as I fly by. I then smell the scent of sage wafting up from the abalone shell that holds a bundle of smoldering sage. The shell rests on my medicine wheel painted on a circle of leather lying before me. It brings me back, and I am again part of the grove of trees in front of me. I feel them embracing one another with their auras intertwined.*

As I reflect back on this experience, I feel that going out to the sauna deck first thing in the morning seems very right to me, but I need to do it other times of the day, too. We have a lot of wildlife at our home—deer, bears, coyotes, foxes, groundhogs, many rabbits, chipmunks, raccoons, porcupines, skunks, snakes (including copperheads), and a very large, mysterious gray/black cat that I have seen twice around our place. There are also many birds, including bald eagles. So far, though, I have seen none of these on cold fall days in the early morning. Traveling to the North in this way brings me closer to my elderhood. Sitting on the deck, performing the ritual of cleansing, calling the spirits, and listening to the drumming makes me much more aware of the spirits of the trees and other life forms around the pond and beyond, even at this time of the year.

BRINGING EAST AND WEST TOGETHER

The opposites of East and West frequently come together in a meaningful way, East being the rational, enlightened side of the person, and West being the emotional, darker side of the person. So often in psychotherapy a person may be of the West, that is, overly emotional, and bringing them to their East, the rational and intellectual side, can lead them to find a solution in the balance of the two opposites. On the other hand, many people are of the East, i.e., they intellectualize their problems and need to find balance with their West, their emotional side.

The next four experiences reflect my own struggle to integrate the East and the West within myself in dealing with a diagnosis of prostate cancer. The first three of these four experiences occurred early in my experience with ecstatic trance journeying, during a time when I was trying to understand these experiences in a rational manner, with the left-brain rationality of the East. My right brain, my West, is also well developed, which I attribute to being left-handed; thus my ability to experience ecstatic trance has been good. Yet my left brain had been asking for a rational explanation of the ecstatic postures and the ecstatic trance experience. I can now see how these four experiences have led me to find better integration between my East and my West, my left brain and my right brain—as though experiencing sunrise and sunset at the same time.

The first experience occurred while using the Tennessee Man (see appendix, figure A.21), a divination posture:

> ***12-8-08:*** *I feel like I am ready to spring—like I'm going to fly, ready for anything. Then something, maybe a big cat, comes running at me from behind, and I spring, grabbing a branch in a tree, and swing up onto the branch. I sit there looking around and see ants crawling up the tree. I follow them up the pine tree, climbing up, branch by branch. The ants go into a hole, and I sit on the branch waiting. I then again feel like springing into the air, and I fly out of the tree. After a while I come to the top of a butte and land, sitting on the edge of the butte, facing South. When I turn my head from side to side I can see both to the East and to the West—the sunrise and the sunset at the same time. I see storm clouds coming from the Southwest and lightning striking in the*

valley below. I see a herd of wild horses running toward the West. Again I spring or fly down to the horses and land on the back of one, with my arms wrapped around his neck. He is running as fast as he can to the West. Then the drumming stops. I feel very alert and ready to spring throughout this experience.

From being able to see both the sunrise and the sunset, a healing experience of balance, the energy then moved to the Southwest, with lightning strikes. For me this is the direction of transition from growth to maturity. But then the energy moved to the West, the direction of maturity and the harvest. This early experience with the ecstatic postures was apparently one of finding the balance between the intellectual and the emotional. It was an experience that opened me to greater maturity as I freed myself from the struggle between the intellectual and the emotional. Up to that point in time I had a tendency to be stuck in my rationality, or keeping my rational side separate from my emotional side.

The next experience occurred a little over a month later, while using the Olmec Prince (see page 50):

1-20-09: *I feel myself soaring in a thermal, round and round. Below I see a high railroad trestle. From the North end of the trestle a train is coming out of a tunnel. As I go round and round I can see the Sun rising in the East and setting in the West. This reminds me of seeing both the sunrise and the sunset at the same time, as occurred in last month's journey. I go into my head, the East, to try to better understand this image. First I think of the sunrise and sunset as being times of transition, then of bringing the East and West together.*

During the previous months of dealing with cancer, my West experience was with the Bear. In this experience, I was sitting with the Bear as the spirits circled me, throwing sparks at me that destroyed the cancer cells. This action of something being done to destroy the cancer cells was more rational in nature, more East. In the journey above of soaring in a thermal, the eagle, the totem animal of the East, was teaching me to be at harmony with my emotions, a more West experience, a more balanced experience. Thus, the eagle was showing me how to integrate East and West. It occurred to me then that in this experience I brought the two together, but now, in reflecting back from a greater perspective, I understand this integration more deeply. Bringing the East and West together is truly a healing experience.

The following month, while using the Tlatzoteotl (see appendix, figure A.22) for healing, I had the third in this series of experiences showing me how to integrate East and West. Here I found myself in the chapel of this goddess:

> ***2-3-09:*** *Tlatzoteotl tells me to journey to the East and to the West. I first go to the East Coast and stand on the beach watching the sunrise. Then I turn and go West. I see a number of sunsets, and I turn to watch the sunrise, but I turn again and continue West, with an eagle flying along with me. I get about halfway there when the eagle brings me to a bear, and then it leaves me. I walk along with the bear, with my right arm around its neck. Eventually I get to the Pacific Ocean, to my brother-in-law's house overlooking the ocean, and we watch the sunset. It all feels very harmonious and peaceful.*

This healing posture, as well as the two previous experiences, again unified the East and the West, bring the two directions together as well as the animal guides, the eagle being the spirit of the East, and the bear the spirit of the West. This indicated that by finding the balance between the intellectual and emotional aspects of myself, I could have a more balanced experience in dealing with my cancer.

This series of four journeys reached completion two months later when I used the Cernunnos, a metamorphosis posture (see appendix, figure A.3). For this posture I wore a set of deer antlers, as is recommended. As the drumming commenced, I quickly found myself on this journey sitting in an oak grove:

4-29-12: *It is dusk. Others—young women and men—are running around chasing one another. Then an old crone crawls up to me and reaches out, cackling as she touches my knee. My legs become roots that grow deep into the ground, and I become an oak tree growing upward, higher and higher. I feel myself standing taller and taller. At first my eyes, high up in the tree, are looking East, but my eyes are also on the opposite side of the trunk looking West, such that I can see the sunrise and the sunset at the same time. I then realize that the tree feels more alive in the daytime, with its leaves collecting the light from the Sun, but at night the leaves droop with no sun to reach out to. From sunrise to sunset the tree is intense, alive, and awake, but at night it is asleep. In the daytime I can see great distances since I am a very tall tree among the other trees.*

This shape-shifting experience of being a tree, of learning from the tree spirit guide, showed me the unity of finding balance between my East and my West, my intellectual and my emotional sides, I experience what it would be like being a tree during the daylight hours and the hours of darkness, feeling the different day and night energies of a tree.

ABOVE AND BELOW

From the vantage of standing in the circle of life, Above is Father Sky, Sun, and Moon—weather, sunny skies, thunderstorms, wind, clouds, energy, light, cold, and warmth. Below is Earth, our Great Mother and all that she encompasses. It takes the gifts from both the Earth and the Sky for life to survive. We need to be stewards of the Earth, Sky, and all our relations, including the four-legged ones, the winged ones, the crawly ones, the swimming ones, and the mountains, trees, rocks, and rivers to ensure harmony.

I had several experiences that brought home to me the relationship of Above and Below not long after seeing the BBC documentary series *Earth: The Power of the Planet,* narrated by Scottish geologist Iain Stewart. In the episode titled "Rare Earth," Dr. Stewart described how

Jupiter protects Earth from collisions of meteorites because of its size and greater gravitational field. Though this film described interdependence on a more intellectual level, I knew that to really grasp this sense of oneness of the cosmos I had to understand it on a deeper, experiential level. Ecstatic trance journeying allows us to do just that, integrating experiences on a deep, unconscious, archetypal level of being. While using the Venus of Galgenberg (see page 47) for journeying into the Sky World, I had this experience:

> ***11-17-13:*** *I find myself watching, then catching and riding a shooting star. The shooting star travels in a large arc, swinging around the Sun and then heading back to Earth. As it heads toward Earth I can feel it being pulled off course toward my left, toward the largest planet of our solar system, Jupiter. As it flies toward Jupiter, moving faster and faster, I leave it before it smashes into Jupiter, and I return to Earth.*

I suppose I was still under this influence of this powerful Above-Below experience, because a few weeks later I decided to journey again, this time with the Calling the Spirits (see appendix, figure A.2), a celebration posture. As described on page 118, this experience began as one of the South but flowed into a deeper understanding of Above and Below. Midtrance, however, the posture morphed, and I found myself standing with my arm raised, once again in the posture of the Venus of Galgenberg. The Venus wanted to take me to the Sky World, evidently. During the period of quieting my mind I saw myself standing on the North side of a pyramid facing it to the South. I could feel power coming from the pyramid, and I raised my left hand toward the top of the pyramid, thus choosing the stance of the Venus:

> ***12-23-11:*** *I am pulled from the South to the top of the pyramid, feeling great warmth coming from it. Then as I stand on top of the pyramid, energy from the heavens continues to pull me upward. I feel myself pulled as if by a magnet toward the Moon that was on the South horizon. As I*

reach the Moon and turn to look back toward the Earth, I continue to feel a great pull of energy between the two—the pull of the Moon that causes the tides of the ocean to rise and fall, and also the pull of the Earth pulling back with its gravity, so the two are in a steady state of equilibrium, steadying each in their movement.

With my intention of becoming one with the Earth, I have been thinking of that which is of the Earth, but I realize that what is beyond the Earth—above her and all around—is also part of the interdependence of things, Gaia consciousness. The pull of the Moon on the Earth is important in this interdependence of maintaining the Earth and all life on it and of it. The Above-Below relationship was vividly underscored by the change of perspective in this posture: from the Earth, one looks Above, to the Moon; from the Moon, one looks Above to the Earth. So which is Above and which is Below?

Brian Swimme's book *Journey of the Universe* taught me that all the elements of which we are composed were first created in the formation of the stars as the hydrogen and helium gases were compressed into the matter of which the stars and we humans are made. The cloud of helium and hydrogen is compressed by gravity, and at the same time an equal force of expansion is caused by the energy of fusion, fusion that creates oxygen, carbon, iron, and the heavier elements. As this process continues, the temperature of the core increases to billions of degrees. Eventually the core is compressed to a single dot, which explodes as a supernova, disbursing the elements into space, whereupon they begin to cohere into small balls that grow to eventually become the planets of our solar system.[1] This simplified description of this complex process is what led to my next ecstatic experience, which brought home in a very visceral way my connection to the stars, making me truly understand the truth that they are my ancestors—as Above, so Below. In this experience, which perhaps significantly occurred on the Winter Solstice, I used the Tanum Sky World posture (see page 46):

***12-21-13:** I travel out into space, into a cloud of helium and hydrogen, where as I inhale I take in the gases, and as I exhale the gases are compressed deep inside me at my* dan t'ian, *my center of harmony. I am aware that in the creation of the stars, these two opposite processes, the pulling in the gases with gravitation and the force of expansion with their fusion, grow in strength and occur at the same time, but in physically placing myself inside this creation process, in becoming one with it, my inhaling and exhaling is a close-enough metaphor. I can feel the heat increasing in my abdomen eventually to the point that I explode, and bits of me fly throughout space. These bits then begin to come together, to cohere into larger pieces of me, until they again form me.*

An experience of going deep within and below the surface of the Earth came after reading Aldo Leopold's *A Sand County Almanac.* It was here that I learned that our extermination of the wolves in the West caused an explosion in the deer population, and this in turn caused the defoliation of the mountains and the subsequent starvation of the deer. As Leopold so aptly says:

> Since I have lived to see state after state extirpate its wolves . . . I have watched the face of many a newly wolfless mountain . . . I have seen every edible bush and seeding browsed, first to anemic desuetude, and then to death. I have seen every edible tree defoliated to the height of a saddlehorn. . . . In the end the starved bones of the hoped-for deer herd, dead of its own too-much, bleached with the bones of the dead sage, or molder under the high-lined junipers. . . . I now suspect that just as a deer herd lives in mortal fear of the wolves, so does a mountain live in mortal fear of its deer.[2]

Leopold's metaphoric way of writing tells me he has integrated his experiences with nature so deeply within that he feels one with the Earth. Several weeks after reading his book, the images of the wolf, the deer, and the mountain continued to haunt me in a vivid experience of Above and Below in which I used the Lady of Cholula divination posture (see appendix, figure A.9):

> ***12-12-13:*** *I find myself on the other side of mountain that rises above our home in Pennsylvania, an area that burned in a forest fire a number of years ago. Sometime after the fire, a forester took us on a tour of the area and showed us an experimental area that has been fenced in to keep the deer out so that the new growth would have a chance. The difference was vivid; the fenced-in area was greener. I then am brought back to the drumming and find myself in an Indian village about 600 years ago, which is a place across the creek from our home. This site is now a popular place to hunt for arrowheads and spearheads. We are dancing to the drumming around a fire. The next day a hunting party leaves. Wildlife is plentiful—deer, wolves, elk, buffalo, bears, coyotes, turkeys, and many other smaller animals. I find myself watching what is going on from the "below" vantage point of the mountain. I can feel the soft, padded paws of the wolves running across me, and the sharper hooves of the deer that dig onto my dirt. I am this same mountain 600 years later, when most of these animals are gone. What remains now are deer, a few bear, and coyotes, along with turkeys and other smaller animals. The area on me where the fire burned is now eroding, and the deer hoof prints are adding to the erosion. There are two deer paths across our property, and they eat everything they can find. We need to fence in our garden to protect it from the deer. Except for hunting season, there is nothing to control the deer population except for a new developing problem, a chronic wasting disease that is threatening the deer population. We are very much out of the balance that existed before white man came to inhabit this area.*

This experience brought Leopold's haunting image home to me. It made the problems in our environment a felt experience for me. The interdependence of all things is an incredibly complex concept, and making it real at a deep level is very important to me right now.

THE CENTER: THE UNITY OF ALL

The Center is the center of the wheel representing the self and the Tree of Life. This is where it literally all comes together, as the wheel spins from the Center. Looking East we see the realm of the beginning of life, of a new consciousness, with its potential to initiate intention and understanding. To the South is the gift of growth, evolving toward maturity. Turning West we find the teachings of the mature heart and the fluidity to continue growing and changing. Looking North we see the fruition of this evolution from birth to death in preparation for a new birth in the East. Below our feet is Mother Earth, the experience of nourishment in the Community of Life. Above is Father Sky who placed Earth in its position with respect to the Sun and with a destiny to sustain life. The perfect circle of life is a sacred balance between Earth and Sky, awareness spiraling inward to the Center, the personal self moving through the cycle to one day become a fully aware human being who begins to understand the interdependence of all things.

One of the most obvious and prosaic examples of interdependence can be found in the chain of what eats what. Faye's experience while using the Jama-Coaque Diviner posture (see page 43) is a stark description of the basic food cycle:

> ***3-20-11:*** *White Bear is sitting and is translucent. I am sitting and watching him/her. I am a black bear. We are both young bears. The bear spirit is watching us both, smiling, looking down on us from the heavens. Then the black bear merges with me, and the bear spirit merges with the white bear. I shine with light and delight. I begin to walk. The scene around me is beautiful, a beautiful lake, trees, and flowers. I feel like I am suddenly in a dark cave but then out in the environment again, frantically digging into the soil, looking for something. I dig deeper into the Earth and find grubs and eat them. Then the trees—honey! Oh my gosh! It is so delicious. Yum! It melts over my tongue, dripping, the comb too. I keep eating and*

eating in pure delight. Then I start dipping the grubs into the honey. They are squishy and their juice with the honey is sooo delicious! I eat and eat and eat. Then, satiated, I go to a babbling brook and drink. The delicious water is clean and pure. The father spirit bear from above is teaching me. Then, I am a white bear in the far North, eating big and delicious fish right out of the water. So nourishing! I eat and eat. Then the bear spirit says they are going to feed my spirit. I stand up and am infused with light. I start to feel that I am running out of time and want to hurry, but realize I have to infuse my third eye and ears really well before going on. The spiral with infused rainbow colors is spiraling through me, permeating my whole being, through my veins, my colon, out my anus, into the Earth. I head into the sky, and then the shaking stops. I am almost finished. I am in some kind of training. My question has been to know God.

For Faye, experiencing what the bears eats, grubs and honey, and the fish was a deep spiritual experience, an experience that took her into a deeper spiritual consciousness of the Center, or unity of the self, with the elements of Above (bear spirit looking down from Above), Below (food for the bear is of the Earth), and all around (the spiral motif).

We who live in the so-called civilized world rarely think about where our food comes from; we simply go to the grocery store. In traditional societies, the life cycle was, and is, different. When hunting, the Indian leaves a token of thanks to the animal that gives its life to be food for the human being, possibly a pinch of tobacco or cornmeal, or a prayer of thanks and appreciation. The Indian, who innately understood his interdependence with nature, also held the attitude of "This is a good day to die," recognizing his participation in the cycle of life and the unity of his individual self with all things.

On my 2013 trip to New Mexico, first to Taos and then back to the Cuyamungue Institute outside of Santa Fe, where I was to spend a few days, I had several experiences that directed me toward a deeper understanding of the Center. In the first of several ecstatic trance journeys

I very viscerally experienced the importance of the juniper tree that is so abundant in New Mexico as my external lungs, allowing me to complete the cycle of breathing. I also sensed the junipers' miles of root hairs that take in the moisture of the Earth—moisture that may not be very apparent in this part of the arid Southwest. I had read about the junipers' incredible network of roots and root hairs in Jeff Lowenfels and Wayne Lewis's *Teaming with Microbes: The Organic Gardener's Guide to the Soil Food Web.* Again, though I was knowledgeable (East, left brain), for this knowledge to come "down to Earth" and become part of me at an experiential level (West, right brain), a trance experience was necessary.

While at the Rio Grande del Norte National Monument, at Wild Rivers, near Taos, I hiked to the lookout above the Red River, on the Pescado Trail. Sitting on a low rock under a piñon tree among the junipers and sagebrush, I took the opportunity to go into an ecstatic trance using the Lady of Cholula (see appendix, figure A.9), a divination posture, and using two sticks to softly beat the drumming rhythm.

> ***9-29-13:*** *I feel myself feeling very small in a large world, recognizing the size of the Great Mother as I sit in this remote place in Northern New Mexico. In feeling very small, and while reviewing my last several experiences, I wonder what do I uniquely have to offer in being an integral part of Gaia. The trees offer oxygen for me to breathe, while I offer them carbon dioxide, but so do all the other animals. I read a sign on the trail that explained how porcupines eat the inner bark of the piñon and thus potentially kill these hardy trees, and there are several dead piñons around me. I can think of many ways I can and do harm to this great Earth net, but with all of my intellect I cannot think how I benefit her. The unique abilities of most all animals, if not all, are inborn or automatic and done without thought. It is our thinking that has created the problems we have right now in our relationship with the Earth. Yet it is just this thinking, if we can direct it in the right way, to be one with Mother Earth, one with all of nature, that could possibly lead us toward finding ways to benefit her,*

or at least given the present state of affairs, to find ways to heal the Earth and help recover that which we have destroyed—to find ways to save the animals from extinction because of what our careless human activities have caused. Yet, the great Mother Earth may be better off without us . . .

This went so well that the juniper reappeared a few days later. While in the kiva at the institute with five other men, we used the Calling the Spirits posture (see appendix, figure A.2):

10-3-13: *As I inhale, I pull the vibrating spirits—in this case, the spirits of the seven directions—toward me. As I exhale they stop but start vibrating more and grow bigger. This continues for quite a while. Eventually as I inhale they are inhaled into me. As more and more of them enter me, I begin to vibrate as they are vibrating. As I vibrate more and more, my body disintegrates and flows out of the kiva in all directions and becomes one with the junipers all around the kiva. I, as a juniper, am vibrating, and the vibrating energy flows into my branches and into my berries, and the berries vibrate and grow bigger. Then a coyote comes to the juniper and eats some of the berries. The coyote soon stops outside the kiva and howls for a while before coming in, where he is one with me as I stand in the kiva howling. Soon my body quiets, and the spirits are now outside of me and around me as the drumming ends. I feel the circle of the spirits from me to the juniper to the coyote and back to me.*

This was a time that my thoughts of this book were germinating within me, as I became one with all the junipers, then a particular juniper, and then the coyote, two of my important spirit guides.

The next day, while using the Lady of Cholula (see appendix, figure A.9), a divination posture, I came to her with a mind cluttered with three concerns, all of which seemed to point to the Center:

10-4-13: *I set two of my thoughts aside and focused on the one concern that was most relevant to our ritual. In considering the spirits, Peter,* *another member of the group, had mentioned that there is really only one spirit, and that the many are of that one. My question is, "What is that one? Mother Earth? How about the rest of the universe? How about Father Sun and Sister Moon? The Lady takes me under the sea. I experience various fish, whales and dolphins, swimming, seeing diffused light during the day and a ball or sliver of light during the night—light coming from beyond, from a universe the fish do not know, but I somehow do. Then I feel I receive the answers to my questions . . .*

The whales and dolphins leaping above the water may have a little knowledge of the cosmos. In our ventures beyond our experienced universe we gain some knowledge, but to the beings of the ocean, the Great Spirit *is* the world of water, and it is all around, Above and Below, and they are one with it. We humans know somewhat the Earth, our Great Mother. There is a universal spirit beyond us that we know more dimly, yet we venerate, as though we are somehow separate. But the Great Mother is part of that cosmic spirit, and we are part of her, one with her. Her nature is that great interdependence, and we too are part of that interdependence with all that is.

I love the experience of ecstatic trance when it brings something that can seem so abstract, like the nature of oneness, to me on an experiential level.

7

BECOMING AN ELDER

When we get out of the glass bottles of our ego,
and when we escape like squirrels turning in the
cages of our personality
and get into the forests again,
we shall shiver with cold and fright
but things will happen to us
so that we don't know ourselves.

Cool, undying life will rush in,
and passion will make our bodies taut with power,
we shall stamp our feet with new power
and old things will fall down,
we shall laugh, and institutions will curl up like
burnt paper.

D. H. LAWRENCE

In Laszlo and Comb's book *Thomas Berry, Dreamer of the Earth* theologian Matthew Fox and depth psychologist and wilderness guide Bill Plotkin as well as others, recognize a deep need at this time for elders who can lead and teach others, especially young people, about the importance of being one with everything of the Earth. We humans have been taught for countless generations, for some 10,000 years, that we are superior to all other life forms on Earth, that our position is to have "dominion" over the Earth and to use all that is of the Earth to our own species' benefit. All generations, but particularly the younger generations, need to break with this pattern of ego involvement, for it is just this attitude that has brought us to the brink of extinction. If human beings cease to exist on the Earth, scientists believe that all that will remain will be insects such as the cockroach. At least the insects, in their oneness with the Earth, have shown an ability to survive. With their ability to survive how can we then say that we are the superior species? Many years ago, Hawk Little John, a Cherokee medicine man who lived in Cherokee, North Carolina, told me that he had found a purpose for the existence of all life except for the black fly and the mosquito. Then one day he saw mosquitoes dancing on the moss that grew at his spring. With this observation he realized that the mosquito was needed to pollinate the moss. Whether right or wrong, Hawk valued all life forms and sought to understand their purpose and their interdependence. Although apparently he has yet to find the purpose of the black fly.

A CALL TO ELDERHOOD

The mouse, an important and early spirit guide for me, helped me overcome my feelings of inadequacy and insecurity. The mouse, which is capable of burrowing and nesting under the snow to survive the cold of winter, is my spirit guide to show me how to insulate my home as it insulates its nest. How can I say I am superior to the mouse? Mice, along with many other microorganisms, tunnel into the Earth, providing necessary aeration and nutrition for the roots of plants. Recognizing these values of mice, how can I justify exterminating the mouse that comes into our house, the mouse that could potentially bring disease into the house? When I trap a mouse I need to show it respect by thanking it for what it has taught me and what it has to offer us, along with apologizing for having to remove it from our house. With apologizing and offering thanks, I can offer something, such as a pinch of cornmeal, as a token of this appreciation.

In dealing with my prostate cancer, the bear, one of my spirit guides, showed me how to nurture myself and heal. The eagle has shown me how to go with the flow and rise above the stressors of life. How can I say I am superior to the bear and eagle? We are dependent on trees and all flora to provide us with the oxygen we need to breathe and the food that sustains us. How can we put ourselves above the trees and the flora? Our young people need to hear such stories from the respected elders of the community.

Besides telling stories that illustrate the importance of our place in the sacred dance of life, elders also need to be good listeners and be able to give advice when others come to them with questions. But they need to provide these answers with humbleness and restraint, restraint such that the answer given promotes further questions. We need elders who live this oneness with all that is of the Earth to teach us and our posterity this oneness. We need them to teach us that we are dependent on all that is of the Earth.

David Korten, cofounder and board chair of *YES! Magazine,* cofounder of Positive Futures Network, and a former professor at Harvard University's Graduate School of Business, regards elderhood as the final stage in human development.[1] Drawing from a number of models of child development, he describes the manner in which we relate to others as we develop into maturity, identifying the first stage of consciousness in our early years as magical. In this stage we are fantasizers; we live in another world and place our faith in magical protectors. This is followed by the stage of imperial consciousness, when we seek power over our world, playing up to the powerful and exploiting the oppressed. Children, beginning around the age of two years, the terrible twos, become demanding and want things to go their way while taking the toys of other kids. Korten sees those adults who are greedy in seeking the accumulation of wealth as being stuck in this spiritually immature stage.

Then comes the third stage, that of socialized consciousness, the stage in which we can be considered good citizens of where we live—in a small world among those who think like us and reinforce our way of thinking. We play by the rules of our identity group, and from within this group we expect a fair reward. As children grow they eventually learn how to get along with and please others. Korten takes this stage beyond the years of childhood when he describes the majority of adults who are the swing voters in determining the direction of our future. This group is the fulcrum between the culture of empire and the culture of a New Earth community.

Those who develop beyond the third stage, into the fourth stage, that of cultural consciousness, are cultural creatives* who live in a world inclusive of others, who may think different from them and yet who affirm their position in life-affirming societies that work for all.

Finally, the most mature among us are those who have attained the fifth stage, that of spiritual consciousness. These people are spiritual creatives living in a complex and evolving, integral world in which they engage as evolutionary co-creators. They are the elders in the new interdependent culture we are seeking to create. It is in this role of the spiritually conscious elder, we are in a position where we can lead others in their personal growth to higher levels of spiritual maturity. Each person's journey is very personal. It is the diversity of these journeys and the acceptance and love of this diversity that is the one factor that leads us into this fifth stage of spiritual consciousness.

Though they have been severely challenged to do so by the colonizing Anglo culture, the native peoples of this continent have never lost touch with their traditional view that they are one with Mother Earth—what Korten calls *spiritual consciousness.* I had the opportunity to spend several days at the Cuyamungue Institute with David

---

**Cultural creatives* is a term coined by sociologist Paul H. Ray, author of *The Cultural Creatives: How 50 Million People Are Changing the World,* to describe people whose values embrace a curiosity and concern for the world, its ecosystems, and its peoples, and who demonstrate an awareness of and activism on behalf of peace and social justice.

Nighteagle, a Lakota Sioux storyteller, educator, and accomplished musician and recording artist. As part of the Men's Conclave at the institute he had much to offer as a respected leader with his stories and music. During my time with David I strived to be politically correct by using the term *Native American,* but David would point at me and ask, "Where were you born?" When I answered "California," he told me that *I* was a native American. He preferred to be called an Indian, explaining that the word *Indeus,* meaning "of God," was used by one of Columbus's ship's crew who first wrote of the native people of the Caribbean Islands at the time of Columbus's visit. Since then I have used the term *Indian* to refer to our native peoples.

To transform to a more balanced society and world we need elders to guide us. These will be people who care for their communities, cultures, and the Earth. They know and share the value of the Earth and the necessity to preserve her beauty for future generations. They honor all living beings and aspects of nature. They model integrity and love, practicing these values while teaching others how to do the same.

Hopefully there are a large number of people of sufficient integrity who recognize the need for elders to promote ways to sustain the Earth and bring us to become one with our Great Earth Mother. It is these people we hope are striving to be such elders. The journey to become an elder is a continual process without an end. There is so much for each of us to unlearn that has been taught to us over the years by the established dominant culture, so many inner conflicts to overcome, and an unending amount of knowledge to learn to guide us on this journey to save the Earth. As we evolve toward becoming elders, each of us has something unique to offer, and this uniqueness provides the movement with its diversity, a diversity that we value because of the breadth of what is required. But this diversity may cause confusion, causing us to question if our unique way is correct or the best. We need to have the integrity, strength, and faith to know that what we have to offer is one important piece of the whole and finding this integrity, strength, and faith is part of the journey. I believe that the use of the ecstatic postures is one unique way to bring us to the spiritual maturity of an elder, and that the following journey of Amalia demonstrates this journey, an unending journey as there is always more ahead of us to resolve and learn.

AMALIA BEGINS A JOURNEY

At the time she became involved with our ecstatic trance group in 2009 Amalia was an emotionally strong fifty-six-year-old woman who had spent much of her early life in both the United States and Israel. During her early years she completed college, and in 1984 she graduated from the Parsons School of Design with a master's degree in art. She then returned to Israel, but in 1988 she moved back to the United States with her husband and her daughter just before the birth of their son. In 1990 they moved to State College, Pennsylvania, where her husband attended graduate school. Their marriage soon ended when Amalia's husband left her for another woman. Between this time and when she joined our trance group she had been in two other relationships, both of which had ended.

The first ended tragically when her partner died. The second had been with a married man, and had ended about a year before she joined our group when out of frustration with the situation she revealed the relationship to the man's wife. The wife gave the man an ultimatum—that his extracurricular relationship had to end or the marriage would—and as a result, Amalia's relationship with the man ended. As a result of her life crisis and the fact that the important age of sixty was looming on the horizon, Amalia felt she was at a turning point in her life and was ready to dive into a process of transformation. This was when she joined our group, and her experiences took her on a spiritual voyage that brought self-knowledge and a sense of her place in the cosmos, setting her on the path to elderhood.

As described in my book *The Power of Ecstatic Trance,* I have found that the basic three-step sequence of (1) a divination posture (to define a problem or answer a question), (2) a journey into the underworld/the unconscious mind (to find a solution or answer), and (3) an initiation/death-rebirth posture (for integrating deep within the solution or answer) is the most effective process for promoting personal healing and growth. When Amalia joined our ecstatic trance group, she was eager to dive into the work using this sequence of postures. Over the next nine months, this turned into a healing journey toward spiritual consciousness. About a year and a half after Amalia underwent this series of experiences, she and I reviewed them in considerable detail to trace her fascinating narrative. As well, the process of finding understanding in one's ecstatic experiences takes time and perspective, and so reevaluating the experiences from a greater distance allows one to see the growth that has occurred.

Amalia's first foray into ecstatic trance posture work began with a divination posture, the Jama-Coaque Diviner (see page 43). She titled this experience "Finding My Beloved":

> ***3-20-11:*** *I am a strong young warrior man, and I see a close-up of a large branch with one leaf, a ginko leaf. For a while I experience nothing except words and certain sensations:* owl, five, footprints . . . *I then squeeze through an entrance, like between two sheets of glass, squeezing in sideways. I dive into the ocean and walk along the bottom. I really like breathing underwater. I then come up in bubbles to the surface. Maybe I see the shadow of a big fish. At the surface of the water I find a rock to stand on and look out to sea, where there are birds, maybe a female peacock, on my right. Ships come in. I think maybe I am a native watching the return of the pilgrims. They are coming from the West to the East, as if arriving in Spain or France. A young woman in a long dress and bonnet comes off the ship. She is my beloved. We hug and there are gifts. We go into the forest, to a big bonfire, and begin dancing all around, jumping over the fire. The fire may also be the burning of a witch. Then we lie down on the ground and roll around on our backs in delight. After rolling around I sit with my beloved on a mossy rock, away from everyone.*

The Jama-Coaque Diviner allows us to come with unstated questions from the unconscious mind. The diviner knows what is most important at the time, what needs to be answered. Sometimes, as in Amalia's experience, the diviner addresses something the person is not even considering at the moment. In trance she saw a single ginko leaf on a tree branch. She considered the ginko a very beautiful tree and saw this image as representing the end of a beautiful season—the end of her relationship with the married man. She felt the strength of a young, half-naked male warrior, perhaps symbolic of the strength it took for her to overcome feeling decimated by the end of her relationship. Though at first she was held back by having to squeeze between the plates of glass, she then dove into the ocean—her sea of emotions. Amalia interpreted her going from the West to the East as a metaphorical pilgrim as indicating her return from exploring the unknown lands of the emotions of the West to the more rational side of her, represented by the East. As the primitive male native, she hugged her beloved self, her socialized self, who was dressed in a socially acceptable manner. They came together and united. "I think the beloved is my heart that went on a journey to unexplored territories, like the pilgrims who went to America. They went with great hope and idealism." The peacock and the ship's arrival signify prosperity. She found her beloved within herself, in the union between the primitive, nature-connected male and the socially defined female. This divination experience suggested that she was journeying to find herself as a whole person.

Later Amalia further refined her thinking and understanding of this initial experience:

I have experienced this struggle as a fight between the male side of myself that is connected to nature and the wilderness, and the female side that wants to create a home and an internal space that is protected and safe. I saw these two parts as being at odds with each other, not because they held each other in contempt, but because their nature was different and they needed different things. I associate this with the different roles that the male and the female have played in society since the hunter-gatherer times. The women were more in charge of the encampment, while the men were in charge of the hunting and had a lot of time away from the camp, in the wild. The women were in charge of domestication. Entrapping men in this domestication has given them the ability to make rules and have control—a very bad exchange for both sides. In this image the female is willing to come back and give up some of her need for domestication and socialization in order to connect with the male's free and natural energy. I think it is relevant to our place in the world and our connection to the Earth.

In her next experience, Amalia used an underworld posture, Jivaro (see appendix, figure A.8), to find needed answers in her subconscious mind. She titled this experience "The Deer Man."

3-27-11: *I am lying on my back, going down head first, flipping over as if under the surface with my belly down. I am walking down steps in a cavernous hole, going deep into the Earth, down many flights of steps along the inner side or wall of the hole. Then nothing happens for a while. I then fall deeper into a blackness without a bottom. I find myself lying in this posture in a boat going down a river. I stand up, and then I am a man wearing antlers, walking in a very old forest with enormously tall trees. I am wondering why I am a man again, wondering if maybe I am gay. I am then in a stream with a woman like a dryad in a colorful fabric dress who invites me to swim with her. She is very graceful, while I am clumsy with my antlers, but we unite. She then turns into a gleaming fish and I try to follow her, but I find it hard with my antlers. I get frustrated, take out my knife, and kill the dryad. But I am sorry and try and put her together again. I manage to put her together, but she is an old woman now and leads me out of the forest to the edge of the ocean. I enter the ocean and transform into a polar bear. The ocean is frozen, and I run off to play on the ice. Now I am the old woman returning to rest, lying on a hammock, but the hammock catches fire and like an insect I burn with the hammock* *folding inward. I am then a brown bear coming out of the forest with a heavy winter fur. I reach the ocean but do not go in. I burrow aimlessly on the shore, not really knowing what to do. I turn back into the forest and start climbing a rocky mountainside. Moving faster, I reach sunlight just as you finish drumming.*

In discussing this experience with me eighteen months later, Amalia recognized that in going into the underworld she was again experiencing her strong masculine energy, the strength to fearlessly face her conflict. In considering the thought that she might be gay, she realized that she identified not with being gay sexually, but with her "masculine wild side" that is in conflict with her "domesticated" side.

I had to be strong but felt awkward or clumsy with this rutting masculine energy, unbalanced in wearing the antlers. The fish I killed was out of the frustration I felt in the relationship with my soul mate, a fish/dryad that was alluded to in my earlier experience, in the image of the shadow of fish. I felt bad about the destruction and tried to put her together again, but she came back as an old woman, a crone. The crone represented the end of my commitment to my love affair, as signified when she burned in the hammock. To avoid facing my intense emotional pain I became a playful bear on top of the ice of frozen or denied emotions. As the brown bear, centered and strong, I again went out to face my emotions, the ocean, but I did not go in, again avoiding my emotions, holding them at bay, protecting myself from the pain. But burrowing aimlessly in the sand, I felt very aimless. I then left all this behind and climbed to new heights, reaching for the sunlight, that is, to overcome this aimlessness I needed to begin on a new spiritual quest to find myself.

After journeying into the underworld, which generally reflects the processes of the unconscious mind and uncovers material relevant to the issue at hand—in this case the death of Amalia's affair and her feelings of loss and aimlessness—using a metamorphosis or initiation posture for

The mother and child unite

a death and rebirth journey was indicated. Amalia chose the Cernunnos posture (see appendix, figure A.3) because the Cernunnos image wears antlers. For Amalia's underworld journey I attached a set of deer antlers to a hard hat for her to wear in this posture. She titled this experience "The Mother and Child Unite":

> ***4-3-11:*** *I start with a very strong sense of the posture. In the beginning I am with many people dancing ecstatically in a Celtic Beltane ceremony. I am then sitting forever in the posture as the sacrificial king, with people bowing to me and asking for justice. I cannot get out of the posture, I have to sit in it. I am very much a ritual king who will eventually be sacrificed for the fertility of Spring. Two figures come, take my antlers, and help me up because I cannot walk. I think,* Oh, these are the helpers, *but*

they throw me into the fire and I burn. I connect this burning to witch burning. The two figures start laughing as if this ritual is all a joke. They are like black-faced vaudeville men in the way they are joking. Then they start digging in the ground, and as they burrow into it they become two rabbits with white tails who then hop away. I am back in the posture, feeling it very strongly. Then a female deer comes out of a thicket straight in front of my nose and I become the female deer, full-bodied, with an acute sense of smell. I am then back in the posture with energy entering me through my third eye and my heart. I am feeling my roots growing through my perineum, and I am becoming the World Tree. The energy is coming out of my vagina and my breasts are full. I am giving birth to the things of the world. Then a young naked woman passes by and passes by again, as I am not paying attention. She then turns into a young girl, runs away, and sits in the dirt. I understand that I can be the mother and the young girl at the same time.

A few days after this third experience Amalia reported,

It's working like magic. It's so amazing that we act on the personal, the mythical, and the energy of the cosmos all at the same time, each influencing the others. I feel a buildup of my sense of being able to be in a place of authority without losing the girl or reverting back and forth, being in both at the same time. I sense a lot of changes. I am allowing myself to feel more emotions without suppressing them, and today in a Reiki share I allowed myself to receive and accept that I don't need to take care of everything, that God is there to do it.

In our discussion of this experience eighteen months later, Amalia recognized that she was the sacrificial king in the Celtic rite who was to die in order to promote a new birth. "I first thought that the two black-faced figures were there to help me get up and were going to help me, but like in a vaudeville parody, they appeared to be something they are not. What was sacrificed was the love affair, which I hoped would not happen. I was put into a role I did not want to play." Then the female deer came to her and she became the full-bodied deer with an acute sense of smell. "I was then reborn into the natural world." With this rebirth, Amalia's new self was reconstructed around a new spiritual center, the World Tree, with her becoming the World Tree. She became the creative energy of her new world, gathering into her psyche all her parts that had been at odds with one another. She was becoming a completely new person in a spiritual sense—she was the child and the mother at the same time:

> *These are the parts of me that I need to internalize. I am not yet ready to deal with the naked young woman, but I am able to deal with the mother and child. . . . My personal myth of joining with a soul mate was shattered, so I moved toward a more collective or universal myth of pursuing a new realm, that of spirituality.*

In our discussion we tried to consider the possible meanings of the two men, their laughter, and then their turning into rabbits. A few days later, Amalia e-mailed me with her thoughts:

> *I think the power of the sacrificial Beltane king is a social power given to fulfill a role that will allow the people to thrive. But the role, although it has power, includes in it its own destruction. I think in my love affair I was given such a role, one of power but at least from my lover's point of view one of a limited time span, which included its destruction at the end. The helpers I think were people who knew about the affair, who I thought would be supportive of me, but in the end helped in the "witch" burning, saying it was for the best and so on and so forth, instead of understanding the depth of the devastation and the sacrifice it had caused me. They became like the black-faced comics who made light of the devastation and scuttled off like rabbits. The burning of the witch in the first and third experience was me feeling that I had been burned by the community.*

This three-stage sequence of postures concludes with a journey into the sky world, a journey that usually provides a peak experience, a feeling of ecstasy that consolidates or integrates the results of the whole sequence. Thus for her third journey we used the Venus of Galgenberg posture (see page 47). Amalia titled this experience "The Lord of the Winds and the Tree of Life":

> ***5-1-11:*** *I am running up a high mountain that seems like it is in the Himalayas. On top I shout to the winds to let me fly. I am taken up and fly to the clouds. I am then running to a castle. At the entrance I am quickly robed in red and gold, with a red and gold headdress. I go inside, and on the throne sits the lord of the winds, also wearing red and gold. I bow to him. I am one of his court, and we take off with the wind and with a few others joining us. I am on his right. I am aware of another wind lord on the left, and there are others behind us. We fly high, leaving the atmosphere, and go into space, making a stop on the Moon and then the red planet, Mars, where we plant a tree and things begin to turn green. We don't stop but fly on back to Earth and the mountain. There is a separation in colors as we approach the Earth, between the dark brown of the Earth and the white of snow or feathers of the mountain peak. I am not sure which way to go. In the end I descend toward me, standing in the posture, and I bow to me. I plant a seed between my feet. There is a strong sexual feeling in my vagina. The seed merges with me and I begin to grow into a tree. The posture feels like a tree. Then I go in the other direction, into the clouds to the mountain peak, and I am given a bowl of water, and I am blessed. The water is poured over me and I descend with the blessed water to the tree and pour the water down into its branches and trunk. The tree flowers in white, and for a long time this is all that happens, the coursing of life through the tree, very rooted, growing toward the Sun. The buds turn red, becoming more luscious, and then fall. The fruits begin to ripen. All this takes a long time. A squirrel finds a crack, climbs up the tree, and makes a home inside. Nothing happens for a long time. Then an enormous and slightly menacing crow lands on the tree and stays there.*

A few days after this experience, Amalia e-mailed me:

What strikes me in my second reading of this experience is the amount of energy in this experience! The running and the wind energy is very powerful and fast. Even though the tree doesn't move and nothing happens for a long time, the coursing of life through the tree is very strong and fast. There is stuff happening all the time, even when nothing seems to happen or it takes a long time to happen. I really liked the lord of the winds. Maybe I'll find that headdress somewhere.

In our discussion of this experience eighteen months later, Amalia suggested that this experience defined her place in the world as being in the retinue of the lord of the wind, a big mover in creation. He is motion and the cosmic winds. He brings life to where there is nothing. He is qi, the portal for energy spinners. "I am here because he is teaching me about letting go," Amalia said. "This is my place in the universe. I feel blessed and united, internalizing what I learned from the relationship. I become the creative energy of the Tree of Life."

After this discussion I did a computer search of *lord of the wind* and found an association with the Hindu god Vayu. A picture of him shows him wearing red and gold, matching Amalia's image, yet she had not known of this Hindu god who is called "the lord of the wind."

Several days after our discussion Amalia provided more insight into this trance experience:

We have illusions of things that will hold strong for us in life. With my husband I thought that the power of the institution of marriage and parenthood would hold us together and that it would help us overcome his passion for someone else, that the social institution would hold because otherwise why have it. That was the crack in the tree, because it turned out to be an illusion. . . . With my love affair I thought passion of the heart would triumph and that also turned out to be an illusion.

She also revealed, "I did not embark on this love affair easily. It took about a year of "courtship" before I crossed the line, the reasons being that I did know what was at stake. One of the first things I did get through was a release of a great deal of my anger toward my husband and the woman he had left me for, whom he later married. I could see how difficult it is to resist the power of connection once it is activated, once the line is crossed."

Thus, to bring these four experiences together:

From the initial divination experience Amalia learned that after having lost part of herself in the love affair she now needed to unite that part of her that represented the socially acceptable, domesticated part of herself, with her more physical, natural, earth-connected self. But then she needed exceptional strength in order to go into the underworld, her unconscious mind, to face the demise of her affair, that is, her killing of the graceful dryad. She felt bad about the death of her affair and tried to put it back together. It didn't want to die and came back as an old woman who again died in a fire. To deal with this emotional pain, Amalia needed to let her emotions freeze so that she could dance and play, and when she returned to face them she felt aimless. So she left her emotions behind in order to begin her spiritual journey to find herself. Amalia's painful emotions continued to linger below the surface and inhibit her ability to move on to find unity in her new life.

To resolve this interference from her emotions Amalia next used an initiation posture, in which she died the ritual death of the Beltane king in order to insure a rebirth for a fertile Spring. Emanating new strength and energy, she was reborn first as a female deer, then as the World Tree, before finally giving birth to a young girl as the creative mother who brings her to a new and natural world. A few days after this experience, which she described as magical, Amalia found that she could feel her emotions without suppressing them. She felt she was in charge of her world, in a place of authority, with a new creative and spiritual energy. To internalize this newfound strength, she journeyed into the sky world and found herself flying with Vayu, the lord of the winds, and once again she found herself rooted as the Tree of Life, reaching for the Sun and producing the fruits of creation.

These four ecstatic experiences pointed to the direction that Amalia's future work would take as a result of the hole left in her by her earlier divorce, as well as the threat of the menacing crow of old age as she approached her sixties. Though she found in her affair with the married man a release of her earlier anger toward her ex-husband, still to be resolved was finding the balance between her valuing the social institution of marriage and her natural inclination to throw herself into love. Amalia concluded, "Moving to a higher spiritual path is, in a way, an easy way out, but it hasn't yet brought me into the balanced relationship with myself that I would like to have." It was to take a few more sequences of posture work for this to happen.

AMALIA'S EVOLUTION

Amalia's next three experiences with the sequence of divination, underworld/Realm of the Dead, and initiation/death-rebirth postures brought her to a new and higher level of spiritual awareness. To start, the question she put to the Lady of Cholula diviner (see appendix, figure A.9) was reflected in the title she later gave this first experience: "Are you Here or There?"

Having lived the first part of her life in both Israel and the United States, Amalia confessed that she had felt divided, as though she belonged in two places or was binational. She felt she needed to decide where she belonged. Being the eldest daughter, she had a certain status and was a central figure within her family circle in Israel. She had an older half-sister and two younger siblings. Amalia gave three reasons why she believed she had to stay in the States: She did not want to move again and had recently bought a house to this end; she felt that there was greater religious freedom here, while in Israel religious beliefs were very dogmatic; and she recognized the "imbecility" of the Israelis' way of relating to the Palestinians and how she differed from her parents in holding this viewpoint. In the end, in her trance experience she expressed a resolute decision to be "here."

> **4-17-11:** *I start walking down a path through hills patch-worked in colors of green and yellow, a little like a fairy tale. An old man with a crooked, pointed hat and a stick points the way to me, and I reach a village. A woman is sitting on the ground outside a house. She is young, but she looks worn out or stoned. She beckons me to sit next to her and pours what she is holding in her lap into my hands. It is a necklace covered with wet seaweed. I put it on and am covered with green seaweed. She gives me a hookah to smoke. Then I pass through a house that is like a saloon full of men in a Western movie. I do not look at them and do not stop. The air is hot and it dries out the seaweed. On the other side of the house I come out to a great expanse—I am not sure of what, but it turns out to be a desert. I walk forward in the heat, through the entrance of an Egyptian pyramid. I walk through the corridors inside the pyramid to the middle room, where I lie down in a sarcophagus. The lid is shut, and I travel on water to the afterlife. There I get up and see a throne way up high, at the top of many steps. I go up, thinking this is my throne, but there is an old woman on the throne and she asks me if I am "here or there." I tell her I don't know, and she tells me to go away. I go down but then decide to go up again, feeling more resolute. I say, "I am here," and she immediately gives me the throne. I sit on it and find I can command things to happen—rivers to move, and many other things. As I get tired of this I notice that from the throne there is a ladder. I climb up the ladder into the blue, and it's like blue fabric that I can float on. I climb some more steps to a door, and an old man, a little like Dumbledore, is sitting there. I ask him to explain everything to me with all his charts. Instead he puts me in a chair with a crown tied to it. I fall backward into an unending void, becoming smaller and smaller. At the same time there comes an enormous bird with red wings flapping, a bit like in the movie* Avatar. *I am one of the children flying with great*

joy with these birds. I then become a woman in a village in a circle of women grinding corn in South America. There I have my legs wrapped so I cannot walk, so I burrow like a snake into underground passages. I end up in a blue cavern. I go even farther down one of the passages and give my offering to the goddess. She takes me on her knee. An ugly imp, like a court jester, then takes me up, and I come back on the same path I started on, now toward myself. I ask if I will have a partner, and the woman returning toward me says, "I am your partner."

Amalia offered an interpretation of this experience some eighteen months later, though she expressed some apprehension about analyzing it, feeling that it could limit or restrict her future journeys and could inhibit the freedom she found in trance journeying. I understood her doubts, but we agreed to review this experience with an open mind. The necklace covered with seaweed indicated a connection to the sea—Amalia's sea of emotions that had been frozen, yet was a source of beauty and power. The journey then took her into a village, where she passed through a Western saloon full of men—an archetypical masculine place that she found menacing and primitive. "It is a place I don't really belong," she said. The next stop was at a pyramid in Egypt that she entered, lying down in a sarcophagus, which took her to the afterlife, a death-rebirth experience. There she found her throne, designating her high rank. When she was asked if she was "here or there," her answer, "here," represented her resolve to break her emotional ties to Israel. Amalia believed that the essence of this experience could be found in this question.

From the throne Amalia journeyed to the three worlds before she returned to find herself. She felt majestic now that she could rule her own life, but then she climbed up higher, into the blue. From there she fell into the great mystery, where she experienced the childlike joy of flight as a bird. Then, having finally arrived in the Middle World, she received the earthly spiritual gift of corn and became snakelike, burrowing into the underworld. This snake represents life's transformations.

From the snake she became a princess who gave the goddess a gift. The union resulting from journeying through the three worlds allowed her to become the princess. In the end she was back on the path where she started, and was told that to attain a higher level of spirituality she must partner first and foremost with herself, as awareness cannot come without self-knowledge.

A week later, Amalia used the Hallstatt Warrior (see page 53), a realm-of-the-dead posture:

> ***4-21-11:*** *I am a boy. A girl takes my hand, and she says "Let's jump." I am kind of dull and she is lively. We jump and play and tickle each other, rolling around on the ground. I say I have to go into the underworld, but I don't really want to go down there. We dig a small hole with sticks but it isn't really going down. It's just big enough for a marble game. Then a bear cub joins us in our games of tickling and rolling. The little girl is no longer there, or maybe she is now within me as the dull boy. The bear cub climbs a tree but I can't get up. He is on top of the tree looking around at a vast forest. I can see through his eyes. Then he climbs down to lead the way. We still frolic until we reach a cliff with a tree trunk that is barely sticking out over the edge. We climb out onto it, and an eagle flies in to join us. I still worry about going underground, because I don't want to go. The eagle puts a skull necklace around my neck and we all dance to the beat of the drum. At some point it is as if he/she is a skeleton dancing, connecting to the drum beat. We then climb down the cliff into a stream. There, a mother bear, a huge grizzly bear, stands on her hind legs and smacks both me and the cub around a bit as if we have been naughty. Then I transform into a male deer and we go to a council of animals in the forest. The bear is sitting on the throne. I am the deer and I don't know what the other animals are but they are there. I still have a nagging feeling that I should go underground. The deer sleeps, and from it a woman rises up and goes underground as in the "Twelve Princesses" fairy tale. Then she comes up from underground and returns as the deer. The council continues, and there is a figure in the middle of the group with a fan headdress. I am not*

sure what it is. A saber-tooth tiger comes into the circle, and though he is very ferocious he doesn't hurt anyone. We climb up the long pole and into the upper forest, and two children ride the tiger.

When Amalia and I met about eighteen months after this trance journey to discuss it, she offered some insight. At the end of this experience she became the diviner. To be a diviner requires letting go of one's intellect, she said, because the intellect interferes with seeing beyond oneself. Entering divinatory situations requires an empty or "dull" mind—which was why she hesitated to analyze her ecstatic trance experiences. A day or two later, Amalia e-mailed me to say that she thought the dull boy in the trance was somehow connected to her awakening her authentic self:

I think I am a bit "dull," in the sense that I am slightly socially awkward, have a difficult time talking, and many times don't know the right social response. When I was a young child my parents took me to a doctor to see if I was deaf because I wouldn't respond when called. I was pretty shy, afraid to knock on doors, even when they were our next-door neighbor, though that might be too much to expect because I was quite young.

Amalia's feeble and unsuccessful attempt to go into the underworld by digging a shallow hole that was only deep enough for playing marbles again reflected her resistance to going within. The bear cub perhaps signifies playfulness, a way of avoiding going into the underworld where she does not want to go. She is given a skull necklace by the eagle. This is a gift of power that shamans traditionally wear, indicating Amalia's movement through her repeated cycles of death and rebirth as she journeys up through the hierarchical levels of spirituality. When she finally goes into the underworld, like the twelve princesses, it is again just to dance and play. The skeleton dance reminded Amalia of the Mexican Day of the Dead celebration. She said that she does not fear death, that "death has become a friend." In being given the necklace, the repeated cycle of death and rebirth is "already done," and the skulls signify her metaphorical death as she transforms into higher consciousness.

The other significant elements of this journey are the bear, the deer, and the tiger. The bear, a spirit guide for Amalia, is an animal of the West, of the mature adult, an animal who can take us through some tough times and illuminate life circumstances. The bear teaches patience and connection, confidence and inner authority, nurturing and protection. Just as the deer has an uncanny sense of where to find the green freshness the Earth provides, we can ask the deer within ourselves to seek out our inner treasures in the depths of our soul. Amalia related the experience of riding the tiger to the t'ai chi form known as "ride the tiger," to represent her overcoming what has been limiting her by taking control of the energy in her life so that she can freely do what she is supposed to be doing.

Amalia's next experience involved the Feathered Serpent posture (see page 52). This is a death-rebirth posture:

> ***5-15-11:*** *I started in the posture as a rooster, a fighting cock. The posture feels like it has that open chest and wings. There is also a hen scratching around for corn. The rooster is sacrificed, its skin is shed, and its blood penetrates the Earth. Inside the rooster are spirits, and they are whitish yellow forms, human-shaped but with no features, and the quality is like meal-mush. They dance on the Earth, and I realize they are the spirits of corn. I feel a very strong and important connection to corn. This is the fertility ritual for the growing of corn. As I think this, the corn sprouts, grows, and becomes a big green stalk. This is probably somewhere in Mexico, as there is a temple on top of a pyramid or large building. I am not sure if I should go there but I do, climbing up and entering through a golden door. Inside it is a peaceful, cool blue, with many large live tree posts as columns, as if it is maybe a jungle but calmer. In the middle there is an enormous ancient tree that reaches into the darkness of space. I climb the tree*

to the canopy, with its many large leaves, and then the leaves become dragon mouths, colorful like sculptures. The center of the tree splits, and I descend into the center, back into the Earth. This time I emerge as a woman with black hair in a many-layered dress, again ascending to the top of the tree. Again there is a split, with the bark separating like a banana peel and the inside white. Again I descend, emerging as a couple of peacocks who strut around and relate this to Krishna consciousness. Finding myself among peacocks reminds me of the Hare Krishna farm and temple in Port Royal, Pennsylvania. They fly away and come back with a plant that they put in the ground. There is a man drumming on a large standing drum. The plant grows and again splits, this time regenerating through me. A bird pecks at my back, giving me divinatory knowledge. I end as an old woman diviner with a Chinese turtle shell.

This journey provided Amalia with four initiation or death-rebirth experiences. The first was the blood sacrifice of the rooster with its gift of sacred knowledge, taking her to the source of life through the corn fertility ritual. Second, in climbing and going through the golden door, she entered a calm junglelike place with a giant central tree, the calm natural world. There she climbed the tree and it split. She descended into the split into the center of the Earth, from where she emerged or was reborn as a black-haired woman who reminded her of a flamenco dancer, suggesting the gift of passion—the second gift. She again ascended the tree, which opened like a banana peel, and she descended, emerging as a couple of strutting peacocks, connecting her to Krishna consciousness, the all-knowing, sustaining energy of the universe—the third gift. She felt a bird pecking at her back, giving her divinatory knowledge—the fourth gift. The experience ended with her becoming a crone. In this experience Amalia became part of the natural cycle of regeneration, and with each regeneration she received a gift of wisdom that she could share with others.

AMALIA'S BEAR SPIRIT GUIDE

Amalia became acquainted with her bear spirit guide when she embarked on a third sequence of trance experiences. Relevant to these experiences is the fact that the man she had partnered with after her marriage had ended—the man who died—was an American Indian.

Amalia began this sequence with a divinatory posture, the Mayan Oracle (see appendix, figure A.12), to ask what she should be working on next:

> ***8-14-11:*** *Going into trance, the first animal that comes into my head is the grouse, and I think of the significance of the grouse as an invitation to join the dance. I start in a meadow but then find myself walking with heavy boots on a black paved road. The road is going on and on with the telephone poles along its edge, going Northwest. On the right I pass a couple of buildings and wonder if I should stop or continue. I decide to stop and go in a coffee shop where some men are sitting. They give me coffee and kid around with me about my long journey. It is a nice stop. Then I am on the road again and walk uphill toward the trees and higher ground, when a bear comes out from the left with its claws out. It is kind of scary and I wonder if I should stop or not and decide "yes," if I am to learn the lesson of the bear. The bear then becomes very gentle and cuddly and lets me ride on her back, resting my head on her back as she walks through the forest. We get to her den, go in, and there she has me meditate and find my place. There are bats flying around in the cave. For a minute I think of Goldilocks and the three bears. Then I fall asleep, cuddled in the bear's fur. I wake up and find I am transforming, walking on all fours, with my back curving. I am a bear cub coming out of the cave, frolicking and running in the meadow. My bear mother is following wherever I go, and every once in a while I go back to her for comfort. I again pass the buildings, but this time I circumvent them. I continue back to where I came from before as a human. I reach the ocean, play in the waves, get bit by a crab, and taste the saltwater, but then run to*

my mother and cuddle in her fur. I can't cross the ocean. After sleeping I awaken and go back to the meadow, running after butterflies. I then climb a tree, which falls over, and I scramble back to my mother, who is always there.

Amalia associated the grouse with the dance of life and an invitation to this dance. She then continued on her journey to the Northwest, the direction of maturity (West) and wisdom (North). At the coffee shop, unlike the Western saloon of her earlier trance experience, the people were friendly and welcoming. She encountered a big bear, an animal of the West, but decided to be fearless so as to learn from the bear—a fearlessness that she related to her training in t'ai chi. She was instructed by the mother bear to meditate—a very bearlike request—whereupon she awakened as a frolicking bear cub. Together mother bear and bear cub go Southeast, back past the coffee shop and on to the ocean. The South represents childhood and the energy of the Sun and Summer; the East represents the beginning of a new cycle.

Two weeks later, Amalia continued this sequence with a metamorphosis posture, the Chalchihuitlique posture (see appendix, figure A.4):

8-30-11: *I start as the male bear cub following my mother, who is teaching me the way of bears. She is growling and roaring, a strong energy, and then digs in the Earth with her claws looking for ants. Then we climb a very tall tree. By the time I get to the top of the tree I am an Indian scout with beautiful feathers in my hair and I think war paint, kneeling at the top of the tree looking out. After that I am an Indian chief in the middle of a village in front of my tipi, sitting by the fire as part of the bear tribe. The mother bear (I am the bear too) comes through the tipis, steals some food, and ambles out to urinate and defecate on the perimeter of the camp, but the chief continues sitting in peace. There are other Indians in the circle smoking the ceremonial pipe, sending the smoke up to the Great Spirit, creating and asking for harmony. Then the chief goes into his tipi* *and cuddles with his wife and child. There is a great sense of peace and harmony in this way of living. Then I am the bear cub following his mama again, and as a bear I feel myself relaxing into the natural state, hearing, smelling, and being in tune with the forest—a very nice feeling. I go down near a stream to drink and maybe catch fish, a playful gamboling between mother and son. A fox comes by and is groveling a bit, wary. The last image is of licking the white sap of a plant that I think is hallucinogenic.*

In teaching the bear cub, Mother Bear taught the skills needed for maturity, but Amalia is still a beginner, a cub. Amalia suggests that the Indian warrior represents her resistance to sacrificing herself to the tribe. She finds the harmonious ways of the chief of the village, so in tune with Mother Earth, very compelling, as indicated by the peaceful scene, but she had to reconcile this pull with her Israeli-Jewish heritage. The fox adds a sense of wariness of something that is not yet resolved, possibility the lack of resolution to sacrifice herself to the community.

A month later our group used the Lady of Thessaly (see appendix, figure A.10), an initiation posture. In our later discussion of this experience Amalia wondered what might have interfered with the continuity of her sequence since the bear was not part of this experience, which she titled "In the Middle of the Spiral":

10-2-11: *The first thing that comes to me is that this pose creates an impetus for an upward clockwise spiral. At first the experience begins with feathers and a big owl sitting on a branch, some reddish brown feathers and white—a very large owl. I am waiting, not as frenetic as I usually am. In the North in the distance are evergreens. It is cold, and a stream is coming down, cascading down a precipice covered in green. At the bottom are water buffalo, one licking and nuzzling the other as if kissing very lovingly. I am both the buffalo and the owl. As seen from above, the owl's point of view, the owl is flying West over a great city into the sunset. Then a red, white, and black snake climbs up me, and I am ready for the bite and death, but it takes its time. I am then reborn as a deer and other animals* *are running in the ribbons of the spiral, around and around toward the heavens where there is a castle of light. The rest of the time is spent being at the center of the spiral that is moving around me like a ribbon. The spiraling ribbon is a little like Dali's painting of his wife. I have a very strong physical sensation of the posture and a sensation in the mouth and tongue.*

In this experience Amalia was both the owl and the buffalo—the owl farsighted and the buffalo full of love and affection. The stream flows to the South, and the owl flies to the West, suggesting feelings of comfort coming from the childlike spirits of the South and the adult self of the West. Amalia's resignation to being bitten by the snake—the totem animal of transformation—signifies an expression of quiet readiness to die and to be reborn. What part of her died she did not know, but the rebirth was again into a birth of her growth in accepting the cycle of nature and her spirituality, being reborn as a gentle deer and running with the animals. The spiraling energy is the natural cycle of spirituality and indicates unity, coming together, as in the seventh direction in calling the directions; it signifies oneness, the aim of her journey.

We concluded this sequence a week later with another initiation posture, Sekhmet (see appendix, figure A.16), which signaled a return of the bear to Amalia's experience, as indicated by the title she gave this journey: "Bear—North."

10-9-11: *A wolf on the hill, with a few other wolves, is howling at the Moon. I am the bear. From inside the bear I walk North, toward the wolves. I feel the posture in my throat. I meet the wolves, who welcome me, and I lie down, the wolves on top of me. I die and become a bear rug for them to play on. I'm kind of upset that I'm dying, but I am sacrificing myself to the tribe and sinking slowly into the Earth. At the end, after many years, I'm only the skeleton that is left. Then many years later I am a bear again, passing through the skeletal remains and continuing on to a stream. First I stand and stretch against a tree, and then sit—somewhat*

Bear—North

similar to the posture. I feel the posture in my stomach as the energy comes in and the bear spirit expands beyond me, connecting to the oneness. Then I feel it in the back of my neck, and I am an elk brought down as if bitten or caught by the neck, maybe by the bear, I'm not sure. Then I am again the bear, completely unified with the spirit of the bear. The bear is in trance.

Amalia felt that the Sekhmet posture represented openness and acceptance. As the bear, the spirit animal of the West, she continued on her spiritual journey to the North, the place of the elders, where she joined in the sacredness of nature in greeting and being welcomed by the wolves, an animal of instinct, intelligence, appetite for freedom, and awareness of the importance of social connections. The wolves lie on her as they sleep, and she dies to become a bear rug for them to play on, sacrificing herself to the tribe and in this act acknowledging the cycle of life. Though she was initially sad at having to die for the tribe, in so doing she found a higher level of spiritual connection in her relationship to nature and to the Earth's natural cycles as she returned years later, again as a bear, although she had lost much of her individuality, as seen in her sacrificial remains as a skeleton. What it means to become a bear is to take on the energy of bear. Bear is emblematic of grounding forces and strength. This animal has been a powerful totem in numerous cultures and times, inspiring those who need it the courage to stand up against adversity. As a spirit animal in touch with the Earth and the cycles of nature, bear is a powerful guide to support physical and emotional healing. In this case, bear sacrificed itself for the whole, sacrificing the individual physical to expand into the unity of the spiritual. The appearance of the wolf is also significant, as this animal can also symbolize fear of being threatened and lack of trust. In an e-mail several days after our discussion of this latest sequence of postures, Amalia expressed that her resistance to sacrificing to the tribe

> *. . . has more to do with my ambivalent relationship to Israel, where the Jewish mentality puts the community ahead of everything else. Take as a prime example the circumcision ceremony that gives an eight-day old infant to be cut in a public ceremony in the hands of the father. This makes this baby part of the tribe even before he is weaned. It is a drastic trampling on the instincts of a mother. In preschool in Israel there is strong attention to the group and group activities, versus the individual attention placed on children here in the U.S. I have my sense of tribal connection in Israel, but I escaped that by choosing to live here, so I am not sure that I want to reconnect with that.*

We discussed her trance experiences again about eighteen months later. Amalia admitted that there are parts of her that still have not matured fully that she wants to continue working on. She realized that there is a part of her that resists letting go of her individuality in favor of embracing unity consciousness—which relates to the appearance of wolf in the previous trance.

I find there is a fear of annihilation, of the loss of the personal that I am not yet completely ready to do. Maybe I am not completely ready for the sacrifice. I feel that I am learning that not all sacrifices are necessary, and some of my fear relates to a lack of trust in the ability of the young or the tribe to survive without the sacrifice. In this experience, the physical sacrifices itself, with the passage of time, is regenerated and meets its own history. Then instead of dying it kills, but the killed and the killer are the same—the bear returns to oneness, a larger consciousness, where there really is no sacrifice.

RESOLUTION

Amalia began a final sequence of postures on this journey of self-knowledge by joining with the group's intention of seeking an animal spirit guide. This time Amalia rattled for the ritual, the first time she was taking on a leadership role in the ecstatic trance group. We used the Tennessee Man (see appendix, figure A.21), a divination posture. Amalia quickly found herself face to face with a fox:

10-30-11: *Immediately a fox looks at me, and I go into a forest glade with it. I am somewhat preoccupied with rattling. I walk down a wide forest path with a cool green light coursing down. At a crossroads, with the fox as my companion, I stop to make a fire. Then we go down the left path, which leads to the small entrance of cavelike stone building. There an old man greets us and takes us down long winding steps, deep into the Earth, to his cave room, which has round blue pool in the middle and is surrounded by shelves with tinctures and magical but unknown potions. There is a big table where the man sits like a philosopher or a magician. I drink from the pool along with the fox and we gambol a bit on our backs. I ask the man what I need to do, and he just indicates I*

The fox

should be with the fox. Then I go into the pool, which is pretty deep, and slowly turn into a fox, beginning with my ears. After the transformation we go out the door into a thicket of rhododendrons, but now I am seeing everything from much lower. This is Shingletown Gap. We cross the stream, drink from the water, and climb up a waterfall. The path leads to a cliff overlooking Happy Valley. We just sit there awhile, enjoying the view, and then continue in companionship through the woods. A wolf howls, but we continue walking.

For Amalia the forest glade and the wide forest path are magical places of nature, and it is in this setting that the fox shows itself. Fox symbolism is varied. Many cultures see the fox as a wise messenger who can guide you through the wilds of the woods. The other significant motif in this trance is the crossroads, representing a life decision, with the fox as her companion. She took the left path, representing feminine energy. She receives instruction from a guide or teacher, the old man, who tells her to play, that is, become one with, the fox. She then emerged into one of her favorite real-life places for hiking, Singletown Gap, only with the perspective of the fox. The waterfall motif represents flowing emotions, which is coupled in the vision with a scenic view of the valley where she lives. The menacing howling of a wolf portends danger. In discussing this aspect of her experience, Amalia thought of the threat of danger as a common theme in Jewish history, the cultural belief that there is always some sort of menace just around the corner, a sense of paranoia about life.

Two weeks after this experience with the fox, Amalia went on a journey using the Olmec Prince (see page 50), a metamorphosis posture, in which she once again found herself with her fox guide:

> ***11-15-11:*** *I start where I left off before, but this time I have only the sense of a fox's nose, then a very slow transformation into a fox, first with the nose, then the ears, and then the tail. It feels like nothing is happening, and I even go again to the old man in the cave to get advice. The transformation slowly continues now with the back, the tail, the nose, and the ears. I meet the bear. Then with the stomach transformed, I lope down the forest path, while at the same time seeing myself as the fox from above, as a hawk holding a kernel in my beak, swooping, after the fox. I am not sure if the hawk will grab the fox in its talons. Thoughts about foxes pass through my mind: the I Ching fox that got its tail wet crossing the river; the gingerbread man and the fox. Finally I get the heart of a fox and immediately my mouth turns into a smile. I am sitting on a ledge above a valley in the moonlight next to my den. I am yipping and howling at the Moon. There is a wolf nearby and I lick its ear and nip it. It is howling, and I am lying in a little furrow I have dug, looking over the valley. Then as the fox I am walking near a green place with a waterfall and pool, drinking from the waterfall and walking through the woods as a fox seeing everything, my belly close to the ground.*

In this experience, the fox encounters a hawk. The hawk can provide perspective, the exceptional vision and vigilance encompassed in the raptor. Though there is something of a threat in the way the hawk observes the fox, this "threat" can be seen as a push toward spiritual awareness. Then the fox reaches out to the wolf in friendship, the wolf symbolizing courage to stand up against adversity. After receiving the heart of the fox, Amalia's transformation is complete, and the fox spirit smiles with happiness. In our discussion Amalia described the green place with the waterfall and pool as "Arcadian," that is, a Garden of Eden. *Webster's* defines *Arcadia* as "a region or scene of simple pleasure and quiet."

Two weeks later, our group journeyed into the Danish Realm of the Dead (see Hallstatt Warrior on page 53), where Amalia had another visit with the fox in an experience she titled "The Fox Fight":

> ***11-27-11:*** *I feel a need to move out of the group to the outskirts, facing out. I find myself as a fox in a fight with a big creature that I cannot see, all snarls and bites, and I am injured, curled up and hurting. I realize that being curled and hurting is the feeling of the posture, protecting an injury to the guts or liver. Then as the injured fox I am in the middle of a council of elders, I think mostly consisting of foxes. There is no talking, but one of the council is laughingly transformed by movement into a beautiful blue peacock, pecking and spreading its tail. I am still the injured fox in the middle of the circle. The peacock is moving on the path through the woods toward the bright white light. The council follows, and their movement transforms into a snake. Then a donkey or ass comes into the circle, reminding me of* A Midsummer Night's Dream. *All the time I am aware of myself as the fox with a wound under my arms, with my guts spilling out. Then there seems to be a healing, and many little foxes yipping at my feet as I stand in the posture and smile. I come down and play with them, and they jump all over me with their tails brushing me. I am dressed like the peacock in blue, wearing feathers and a blue mantle, and as a woman I start dancing to the music of the drum. The foxes lead me down the stairs. I gain a crown along the way, going down the stairs, into the*

forest. I anticipate meeting someone or something, but I don't know who, as we reach the end of the drumming.

Wolf again made an appearance in this fox experience—an animal that expresses an appetite for freedom and social connection. As a wounded fox, Amalia's healing takes place in a setting of transformation and playfulness, in the council of elder foxes. The beautiful peacock makes an appearance, often a symbol of integrity, the ability to show our true colors. The transformation continues, into the body of a snake, symbol of transformation and enlightenment. The donkey also makes an appearance, donkey being a "beast of burden" but also light-hearted and humorous with its silly braying, willing to make an "ass" of himself. This transformation leads her back to herself as a woman standing in the posture, but as a woman of nobility with the faerie energy of magic, signifying that she has been given gifts of knowledge from all these spirit guides.

When our group met two weeks later, Amalia experienced the final posture of this sequence, the Feathered Serpent (see page 52), a death-rebirth posture:

12-11-11: *In the posture I first feel my head wanting to go down, to become the serpent crawling in and out of the Earth. There is a bush with red berries, and I as a girl am sitting under it eating the berries. The serpent comes, eats from the berries, and then crawls on the girl to bite her on the left side of the neck. She lies down and dies, and her spirit rises and departs into the sky to become an angel in white looking down from the clouds. As that happens my head no longer goes down; the whole posture changes and I stand very erect. Then from the angel an eagle flies straight at me and lands on my left arm, whispering in my ear. We are looking out together and I now am the World Tree, extending upward and becoming one with the heavens. This also feels like a change in the posture, as if my head is leading that expansion into becoming the sky and the heavens. At my feet are animals—wolves, beautiful, playful with gamboling cubs, and* *also the fox, who is hiding in a den at my roots. The wolves are gathering and starting on a long trek. They lope along the side of the mountain on a trail on a precipice, a very long distance. As the heavens, I open my mouth (literally) and red fruit comes out to feed the wolves and the eagle who take the fruit directly from my mouth. A skunk also comes to feed. In the meantime the fox comes out after everyone is gone and also feeds and wakes the girl. The fox takes her on a much easier and slower path than the wolves. I am all of these at the same time. In the distance a volcano erupts. As the heavens I can cool it and ice it. I am also the World Tree, the wolves on the trek, the fox, the girl, and the eagle messenger.*

Amalia's report of this experience is full of all the images of the universe coming together in the Center, which is the World Tree that unites all the sacred directions. Appropriately, many different kinds of animals are gathered around in this image of interdependence.

In our subsequent discussion, Amalia reported that the posture feels very strong for change and transformation, with many levels of learning and development. The serpent initiates this transformation of rebirth with a bite and death. She becomes first an angel, then the messenger eagle, before becoming the World Tree, whose canopy becomes the heavens. As the heavens, Amalia opens up to feed fruit to all creatures—the wolves, eagle, skunk, the fox, and the little girl. In comparing wolf and eagle energy to that of fox, Amalia recognized that the fox is not part of a clan or pack as the wolves are, but more individual, reflecting her preference for this fox spirit's individuality and her own resistance to sacrificing herself to the tribe. At the end she felt the enormity of her being, of learning to be all things, the union of all things above, below, and all around.

Amalia's progression through each of these four sequences of postures brought considerable healing and spiritual growth. Yet the path of spiritual growth always involves continued work, to bring ever-greater awareness and greater resolution to personal conflicts. This recognition is wisdom. Life is a collection of dualities, of the ego meeting the shadow, the yin meeting the yang, and though we may seek the unification of such opposites, they are always with us. It is the path of wisdom to seek balance. For Amalia, the central duality was her valuing her individuality on the one hand, and her valuing being part of the tribe, the collective, on the other.

In becoming elders, human beings have a unique contribution to make to the Earth. Most everything of the Earth functions instinctively, without conscious awareness, while humans have conscious awareness and the ability to choose. This conscious awareness can, as it has for the past 10,000 years, take the world on a downward path of destruction. Or, with conscious intent, we can acknowledge and participate in the interdependence of life and thereby help facilitate healing of the Earth, lead toward Earth's higher evolution. We may be pulled in different directions, but by valuing the rituals of venerating the Earth, rituals that tie us to being one with her, we can again find paradise on Earth.

8

GRIEVING FOR AND HEALING THE EARTH

Grandfather,
Look at our brokenness.

We know that in all creation
Only the human family
Has strayed from the Sacred Way.

We know that we are the ones
Who are divided
And we are the ones
Who must come back together
To walk in the Sacred Way.

Grandfather,
Sacred One,
Teach us love, compassion, and honor
That we may heal the earth
And heal each other

Ojibway prayer

Sometimes our ecstatic experiences express grief for what we have done to the Earth. These experiences are valuable in leading us to consider how to heal the Earth and support her as we move forward in Earth consciousness.

While using the Olmec Prince (see page 50), a posture for metamorphosis, I had an experience of deep grief for the dolphins off the coast of Santa Barbara, California. While visiting my brother-in-law I had identified a sacred place for ecstatic trance, on a cliff overlooking the Pacific Ocean and Santa Cruz Island, one of the Channel Islands off the coast of California. It was about four in the afternoon and somewhat foggy. I watched two dolphins leaping from the water just a few minutes before I had the following experience. As I sat in the posture I listened to a recording of drumming on my I-touch:

> ***9-20-13:*** *As the drumming starts I quickly became a dolphin swimming so freely and playfully in moving through the water with another dolphin. We break the water twice in our play. As we dive to the ocean floor we turn and shoot up to break the surface of the water. It feels so good and so right. We are just doing what we should be doing, with no worry about food. As we swim through a school of small fish I take several fish in my mouth without much thought. But then I as a human have the thought from the news of several days earlier that dolphins are dying on Atlantic Ocean beaches, and I remember that a short distance down the beach from where I sit a polluted river flows into the ocean, polluted with sewage. I have walked along that river and have smelled its stink. I feel such sadness for the dolphins, swimming in the sewage without an awareness of the danger it poses.*

Only since the fall of 2013 have I used the ecstatic postures with the intention of becoming one with the Earth. Most of the experiences presented in this book occurred before that date and were spontaneous examples of gaining this oneness. This dolphin experience was one of the first times I sought this oneness intentionally. A couple of weeks later, while using the Mayan Oracle (see appendix, figure A.12), again with intention, I experienced sorrow for the Earth again. I was back at home, and it was a rainy morning as I sat on the deck of our sauna, one of my favorite sacred spaces. I asked the Mayan Oracle, "What should I be doing to become one with the Earth?"

> ***10-11-13:*** *Though I feel quiet inside, my mind flits from the many rabbits in the area to the trees. Over the years we have lost both elm and chestnut trees to tree diseases, and now there is a fatal hemlock disease, though it has not yet reached our hemlocks, but the emerald ash borer is killing our ash trees. I think of the negative connotation that some people attach to the term* tree hugger, *yet hugging a tree feels right. I feel the warmth and comfort of the rabbit's burrow lined with rabbit fur. Then my mind returns to the drumming. I follow my breathing for a while and soon go to the spirit of the Great Mother, who I picture as the mountains around us, and I am nestled in the pit of her arm. She suggests I open my eyes so that I can see the trees and life around me, and I first notice the shimmering auras around the trees and how the aura is limited on one branch of a tree near me that is dead. I feel that these auras are speaking to me about the health and wellness of the trees, and the hemlock's auras seems full. I feel grief for the ash, the top of which is dying, as seen in its fading aura. I feel that the Great Mother is telling me that being out in nature while I journey is the right place to be, and that I am doing the right thing to become closer and one with her.*

I felt such emotional pain in realizing that the dolphins were swimming in polluted water off the California coast, and the trees in our area of Pennsylvania are dying of various diseases. Experiencing this kind of pain is important to me in keeping my awareness on my connection with the Earth. I experienced sadness, but there were also elements of hope in this journey, as seen in the warmth of the rabbit's burrow, the reading of tree auras, and listening to the voice of Earth Mother.

FAYE'S JOURNEYS

One of the elders of our ecstatic trance group is Faye who is in the middle age of life. We often meet in her home, and she is the person who first challenged me several years ago to listen to the trees. She has a keen sense of being one with the Earth and the entire universe through her ecstatic journeys. Her journeys include many experiences of shapeshifting, experiencing the qualities of each animal that she becomes. Her ecstatic experiences are often of grief for what we are doing to the Earth, as well as some experiences of Earth healing.

While using the Jivaro posture (see appendix, figure A.8) to journey to the underworld, she had the following experience:

> ***3-27-11:*** *A group of native people are preparing me for a visionary journey. They paint my body with the juice of elderberry. I drink the deep purple juice and there are some elder flowers in my hair. I lie down with my hand over my third eye. As I face the Sun the open qi point of my third eye absorbs the light into my body down to my naval, and down into the underworld. Then my eyes can see all things. First I am riding an eagle. Then I become the eagle, soaring through the sky, seeing the world from above and looking all around. The journey is just beginning when the drumming stops. In this journey the question comes to me, "What is my purpose and how do I walk the purpose in this life?"*

This experience began Faye's journey through the next twelve experiences to seek ways to heal the Earth, while also allowing her to experience deep pain as a result of the ways we are destroying her. A week later, using the Chalchihuitlique posture (see appendix, figure A.4) for metamorphosis, she became the winged horse that flies through the universe.

> ***4-3-11:*** *I am an ancient man, dark skinned with tan body paint. I am on all fours, looking and waiting, paying acute attention. Then I see a face,*

mine, looking over a large body of water to the horizon. I am looking into the distance, waiting for something. The rain comes and soaks my naked body, cleansing me through and through. The Sun comes, melting my skin, burning me alive, but I don't worry, I have been burned alive in the past and probably won't have to go through this again. Then the Moon comes. I am reborn into a woman of light, moonlight, a big, strong, tall woman of bluish white light. I am birthing lots of balls with something from my belly and out through my vagina. They are rolling onto the Earth and springing up into humanlike beings. I am then a horse with wings, a being of light traveling with the rain, sun, moon, and stars. I go through this universe on to another universe far away. I fly and fly. Then I get to this place with different colors of light, and I just am, when the drumming stops. I know I am from this place and wish I had more time to see what it is like.

In this experience Faye was cleansed of her personal struggle and brought to a new level of energy and a new direction. She experienced a rebirth in feeling this new strength in being a woman and in her goals and aspirations of flying to a higher place, her cosmic place of origin. The winged horse became an important spirit guide to her for several subsequent ecstatic experiences. Over two years after this experience Faye identified this winged horse as her Sagittarius side. Her next five experiences intensified her feelings of oneness with the Earth and the universe and placed her in situations of healing the Earth.

In the next experience of the winged horse, Faye became one with and the keeper of the plant world and the soil. She connected with ancient wisdom in caring for the plant world. More than being one with the Earth, she became one with the universe. Part of her realized that she can get caught up in dwelling on the past—again, her place of origin somewhere in the cosmos—but she was instructed to not waste her time on this. Faye strongly identified with the horse and reported that during the winter when walking on ice she feels as if she is trotting with short steps, as if on hooves, in order to not slip. For this journey into the Sky World Faye used the Venus of Galgenberg posture (see page 47):

> ***5-1-11:*** *The horse comes to me and says I should use the horse spirit instead of the bear to go on this journey. The horse spirit with wings comes and carries me to the Sun. I am sweating pure gold. Then I go on to the stars and out of this universe to another one—far, far away—where I reach a place with plant spirits with blue translucent colors and many other colors. A yellow daffodil comes and licks my third eye, smiling. The plant spirits say I am one of them. I feel sexual energy. My gut opens, and the whole world, the universe, everything, lives within me. Then God comes. I feel the soil of the Earth and God says he made me with soil so I would stay on the Earth and not transcend back to my cosmic place of origin. The soil will keep me on the Earth. I am one of the plants of this place and all live within me. I am one with the universe and a keeper of the Earth's plants. I continue to care and work for and with them. I am not to get caught up on the Earth plane, but to take time to connect with my place of origin. Then my arms and head stay in this place while the rest of my body stretches down, down through the space beyond this universe, down to the Earth's universe, past the Sun, when I once again start sweating. My feet leave the ground and continue down like roots, into the Earth's core. Then the Earth goes inside of me and I wrap myself around the Earth. I am a huge plant, with the world inside of me. The plants move and have smiles on their faces with colors of light. God is just a life-light face. It seems masculine. The soil is dark, cool, and moist. The core of the Earth is hot. The universe beyond the Earth's universe is dark, but the darkness lights up and is comfortably cool. Ayahuasca comes and tells me I am great-great-great-great-grandmother, ancient, and I give birth to many things.*

In Faye's experiences she typically becomes one with the universe.

A few months later, while using the Sleeping Lady of Malta (see appendix, figure A.19) for journeying into the Lower World, Faye felt great concern for the plants and the soil, this time by becoming a root and experiencing the miles of roots and root fibers that exist throughout the soil when it is healthy. The roots bring energy and nutrition to the plants. Faye called the following experience "Plant Roots Travel":

7-31-11: *I am a root of a plant traveling along the subsoil of the planet. I am communicating with all the other plants in this matter, traveling through all kinds of soil, sometimes taking a deeper dive. I came across some devas sitting down to eat. They invite me to join them. I wonder who the devas are, so I join them and we open our mouths and start inhaling energy. Oh, so much life! As a worm I inhale through my skin, absorbing light and energy nutrition. I continue traveling along as tree roots going deeper into the ground, communing with all the trees on the planet, feeling vibrations through the soil. Then I am traveling under the soil of the ocean and the vibrations intensify. The water is a carrier of sounds and vibrations. Then the rattling stops and the journey ends.*

While using the Lady of Thessaly (see appendix, figure A.10) for death and rebirth, Faye again traveled as a winged horse:

10-2-11: *The horse comes and takes me to the place of light, preparing me for the journey. We go to the place of light, where I am transformed into the horse, and I continue on as the winged horse. I realize I am both the bear grounded in the Earth and the horse of the upper world. I become one, full of light, with both the bear and the horse. This journey takes me in two directions at once. My knees and torso, arms and hands go in one direction, while my shoulders and head walk in another as a spirit being. My head is full of the light, light that flows through my body, pulsing in wormlike movements through my core. I am walking between the two worlds on a tightrope, wondering what it would be like if I fell into the darkness below. So I let go and fall on purpose. I keep going down into the darkness. It seems bottomless, so the winged horse comes and takes me back to the rope. I realize the rope is a metaphor and I can just walk between the two worlds. I see animal faces and their noses, especially the dog and the wolf. I realize we all need noses to breathe to be earthbound. So I journey up into the light and bring it back down, bringing the light into the density of the Earth. My body becomes a portal, and I become the light, going into pure nothingness. Then I hear ethereal music intertwined* *between the drumming and rattling. The ethereal music becomes louder and clearer and we all become one.*

In this exhilarating experience, Faye became one with both the Earth and the Sky World, "bringing new life." She continued to show concern for the "density of the Earth," but whereas before she aerated it as a worm, she now breathed air and brought light into this density, in this way bringing her own healing energy to the Earth.

While using the Tennessee Diviner posture (see appendix, figure A.21), Faye had an experience that she titled "Seeking Power Animals":

10-30-11: *First, the great eagle comes, and we fly to where I can see the whole world from above, from a distance. I then sink into the Earth and start swimming through the waters, to the center of a cave. I am a huge serpent. I am living as a serpent in a mystic lake. I crawl onto the land using my tongue to sense. I feel like serpent, using this sense to survive, with the ability to live above and below the Earth, in and out of water. I am then a huge wild black cat, using my ears to sense danger and to be aware of my surroundings. I am then a woman from the waist up and the black wildcat from the waist down, standing on my hind legs. I am then a bear hibernating in a cave, learning how to regulate my body temperature, breath, and food consumption in order to learn how to survive in the coming times. I have a human head and a bear body while dancing a medicine song, being told by the spirit I am a medicine bear shaman. Then I am again a horse, flying to the upper world. I am a half horse waist down, walking on horse legs, and waist up I am human with a bow and arrow, learning how to live between the upper realms and surviving on the Earth. I realize I am learning how to live in the many upper and lower worlds and on the Earth plane, using the different senses.*

In Faye's journey she was learning to live in the worlds of the eagle, serpent, a black wildcat, and a hibernating bear, learning their medicine songs. Again, the Sagittarian centaur makes an appearance, representing the union of civilized thought and primal nature. In learning from and becoming one with these creatures, she experienced the Lower, Middle, and Sky Worlds, learning by sensing with the tongue, then by her ears, and then by regulating her body temperature and food intake.

FEELING HER GRIEF

In this next experience, Faye connected with her grief over how the human species is destroying the Earth. She did not see the Earth and other life forms surviving. At first she experienced survival as hopeless, suggesting that we are too late to save the Earth. But as we shall see, over the next few sessions she began to find some hope.

While using the Olmec Prince for metamorphosis (see page 50), Faye had an experience she titled "A New World":

> ***11-13-11:*** *First I am a cell, pure energy, and I am then a young serpent. My head senses with my tongue, body fluid, and shedding skin. I now am a large wild cat feeling with my paws, very aware of my surroundings. I travel to the center of the Earth by way of water to find the secret of saving the Earth. I'm too late. Then I'm the plant world of my origin. I bring the world of the spiritual plant to the center of the Earth. A portal from the plant world to the Earth center is bright, with colors of light that change, uplifting the Earth's energy. Then the Earth explodes, and I am a wild cat walking in the other world, watching the explosion, unaffected by the Earth's destruction, watching, watching. Then I am a cell again, a fragment of light, a spirit plant, flying around the universe and trailing other sparks of light to create a new world.*

Faye traveled the world with a serpent spirit and a wild cat as guides, who took her to the center of the Earth to find answers. It is too late to prevent the Earth's destruction; it explodes, and she returns, but as a cell, a mere fragment of light, and the spirit plant survives to create a new world.

Though Faye had not read Thomas Berry, her next experience with the Hallstatt Warrior (see page 53), a Realm of the Dead posture, expresses Berry's thoughts of starting change with our youths by teaching them how the world should be:

> ***11-27-11:*** *The bear is sitting back and watching. An eagle is looking at the world, a world of many greedy and self-serving people. How can we keep the human spirit pure? We need to start when people are young, with pure thoughts of how the world should be, and keep them on track so they do good things for the planet and not become selfish and evil like the humans who are controlling everything and destroying the planet. From the beginning of time one person doing evil over others has led to the destruction of the planet, while at the same time there have been humans with the love of light, love, and nature that gives us hope. We are a failed species. Is it too late? Looking at the world, what can we do? The answer is that each and every human must go within and meet her- and himself, soul to soul, every day for an extended period, deep within to be with self, face to face with self, to answer the self's soul purpose with each action, to go within each action, to be one's own judge. We must dive deep within to not let ourselves go so far astray, to know truth and follow it. This is our only hope.*

Thomas Berry believes that to become one with the Earth we must have elders to bring the younger generations into the fold. We need to teach them that the evils of greed and ego-centeredness are causing the destruction of the Earth, and because of this we have become a failed species. For both Faye and Thomas Berry, the answer is to go within, deep within our soul, to face ourselves and our actions and not let ourselves go astray from the truth of what we find there. This experience of Faye's that came from deep within her beautifully expresses Thomas Berry's thinking: "Our present situation is so extreme that we need to get beyond our existing cultural formation, back to the primary tendencies of our nature itself, as expressed in the spontanaeities of our being."[1]

Faye was feeling great frustration with those who are destroying the Earth with their corruption and greed. In her next ecstatic trance experiences she repeatedly died to return to Earth, seeking safety and places free of pollution and toxins. In her rebirth she was given new and increased strength and beauty as a healer of the Earth, but what survived is a speck, a molecule, the spirit to bring to life a new world of beauty, where she is an elder helping to bring back the ancient ways of the hunter-gatherers. While using the Shawabty posture (see appendix, figure A.17) for initiation or death and rebirth, Faye had this experience:

> ***3-4-12:*** *I feel myself folding into myself, feeding my heart core. My heart turns into the Sun. I am burning up, everything about me burns up. Then down through my feet into the Earth sprouts up new little Fayes, coming up like flowers. Balls of light emanate in round discs from my hands, and I start growing up through the universe, a very long distance until I finally come to the place of my origin. There I am with a large light like an aura around my face. About me is the place of my soul's origin looking down at me as I am looking up at it. We then merge, the part of me that is of my origin merging with the part of me that is arriving there. I am merging into myself, going up and facing down, going down. This merging is happening back down through all the universes until I reach the Earth, my head and hands down with my head immersed in light. From my hands emanate balls of light. The balls of moving qi are moving up through my present physical self, working every inch of my body until they reach my head. They move up my spine and back to my third eye. I become the ball of qi, moving through the universe, condensing into what is going to be a star.*

In this rebirth Faye was given energy, qi, as she spouted up from the Earth like flowers, with the light of an aura around her face, a new energy that flowed through the remaining five experiences. She grew up through the universe to merge with her soul's origin before returning to the Earth.

While wearing deer antlers in the Cernunnos posture (see appendix, figure A.3), used for metamorphosis or shape-shifting, Faye had this experience:

> ***4-29-12:*** *Small serpents come from my mouth and from my stomach, lots of them. Then come larger serpents, then a waterfall comes out of my mouth. The water makes a lake, and a very large serpent swims in the lake along with the smaller ones. The serpent carries me. I am riding on it and sink into the water. I am moving around in the water and breathing through my skin. I start to sink into the soft mud at the bottom although I don't want to. I keep going down with all the streams of water carrying me to the center of the Earth. I am swimming around in very clean water and loving it, wanting to be in this crystal-clean water. Then I come across dirty water that had seeped to the center from the toxic waste above. I swim away from it but can see more toxic water ahead so I come back up to the surface. Then I am a serpent tree. I split off and become branches. The big serpent body wraps around the Sun, the Moon, and the stars, and I keep going up and up, to the faraway place of the grandmother serpents. We look down on Earth and I see corruption, garbage, and toxins instead of flowers and animals. The animals are the purest of all. The grandmothers shower me with white light and beauty and my head reaches up into light and beauty. It is permeating my whole being, and I am to bring it back to the Earth, through the dark veil down below. At one point the serpent comes out of my mouth, into my vagina, up through my body, and again out my mouth. Then it reverses direction, going into my mouth and down through my body and out through my root chakra.*

In this experience Faye was the serpent of sacred knowledge looking for crystal clear water but finding only pollution. About two years later when she discussed this experience with me, she identified the serpent coming out of her mouth, into her vagina, and up through her body to again come out her mouth as an act of facing herself, just as the ouroboros takes its tail in its own mouth. The ouroboros symbolizes self-reflectivity, especially in the cyclical rebirthing of itself while facing itself.

REBIRTH AS A HEALER

In Faye's next experience, using the Jama-Coaque Diviner posture (see page 43), she sought a place near clean water, away from people, a place where she could tend her garden in peace. She asked a question of the diviner: "Is this where I'm supposed to live? If not, where?" She received her answer in a vision:

> **3-12-13:** *I am the ocean, lakes, rivers, creeks, and waterfall. I am a floppy water creature falling. I understand that I should live near water, any body of water, and water, for now anyway, is my medicine. I am then an eagle flying around the world looking for water; it needs to be unpolluted and that is not easy to find. I am then on top of a mountain. A ceremony is being performed for me to let go of all attachments. I am naked and starting out fresh. I come into a new space, moving forward. I see myself living away from any town, not too close to so many people, a place where I can continue my spiritual growth. My energy focuses on myself to find this spiritual place where I can grow with the right amount with work, where I can work more on myself than in my practice or my gardens.*

Several weeks later, while using the trance stance of Ishtar (see appendix, figure A.6), an initiation and death-rebirth posture, Faye sought an answer as to why humankind has to be destroyed, though she already knew within herself the answer to this question. As a huge bird along with many other smaller birds and beings, she flew to the center of the Sun:

> **3-31-13:** *I am the goddess, strong and upright. I begin walking the Earth and see people burning. It goes to my heart. I know inside of me that they have to burn, but why? I take off like a rocket, straight up toward the Sun. The dragon comes and says, "You don't know what you're getting into"—a warning, but I have to go. I have to know why and whether the people of Earth will be saved. I continue. I become a huge bird with a large beak*

and large, strong wings, shape-shifting, as I still feel like the goddess. I fly directly into the Sun, and other birds join me. We are all loaded down with smaller birds, representing life. The other large birds that are carrying the smaller beings of life are following me. As the leader, I am the one in charge. I have to go directly into the center of the Sun to find the answer—that is where the knowledge lies, so I go into it, and the others follow. We all get burned, singed, and then we are only molecules of life. Our bodies are destroyed, but our souls and spirits are the molecules of life. I then see why: The people are destroying themselves, with no exceptions. Even newborn babies are reincarnated souls that are part of the destruction created by the decisions they made in previous lifetimes in which they chose greed, consumerism, and luxuries. There are no exceptions. The Sun then sends me back. I am still the goddess in bird form, a big white bird with a huge and beautiful wingspan. Not all of us make it through the Sun. As we are sent back we pick up bits of the universe's molecules to take back to start a new life on the face of the planet. Those of us who do make it through the Sun are sent back to Earth. The Sun gives us a shortcut back. It took a very long time to reach the Sun, but we become part of the water, hail, frozen water, being hurled back to Earth, then rain, heavy rain. Back on Earth, Earth is totally burned. All that remains is smoke. Nothing living is left.

Note the appearance in this vision of the dragon who can be seen as having similar qualities to the snake. Their ability to breath fire exhibits their role as both creators and destroyers.

Following this apocalyptic vision, Faye had a final experience of rebirth a month later while using an initiation posture, the Shawabty posture (see appendix, figure A.17):

4-28-13: *My feet go into the ground. My body fills with worms and sperm with big eyes. My spirit leaves through top of the head, but my feet keep me on Earth. The spirit part of me that is released is flying. The eagle flying, the dragon spitting fire, the winged horse—all are merging into* *one, becoming one creature: an ancient being, the wise healer who can walk on the Earth, fly in the sky, and move through the underworld, while gathering plants, crystal-like objects, roots, and energies to be used for the good of humankind after the men of greed destroyed themselves. So I am one of these creatures and have the spirit of one, the personality of one, but I must remember who I am. Now I can go to all of those places, but only in spirit. The humans can go physically to all of these worlds. I am supposed to remember and bring back the ancient ways.*

In this final experience, Faye's eagle, dragon, and winged horse merge into one ancient creature: the wise healer who can walk the Earth and fly. This being gathers together the beings of the Earth that will survive, the plants, roots, and other good energy, which will be used to heal the Earth after the men of greed have been destroyed. Faye's direction is clear: it is her life's purpose to remember and bring back the ancient ways.

9
RECONNECTING WITH OUR MOTHER, THE EARTH

Wherever you are is home
And the Earth is paradise
Wherever you set your feet is holy land . . .
You don't live off it like a parasite.
You live in it, and it in you,
Or you don't survive.
And that is the only worship of God there is.

WILFRED PELLETIER AND TED POOLE

The ecstatic experiences that I have presented in the previous chapters were taken from my collection of around 2,000 experiences gathered from different groups I have led since 2007. In retrospect I can say that all of these spontaneous experiences provided the journeyer with a greater sense of connection to Mother Earth, especially those that were undertaken with the intention of creating a sense of oneness with the Earth, as the experiences described in this chapter reveal.

The ecstatic postures are an excellent way of giving a person direction, especially the divination postures. And because the postures are derived from the ancient hunter-gatherer peoples who lived their lives so attuned to the rest of creation, they are particularly powerful in connecting us with nature and the Great Mother. I have found at times that by just asking the spirit of a divination posture which posture should I use, the diviner frequently suggests that I change to a different posture. That is why we often begin a sequence of postures with a divination posture. In the pursuit of ecstatic ecology, sometimes what is needed next is not clearly known to the person, and so asking a question like "What do I need to become more one with the Great Mother, the Earth?" can provide a clear answer.

ASKING FOR DIRECTION

Our regular ecstatic trance group uses the Olmec Diviner posture (see appendix, figure A.14), a posture for divination. Amalia had the following experience, which she titled "The Earth Loves the Sun."

> ***2-23-14:*** *The first thing I see is the fireball of the Sun with flames coming out of it, with the Earth looking on. It is maybe one of the first sunsets with wispy clouds, and I realize that the Earth loves the Sun and yearns for it and its heat. I see the first tree—again, a wispy thing—and great broad landscapes of the Earth before the time of living creatures. I then see the stars and especially a very large white star, a birth star to which we are connected, maybe our origin. Maybe it explodes, but that might just be a thought. There are many falling stars in the night sky, and there is the deep sense of yearning in the Earth to respond, to show the Sun how much she loves him and basks in his warmth. She makes herself beautiful with mountains and oceans to reflect the Sun and dresses herself in green, all beautiful, with all the plants yearning and growing toward the Sun. Then I see us dancing and participating in this worship. I see celebrations and Stonehenge, the Hopi Indians dancing, and the sacred Sun Dance. All the time I feel this opening and yearning of the Earth for the Sun and her joy in bedecking herself for him. The smell and other senses I experience are important and vivid.*

Amalia concluded that the message she received in asking what she needed to do to become one with the Great Mother was to get back to celebrating the Sun. Later she added some more thoughts about this experience:

With the Olmec Diviner I had an incredibly strong feeling that we are creations of the Earth, and our purpose is to help in the celebration of her beauty before the Sun and the stars. I am thinking of the beautiful patterns of light that one can see at night when flying over the Earth. The patterns of light feel like adornments. I am also feeling that immense yearning that we all feel within us that comes from the Earth's yearning. I think my answer is that we don't have to become one with the Earth, because we already are. We just have to accept our place in this celebration of interconnectedness.

During the same session, Julia asked the same question of the Olmec Diviner and recorded the following experience:

2-23-14: *I first see a swan flying across an expansive sky. I see a very large bear walking toward me. I see a blue sky with clouds. I am walking along a river. I see myself as a small child looking up at the Olmec Diviner, and I ask the Diviner the question, "What do I need to be one with the Great Mother?" I then see myself as a primitive woman shaking a rattle over an infant (I'm assuming my infant), and the baby is wiggling to the rhythm of the rattle. We are outside and it is dark. Everything is illuminated by firelight. The scene then changes, and I see a city full of robot people walking in the streets, and every robot person has a cell phone raised to their ear as they all march with cell phones, like an army. I then see myself at my computer using the Internet, surrounded by a bubble. Then I return to the earlier scene, where I see a bunch of primitive people with rattles on their ankles dancing rhythmically around the infant. I see the bear again walking toward me.*

After allowing this experience to percolate in her mind for eleven days, Julia delved into an interpretation:

> *I think the vision of myself surfing the Internet surrounded by a clear bubble represents me being trapped in my own little world. When I think about the image of the robot army all marching through the city, each person holding a cell phone to their ear, I feel stuck. We're so absorbed in our own little world of being in the bubble, sucked into the Internet and sucked into a phone call or playing games on the cell phone. All this takes us out of the real world and into an artificial world. More and more people just interact with technology and less with actual human beings. We're using technology as a means of interacting, which separates us from one another. Social responsibility is declining, yet there are pockets of people who still care. I think people who don't care much about the welfare of other people certainly aren't going to care about the welfare of the Earth. In my experience of traveling to a lot of low-income countries, the pollution and environmental destruction in other parts of the world are even more atrocious than what we see here. I've come to think that caring for the environment is a luxury, and it seems like it's mostly a certain liberal type of wealthier person who cares. I think it's really telling of just how much technology separates us from other human beings and from the natural world. It's so illusory. Many people say that technology is uniting human beings, and that we're now connected to every other human being on the globe through technology, but it's all phony and artificial. Indigenous peoples are seemingly not valued as oil companies displace them or kill them for that matter. Modern people who have the most advanced gadgets are more valued, but only because they have some purchasing power. Indigenous peoples are seemingly more connected to the Earth, knowing and understanding all of the natural world, while most modern people don't have a clue. We rely on specialists, or what information we can find on the Internet. What seems so ironic is that indigenous peoples actually seem alive, like real human beings, while a lot of us in the modern world seem robotic,*

like zombies, and even reckless. So by saying that the indigenous peoples actually seem alive and connected to other human beings and their natural environment, it seems that they're much more advanced than the zombies on the cell phones. Lifestyle changes seem monumental, but it's easier when one first looks at his or her values.

So what do I need to be one with the Great Mother Earth? Spend less time on the Internet? I don't spend much time on it anyway. A lot of people have issues with their parents, fathers and mothers, that they can't resolve or get past, and they are neither capable of forgetting nor do they know how to forgive. Perhaps it's just that I need to love and respect my own mother. In indigenous cultures there's definitely a reverence for elders and ancestors that our modern society seems to be lacking. We don't value aging in this culture. We value youth and beauty. Hence, we're a disposable culture. We always have to have the next new thing.

Julia's commentary reflects her own personal growth as she is challenged to face personal issues in responding to the current crisis on our planet. Only by reconciling these issues will she be able to find oneness with our Earth Mother.

Betty was also part of our group that used the Olmec Diviner on this day:

2-23-14: *My journey is in a mass of humanity. It is dark when I first start. I am in a very rough ocean, and the waves carry me to a beach. About fifty feet in from the shore is a high wall. There is a symbol of a beautiful peacock. I am then met by an ancient man. He is dressed in a beautiful robe and the Sun is setting behind him. His robe reminds me of Aztec or Mayan robes. He is holding a basket of grain. He smiles at me and nods his head for me to accept the grain. I take the grain, and I then see masses of children. The expressions on their faces show that they are perplexed. I then am in space looking down at a planet, a planet unknown to me. I am then back on Earth, and there I am met by a great crowd of humanity. They are very happy, and I have a feeling of peace.*

Betty's experience triggered memories of her Irish grandmother:

I don't know who loved who more. I was six or seven years old. She taught me about nature and instilled within me a love of fairies and the spirits of flowers and elves, but mostly love for the Great Mother. In later life, after she had passed, in my mind she became my "3-M gram": myth, magic, and magnificence, and so much more. She taught me much. I try to walk with Mother Earth always. It's not hard, and the joy is immeasurable.

A couple of weeks later, Betty added,

I really, really liked this! This journey was like a hit on the head! I understand everything this journey holds. Blessings to the Olmec Diviner! Your question of "What do we need to become more one with our Great Mother?" brought me thoughts of my grandmother. She popped into my head immediately. Over the years, as I learned about the Native American culture, I began to understand what she had told me. In this experience the children's look of confusion is what I was meant to see in feeling my heart ripped open, knowing that children around the world go hungry. It was a wake-up call to me to go beyond just thinking about it, to doing something about it. The grain was a powerful symbol to me after I understood this message. The planet unknown to me is the New Earth, where people are happy and at peace. So now there is a new path for me, my new mantra. "One seed can create a miracle!"

Catharine, who was part of the group that used the Olmec Diviner on this occassion, had the following experience:

2-23-14: *When the rattle first starts I see an eagle flying . . . It is flying high over the water, either a large river or lake. Then I am a fish swimming in the water, then a heron standing in the water. I then become a parrot in the trees, and then a rhino. Then I am a bug, and* *then a butterfly. I find myself going into the Earth as an earthworm or maggot, and as I crawl out of the ground I become a flower blooming. I go up to the petals, where I become a bumblebee buzzing around the flowers. Then I return to myself as a human dancing in the rainforest. My arms are butterfly wings, and my feet become fins. I am dancing to the rhythm of nature. At the end of the journey I am again an eagle. At one point I am flying over Alaska.*

Following this experience Catharine reported, "I feel free, connected to the Source, to Nature. As I morph from one being to another I know we are all one. I feel grounded and connected to the Source; calm and at peace in the circle of life." Several weeks later she summarized the message of this experience simply as, "Let go and just be."

My journey in this session with the Olmec Diviner yielded the following experience:

2-23-14: *The diviner immediately tells me that what I need to learn is from the jaguar. I quickly become the jaguar stalking through the jungle, moving slowly, very aware of everything. As I lifted my leg and set my paw back down on the Earth, it is with great intention and care, feeling it slowly touch the Earth and what I am about to step on, testing the Earth beneath my paw. My paws feel extremely sensitive to what they touch as I set them down. I lower them in silence and do not want to harm anything on the Earth beneath my paws, the microbes and other life in the soil. At first I am not aware of my hind legs stepping, but then I become aware of them and realize that this way of stepping is automatic, without thought, and that my awareness is more through my eyes and nose in being aware of everything around me.*

The jaguar features prominently in this journey. All major Mesoamerican civilizations featured a jaguar god, and for many, such as the Olmec, the jaguar is an important part of shamanism, represented visually in much of their art. Jaguar symbolism is confidence, power, and intense focus. Cats have very sensitive sensory neurons in the paws that direct where they step, allowing them to walk in silence.

The lesson I learned from the jaguar is, first, to be aware of where I put my feet in order to harm nothing of the Earth, and second, to be very aware of everything around me at all times, not just when I feel like stalking. The teaching is that I must show constant, continual respect for everything of the Earth.

When we concluded this session, I asked the group what posture we should use for the next session. The word that came to mind was *celebration,* meaning celebration of the Earth, and that is exactly what we did, by going back to our earliest memories of bonding with our Great Mother.

EXPERIENCES OF CHILDHOOD ONENESS

Children very naturally experience nature and the Earth with a great sense of oneness. They just innocently live this way without trying to put it into words. Then the various institutions—educational, religious, and state—try to take the child away from this natural, in-born, magical sense of oneness. These institutions have other ideas as to what is important; they attempt to mold the minds of young people, asking them to abandon their innocence and sense of oneness in order to conform to social norms. That is why, as an adult, bringing alive these early, innocent childhood experiences can be a very liberating experience in regaining our sense of wonderment and connection with the world around us.

Our local group decided that in our next session of April 6, 2014, we would use the Calling the Spirits posture (see appendix, figure A.2). A week before our group was to meet, in preparation for this journey, I decided to use the Calling the Spirits posture myself at home. To connect with the spirits of my youth I faced South as I stood on our sauna deck next to our pond:

4-6-14: *What first comes to mind is the feeling/thought that I need to call the spirits of my youth. Recognizing the child's natural ability to explore the Earth and my own childhood experiences of exploring the terrain of a small area in the San Bernardino Mountains near the village of Running Springs, California, I feel I need to explore further the origin of my feelings of becoming one with the Earth. I quickly see and become my younger self sitting next to the street curb in front of our house, my childhood home, watching a stream of water running alongside the curb. Someone up the street is watering their lawn, and the runoff is running along the curb. I find a leaf or a piece of paper lying nearby and put it in the stream. I then run along the curb and down the block in front of the homes of our neighbors, watching the leaf float to the end of the block and then down a sewer drain. I run back and put another leaf in the stream, this time with an ant on it, and I watch the ant make its journey down the stream. After doing this several times with different boats and passengers, I have the adult thought that this is showing me the journey of life, of floating along with the stream, but at the level of a childhood experience this is one more of those early experiences of connecting with the Earth.*

This experience clarified for me the importance of reliving and internalizing at a deeper level my childhood feelings about nature—the simplicity and naturalness of my connection, and the sense of wonder invoked by it. I vowed to work with these feelings again the following week, when our ecstatic posture group met. I recommended that we all face South while using the Calling the Spirits posture and suggested that we enter the experience with the intention of reliving, honoring, and celebrating our childhood experiences of being one with the Earth.

In this session Amalia had an experience she later titled, "The White Dove":

4-6-14: *I am in a playground sliding down a slide in a game I had utterly forgotten, in which many children hook together, one after another, to go down a slide like a train, ending up as a pile of kids in the sand at the* *bottom. I must have done this many times but I can't remember a specific memory, just the sensation of togetherness and the touch of a tangle of kids. Then I am flying in the air on the back of a white dove. I am very small, like Nils Holgersson.* I am holding on to the dove's neck, my arms wrapped around her, and I feel very close and snuggly. We are flying over a forest toward a high snowy mountain. Then we land at the foot of the mountain at the edge of the forest, and I get off the back of the dove. I am like Tom Thumb, as high as the blades of grass, peering through, a little scared, but ready for adventure. I am holding on to the dove with a looped string that is tied around the dove's neck. I am wondering if that is because the dove is captive or for another reason. It seems that the reason is my need for connection with the dove. We venture through the forest of grass into the real forest, with its enormous trees, where we hide and watch. There is a fairy-tale cottage and a road with a bridge. We watch as a man on horseback crosses the bridge and knocks on the door. A woman opens the door and he goes in. We stay hidden and then follow the path that leads into the open, to a castle far in the distance. We fly to it and land on the ramparts. The Sun is shining and there are fairies flying all around. We look down into the depth of the castle and there we descend. At the bottom there is a small pond, and I peek in it to see my reflection. It is me as a young girl with short hair. We stop and stay there awhile. Then we fly into the light. We come to this great fairy woman who is all light and we sit in her lap. She comforts us. Then we continue flying in the light and back into the forest. The connection with the dove is familiar, like in* The Golden Compass. *We land on a boat on the ocean on top of the mast, looking down at the people below on deck with a shimmering sun on the waves. We reach the shore, the beautiful beach of probably South America. Then I dig in the sand and bury myself while I am still cuddled and connected to the dove.*

*Nils Holgersson is the hero of an early-twentieth century two-volume tale *The Wonderful Adventures of Nils* about this young Swedish lad whose "chief delight was to eat and sleep, and after that he liked best to make mischief." He is reduced in size by an elf and as a result is able to talk with animals.

Amalia's experience is notable for its many fairy-tale aspects. A few days after the experience, having given it some more thought, she e-mailed me:

I think the Calling the Spirits posture brought out that sense of connection. The dove, if you remember, is the symbol of peace after the Flood. The dove is white and pure. It is not really loving in the sense of nurturing, but it is connected with a sense of oneness of purpose, a sense of "we," not "me." I am not alone in this Earth adventure, just as I was not alone in the pile of kids at the end of the slide. I think that sense of not being alone and at the same time of being very small is important to my sense of oneness. At the end I am immersed in the Earth. I am safe and connected. It is a physical sensation of connectedness.

Betty reported her experience with the Calling the Spirits posture as follows:

4-6-14: *I am first aware of indistinct shadows of people. I am then in a very tall tree. Always in my childhood I climbed to the tops of all trees. I turn around and am face to face with an eagle. He is angry but I don't know why. I am then on a pontoon boat. Alongside me are dolphins. I am so happy. Next I am in a high mountain range. I can see a huge dwelling and decide to climb to it. I don't remember climbing but I find myself in the courtyard. There are Buddha-like people there, very calm, very kind. I play with a child who is adorable. There is then an eclipse of the Sun. The Sun is huge. I am then by a creek. I always played in creeks as a child, catching tadpoles. I see a snake slide into the water so I leave.*

After Betty's experience she mentioned that she is afraid of snakes. I commented that the angry eagle may have been someone who did not approve of her climbing trees. A week later Betty responded to my suggestion via e-mail:

I think I was born with a need to climb. The only person who didn't approve of my actions was my mother. I had to laugh at the thought of her being the angry eagle. She was frustrated with me but never showed anger. I don't know why I had and still have a strong attachment for trees. They have always brought me joy and peace. I told you about my gram and the things she told me. It was for her that I disobeyed my mother because I could not stay away from nature, it was who I was. My gram knew that, and that is why she chose me to hear her stories. I loved all of it—the sky, especially the night sky; the water, which also talks to me as I sit and listen to it; and the flowers too. They are Mother's art. She gives me so much. I love people, and yet there are times when I seek solitude. She is always with me. I know I speak a lot of joy, but it is a great gift and it sustains me. As for people, I applaud their achievements but do not go by that. I look inside to try to find their heart. It has never failed me. I do know that I march to a different drummer, but that's okay. I like me!

Julia reported her experience of accessing her childhood while using the Calling the Spirits posture as follows:

4-6-14: *I see myself as a child skimming rocks on water at Jacobsburg Park, near Easton, Pa., a park I used to love as a child, and my father would take me there frequently. I see myself on the banks of the creek. I am looking at the stones, looking for one that is flat and will skip well on the water surface. I skip my stone and look down into the water. I see lots of tadpoles. I remember how I used to look for tadpoles as a child. Later I see myself in my backyard looking out into the cornfield that is in back of our house. It is late autumn, the sky is cloudy gray, and the corn is pretty much knocked down. I can see the barn in the distance. Then I see a mass of people marching along to the rhythm of the rattle. They are black Africans, tribal people. They instantly symbolize to me humanity. I see this large group of people as a single organism, humanity, and they are moving together perfectly to the rhythm of the rattle or perhaps the* *rhythm of life. I realize that while every individual human is a separate being, a body/mind, each one is also part and parcel of the whole of humanity and the collective consciousness, and that each individual is playing out his or her part in the divine play of life. It occurs to me for a brief moment how human consciousness evolves as each person is both a participant and an observer of the play, and how our fears get played out before us as an evolutionary catalyst until that performance is no longer a challenge for us. I then see myself as a child again, spinning on the driveway, looking up at the clouds and seeing shapes in the clouds. I see myself playing by my treehouse, making mud cakes.*

Part of Julia's struggle, she said, is in letting go of her individual identity, her ego identification, to become part of the whole of humanity. It's a struggle we all must face as we mature in our spiritual awareness. Her desire to have a closer relationship with Mother Earth by connecting with her natural child self was nicely expressed in the image of making mud cakes.

DREAMING WITH INTENT

This group session went so well that I offered to lead a similar session for the morning workshop at the annual conference of the International Association for the Study of Dreams in 2014 (I led groups in ecstatic trance at this conference several years between this and my first experience seven years prior). The conference program offered the following description of my workshop: "What we are doing to resolve the ecological crisis is not enough. Changing how we experience our Great Mother, the Earth, by becoming one with her is required. This morning dream group will lead us on a series of ecstatic trance journeys to bring us to this oneness."

For the first morning, I chose what I consider to be one of the more enjoyable experiences, by asking the Jama-Coaque Diviner (see page 43) to take us back to some childhood experience with nature. Children in their innocence very naturally experience a closeness with nature, a oneness that is often lost when we reach adulthood, and so when we reconnect with these feelings the results are often quite exhilarating.

The group had twenty participants. The following are the experiences of six of the participants at the first session. What I found most interesting in all these experiences was how many of them found themselves under and/or climbing a tree. The following is David's account:

> ***6-5-14:*** *I go back in time to when I was young, growing up in cornfields and forests in Illinois. I am getting dirty digging holes, fishing, and lying in the fields, watching the clouds passing in the sky. I run through the forest and see the animals, some imaginary ones, coming up from the ground itself and then disappearing. Then I find myself in the fields, creeks, ravines, trails, clearings, bluff lines and sandstone outcrops, shelter bluffs, and forests of Southern Illinois that I know so well. I know all the nuanced shapes and features at various places. Then I move on to Southern Ontario and the lakes region, and finally to Western Australia and some areas of land on the coast near the small town of Denmark, along the wild Southern ocean, with its trails, brush, coastal scrub, sand dunes, and seacoast. I see myself as a child especially when I am in Illinois, and later, in Australia, as only a spirit with no body—a very pleasant experience.*

Such a collection of childhood experiences are often relegated to just the carefree nature of the child and do not reflect the responsibilities of adulthood. Bringing them alive again by reliving them in ecstatic trance and recognizing their importance in the life of a child brings that lost sense of innocence back into the life of the adult, with a new sense of connection with nature.

In an e-mail to me a few weeks later, David, who continues to live in Australia, added that his experience

. . . goes across my lifetime so far, from the beginning of childhood to the present, as exhibited in the narrative. I spend a few hours outdoors most days and always either go for a walk, run, a bike ride, a swim in the ocean, or a paddle on the river. I actually enjoy getting to know the landscape well, with all of its nuances. For the past four to five years I have done a daily outside meditation, affirmation, or belief work exercise that lasts about an hour or so.

On that first morning of the conference another attendee, Marilyn, found her experience with the Jama-Coaque Diviner to be most powerful:

6-5-14: *I immediately find myself as a young girl listening to the sounds of the leaves rustling in the breeze. I am very small, before the time I remember, maybe when I am just a baby or even still in the womb. I see shadows dancing in the light over my body. There is a zooming in a horizontal direction, and my world becomes very wide, encompassing all of the horizon. I am the world around me. There is no separation. The drum becomes my mother's heartbeat. It is dark, and then I see the Earth below me. I am floating in space and looking at the Earth starts a shaking in my legs. I am under the tree in my body, feeling the energy inside me, watching the shadows and hearing the sounds. I feel tears throughout the experience.*

In Marilyn's response to me a week later she reported,

It is interesting to me that the memory first came as a sound. Sound is a very important way that I connect in the world and especially in nature. I have traveled to places with my main agenda being to hear certain sounds, like the sound of wind in the aspen trees, the call of the loon, the fall mating call of the elk, and the howling of the coyote. Visuals for me come second, after sound. I think my experience was about how at one with nature I was as a little one. How open I was to all input from the world around me. How intense it was. But I also don't feel like I have lost that connection with nature. I feel in many ways that I can't live without that connection. I chose to live in the middle of the redwood forest. For this I am grateful every single day. When I go to the city, I immediately locate some little piece of living thing to keep me feeling connected.

A week later, Marilyn added more to her reflections on this experience:

For me this was probably the most important thing that happened at the conference. I feel like it reflects a lifetime of work. It was very spontaneous. While I know I was creating this in my mind, it didn't feel like I was creating it. It felt like it was presenting itself to me. How I relate this to my childhood experiences of nature is that at three years old, I was having to learn that there was a door between me and the world around me, that the oneness that I experienced wasn't experienced by those around me and that I needed to learn about that separation. Developmentally it may have been a necessary step, but now I can open that door again. In fact, maybe it is even my task to open that door again. As we age we are increasingly aware that we are heading home. I've been caring for my 98-year-old mom for several years now. It looks to me like it is definitely her job now to find her way back to where she came from. At 68 I've had an eyeful of what is ahead. This experience showed that in so many ways.

Barbara, calling the spirit of the diviner Jama-Coaque had this experience:

6-5-14: *As a young child I have a big tree in my front yard that I love. It is my friend and I talk to it. I tell it all kinds of things. My grandma lives next door and she has land. On her land there are four-leaf clovers, and I* *sit with my young cousins and look for the four-leaf clovers. We then move away from my friend the tree and the four-leaf clovers, and I have a deep sadness in my heart, so in this meditation I keep allowing myself to go back to my friend the tree. In writing this I feel very much like a child again.*

I often experience a tree as a spirit guide with connections to the three worlds: rooted in the Lower World, growing in the Middle World, and climbing to the Sky World. The tree is an exceptionally strong and rooted spirit guide for children. Also, so many children love the stories of the luck that four-leaf clovers bring them and they spend hours on their hands and knees looking for them.

Brian's ecstatic trance experience while using the Jama-Coaque Diviner brought him to two strong and stable features of nature:

6-5-14: *First, several childhood favorite nature spots come to me. The strongest image is a large tree in an open field on a hill where I spend a lot of time. I see the golden field, the green tree, and the blue sky with some big white clouds. The tree is one of the larger trees in the area. The second most prominent image is a large rock on the Gasconade River near my grandpa's summer home on the river. The rock was used in the 1800s to dock steamships and has an ancient metal ring in it. The rock overlooks a deep hole adjacent to a creek. This place holds some mystery compared to most of the river.*

Brian concluded that this experience of nature brought him back in touch with the rootedness and stability that he needs to be a leader and elder.

Sandy asked the Jama-Coaque Diviner to show her some early childhood experiences of being one with the Earth:

6-5-14: *I immediately go back to my World War II victory garden, when I was five to seven years of age. I am digging in the dirt, pulling carrots to eat, and find amazement in how strawberry plants send out runners.*

> *I look for four-leaf clovers on summer evenings, lying on my stomach in the grass, smelling the grass and feeling the grass on my cheeks and the taste of grass roots. I climb trees, swing on branches, collect leaves, pretend-play with acorns, and catch fireflies. I go on bird walks with my first-grade class early in the morning before school starts, and I find fascination with waterfalls, fast-flowing streams, and much more!*

Most impressive in Sandy's experience of nature is her use of all her senses: tactile, kinesthetic, taste, smell, and sight.

Janet went into her ecstatic trance experience with a beautiful quote by Mary Oliver: "I thought the Earth remembered me, she took me back so tenderly . . ."

> **6-5-14:** *I find myself at the base of a tree between large protruding, mossy roots. In this secret space I explore the tactile aspects of the tree and its roots, its bark, the Earth, my favorite place to play as a child. I dive down into the Earth to follow the roots and explore their essence. I climb up the trunk, enter a knothole, and become the creatures that are nurtured and sustained by this tree—the baby squirrel nesting with its mother and litter mates, the egg being incubated in a nest, and an inchworm eating leaves on the uppermost branches. I understand why humans do not care for one another with love, compassion, and nurturing spirit. They have lost their way because they have become disconnected from this essence of Mother Earth. She teaches us how to support, protect, shelter, and sustain one another, but most of us no longer know her, we don't hear her messages or don't listen, even if we hear her messages, her smells, tastes, touch, sound—senses all so strong throughout!*

Janet's experience beautifully brought alive her childhood experiences with nature, experiences of the interactions of life in nature, and offered her insights and teachings.

The enthusiasm of this group of IASD participants and the fun nature of revisiting childhood experiences was a very rewarding experience and showed me and the attendees the importance of connecting with our authentic natures as human beings at one with and attuned to our world and Mother Earth.

10

RITUALS THAT CULTIVATE OUR SENSE OF ONENESS

Hail Mother, who art the earth,
Hallowed by thy soil, rocks and flora
that nourish and support all life.
Blessed by thy wind that gives us breath
and thy waters that quench, bathe and refresh
all living things.
Holy Earth—as one—we praise your majesty,
grace and wonder.

Bill Faherty

Because of our busy lives we easily become distracted and forget that we are part of the Earth. Most of us live in an artificial world that seeks to control everything, especially the Earth. We need constant reminders to hold the Great Mother foremost in our minds, and these kinds of reminders are best given in the form of a daily or a continuous ritual. Such rituals and celebrations have always been central in the lives of hunter-gatherer cultures, with everyone participating in some way, depending on age and gender.

Ecstatic trance can provide an excellent framework for choreographing a daily ritual that connects you to the Earth. To determine your personal ritual, I suggest beginning with a divination posture to ask for general direction. Here I offer some experiences of members of our regular monthly ecstatic trance group, as well as those of participants in the morning workshop I led at the 2014 IASD conference, mentioned in the previous chapter.

On June 1, 2014, our regular ecstatic trance group journeyed with the Tala Diviner (see appendix, figure A.20). We asked the diviner to inform us about personal rituals that will help us maintain our sense of connection with the Earth. Julia offered her account:

> ***6-1-14:*** *I see myself as a young girl, around five years old. I am wearing a dress with leotards, chasing butterflies in a meadow. I quickly begin to feel like I have wings of my own. A butterfly lands on my hand and I am awed by its beauty. Then everything changes, and I am hugging the trunk of an elephant and petting the elephant's face. I am awed by the elephant's beautiful eyes, when again everything changes. I am now hugging a dolphin, but strangely I don't think we are in water. Again the scene changes, and I see myself sitting in the meadow, where I tear off my leotards and run off laughing and skipping joyfully. I feel that I am looking at someone next to me or holding the hand of a companion, but it isn't clear. It feels like it could be my grandfather. As the drumming continues I see myself still bare-legged and barefoot, spinning joyfully in the meadow.*

Julia said afterward that "this experience suggests that I need to bring more childlike play and dance into my everyday life to be closer to nature."

Betty was the drummer for this session with the Tala Diviner, in which she saw herself as the drummer for a group of Indians:

> ***6-1-14:*** *I first see a very thin cornet or crown. I am then with Indians, sitting in front of them as they sit in an arc in front of me. It is dark, but there is a fire and all are seated. I am playing the drum. The Indians' faces are painted. The way they wear their hair looks just like what I have seen at powwows. I see an opening over us and there are so many stars in the sky. I love playing the drum.*

I got an e-mail from Betty a week or so after I inquired about her experience:

> *I want to let you know where the Tala Diviner sent me. I have planted so many things and find joy seeing them grow. Harvesting brings me a great joy. Seeing what I harvest and going to food banks fills me up. I had the great honor of taking the totes to our local food bank this past week, strawberries, lettuce, and cabbage. All perfect! And to use the word* honor *is precisely correct. The people who receive the food are so grateful, and the children at the food bank I adore. Thank you for teaching me to journey. I know there's more to be learned, and I look forward to it eagerly.*

Tending a garden needs to be a daily ritual for it to be productive. Drumming for a circle of Indians, as in her ecstatic experience, connected her to the joy she finds in her garden, a direct connection with the Earth. As she enjoyed drumming she enjoys the children at the food bank.

When Amalia asked the question of the Tala Diviner, she was told that she needed to dance in a special way in a special spot in her garden as part of her daily ritual of connection:

> ***6-1-14:*** *I dance, starting with stretching and standing on my toes as I face Southeast, on a line connecting the wisteria to the apple tree as the center line of my garden. I'm dancing in a very deep, wide squat, similar to the grinding corn posture of qigong. This is not a very comfortable*

posture as I move from side to side. I walk into my vegetable garden wearing my yellow scarf as a skirt and bow as I enter. I honor the skunk. I walk on all fours and then roll in the grass with my legs in the air, like a pony.

The rituals have been implanted in each person's unconscious, and though they may or may not practice them daily as described in the experience, they are present in the unconscious and practiced mentally. I know personally that sometimes such a change in a person's ways of daily living does not happen immediately, but when the intent has been planted the change starts to happen and eventually becomes central in life.

At the morning dream group of the 2014 conference of the International Association for the Study of Dreams, I suggested we frame our question as "What can I do regularly to keep our Great Mother before me?" We chose the Mayan Oracle (see appendix, figure A.12) for this session, in which Marilyn recorded the following:

6-6-14: *My experience today is all about vibration, feeling the vibration in my body. My arm held up by my face is compelling, as if it is there to help me keep my focus, not to look away. I have the realization that I need to use a sound in my practice, even if it is just going out to my yard to drum each day before I see clients. The drumming is intense, and today it sometimes sounds threatening. I think I am feeling more vulnerable. The message I receive is that I am out of tune and I need to keep my body "in tune." I am experiencing moments of waves of nausea. My arm begins hurting and feels like it takes endurance to keep it there, but it is important to do so. I end the experience feeling many tears.*

Marilyn later added, "Today's experience was darker and a bit ominous. I am not sure why. Near the end I even heard a low growling sound. It may have been real, as if someone in the room cleared their throat. I don't imagine a real growl happened." A week after this session, Marilyn had reflected on this experience sufficiently that she could add to her earlier insights:

The realization that the sound and vibration of the drum was deeply affecting me was a direct message that I need to incorporate sound in my practice at home, and I have. I went from this meeting to the meeting of Dream Incubation with Sound, where Travis Wernet played the dijeridoo and other instruments. I became a salmon swimming upstream. I registered the question as to whether that was wise, knowing what happens when salmon go upstream. I stayed with the salmon, and this took me into an experience of deep, deep grief. This was again a confirmation of how sound keeps me connected to what really matters.

A couple of months later, Marilyn reported that she was still drumming every morning.

Sandy also took her inquiry about finding a daily Mother Earth ritual to the Mayan Oracle:

6-6-14: *I am not able to physically hold the posture for long, but I can hold it in my mind. First, a vision of the first day comes to me, of sitting and lying on the grassy lawn at my parents' home, searching for four-leaf clovers. Then I see a dandelion blossom, which grows until it takes up the whole visual field. My experience then morphs into a recent adult experience of seeing a residential lawn covered with a carpet of huge dandelions about eighteen inches tall. It makes me laugh out loud in waking life and in today's vision. It's why I drove around the block to view it again, and then a third time. I stopped and took an iPhone photo. Today's vision includes Thich Nhat Hahn's poem about dandelions: "I have lost my smile. But don't worry, a dandelion has it." My ritual will include finding the exact poem and saying it aloud daily.*

When so many people wage a continued war against dandelions, her dandelion story is beautiful and a great reminder that there is a purpose for all of nature, and that this war on dandelions takes something from the Earth. The deep roots of the dandelion continually bring to the surface the nutrients needed by so many other plants around it, plus it is an incredibly nutritious herb—a great addition to salads.

Several days later in an e-mail communication, Sandy added:

In truth, Mother Earth is before me every day. Those childhood memories and behaviors linger on. I have been greeting every sunny morning for years with Mary Oliver's poem, "Hello Sun in my face . . ." just as I've been recycling for about twenty years. Being in nature mindfully is important for me every day. But I appreciate the further reminders and will add the postures I learned.

At the same session, Sylvia had the following experience:

6-6-14: *At first I get very warm, then I hear a sound that I can no longer identify. My child self is running through a ripe golden wheat field with my arms spread wide, brushing the grain, which makes a sound like music as they brush together. Then I hear and feel the rumbling and trembling of the ground as a herd of buffalo race forward. This is a buffalo hunt with Indians on horseback, their weapons (arrows) held high. Yi! Yi! scream the hunters. The head of a buffalo is so close to me that I can see his one eye, which reveals that he knows what's going to happen next. Then the kill, and all is frozen in this moment. I am so close, connecting to this sacred beast. We commune somehow, just in the knowing. Then the scene changes, and I'm back in a dream. My hand feels a cold breeze of air. In my dream I am rescued by an Indian driving a chariot.*

Later by e-mail Sylvia offered two related nighttime dreams that provided insight into this ecstatic experience. In both dreams she was caught up in buffalo stampedes with a friend. In both dreams she was rescued or survived, first when she was rescued by an Indian driving a chariot, and then by hiding behind some buildings. In both dreams the friend was terrified and left behind to fend for herself in the stampede. Sylvia offered this interpretation:

My friend in the dream, I feel, is the conformist part of me who resists moving forward, is only interested in being with the part of society that remains unaware of our evolution into a new dimension, a new way of being and living. She wants to be with people who are unwilling to change. Her eyes are closed to what's really coming, not aware of our need to move through this perilous time by doing things differently through the power of the divine feminine. I feel this buffalo stampede, a "blast from the past," is warning me not to be blind, but to learn from history and create a new way that will respect and protect all sentient beings. As Mother Earth is making her transformation, so must we. Tapping into the primal center of my being, getting in touch with my basic instincts, can aid me in understanding what is happening, to face the fear, go with the flow, and find a place within and without, where I can feel support and security.

This experience brought to Sylvia's mind the daily importance of keeping before her a sense of her connection with the Great Mother at a metaphoric, unconscious level of remembering the past and remembering to move forward to a new way of being and living with the divine feminine.

Using the Mayan Oracle posture to identify a daily ritual to keep our Great Mother before her, Paula received the following direction:

6-6-14: *The instruction I am given for a daily ritual to stay in contact with Mother Earth is that I should lie facedown on the floor/ground, using a massage pillow under my forehead to keep my nose facedown lying in an imaginary circle with arms and legs wide like Da Vinci's "Circle of Man." I imagine tendrils like a jellyfish coming from all the cells of my body, trailing down deep into the Earth, to its center. Then I hear a voice, instructional and loud, but also gentle, from an ethereal being at the 1:30 position of the* *clock-like circle around me saying, "EAT YOUR VEGETABLES!" Then it laughs and disappears. It is clear that the vegetables being referred to are those that grow close to the ground, root veggies and greens. I want to know who the spirit is and ask, "Man? Woman? Angel?" Ah! She appears in glowing robes flowing behind her as if she is facing into a breeze. Her golden hair tinged with red is also flowing behind her. She is smiling and joyful. She is the Sun! Farther back, in a wide, clocklike circle around me, from 9:00 to 3:00, are many other ethereal, indistinct beings clapping for the Sun, not with the rhythm of the drum, but as an audience would clap at the end of an appreciated performance. They love her appearance and instruction. I feel happy. I think about creating a circular blanket of material for the ritual, but that would be a barrier.*

In a later communication Paula reported that while sitting in the Mayan Oracle posture she was facing the Sun as she, as the Sun, appeared. She was nourished, not only by the light of the Sun, but with the Sun's instruction to eat vegetables, which she admitted she doesn't do often enough. She reported that she is taking this instruction to heart, especially as it builds on the idea of nourishment from the Sun. Her connection to the Sun is stronger than her connection to the Earth, she said.

In Janet's pursuit of the wisdom of the Mayan Oracle to create a ritual honoring Mother Earth, she had the following experience:

6-6-14: *I am led along what seems to be the beginnings of a pathway. I am outside searching for a special place. I try out a few places from my childhood, such as a treehouse my father built. Eventually I move to a grotto, which in reality is an enclosed circular hiding place at the edge of a wooded property with a cabin that I owned for ten years. But I want a place where I am living now to create a ritual honoring Mother Earth. I am drawn to the small creek flowing through our property, to a bend where a deep pool forms, the only deep section of the creek. I become my little eighteen-year-old dog making my way through the deep grass to get* *there. I step in, go farther, and begin to dog paddle. I can't see too well any more, but the water feels cool and refreshing. But I tire easily and cannot find the bank again. Eventually I am too tired to go on, and I let go and sink to the bottom. My spirit easily leaves my old gray body and scampers off, a puppy once again. My body is worn out and no longer serves me, so Mother Earth has taken me back. I feel the sadness and loss of my human's grief when she finds me, but she is now connected to this location as the bridge between body and spirit. This will be the place to create a new ritual. The creek gives life but also takes it. It is a circle of wholeness, a threshold, a sacred spot.*

Janet's Mayan Oracle experience to honor Mother Earth took her to a special sacred place—a deep pool on the creek that flows across her property, the place where her aging dog died. This is the place she decided to frequent for her daily ritual.

Following this session, our dream group used an initiation or death-rebirth posture to incorporate or instill within each participant what was learned from the Mayan Oracle session. For this we used an initiation posture, the Shawabty posture (see appendix, figure A.17). Here I return to Janet, whose experience with this posture added depth to her previous divinatory experience:

6-7-14: *I return to the water's edge, the creek I visited yesterday, the place where my dog drowned. I step into the water. I go deeper and deeper—knees, hips, waist, shoulders. The water is at my chin. I submerge entirely. A few air bubbles escape, but then I am done breathing. I think of a full-body baptism, of being reborn. I sink down and it is very pleasant. As I drop to the bottom of the pool, a spirit boat awaits. Ah, I realize it will take me to the underworld. Then the boat moves silently through the dark waters. I see the golden-eyed dog guarding the entrance step aside as we travel in. I see a double helix staircase of souls traveling upward and downward. Then I am back in the world above. I see baby Moses floating in a basket of reeds at water's edge. Then the scene changes again. I am* *an egg in my mother's uterus. The sperms are streaking past like comets. Which one will it be? What is my destiny, my DNA? I am excited to find out. I am now a developing fetus inside my mother's womb. I can't recall ever having the feeling of being inside her as she carried me. She is so excited, a second child. She sings to me throughout the day. I realize that this Shawabty pose is also a potential fetal position, and I want to curl up my body. Death/life/rebirth and the flow of water, blood, amniotic fluid are the primary vehicles of life. By returning to the water each morning to honor the Earth I can return to these primal states anew.*

The sacred place by the creek became a portal to Janet's rebirth, beginning with her conception within her mother's uterus, the beginning of life, and the excitement of her birth, just as the puppy spirit of her old dog rose and scampered off, leaving its tired old gray body in a place that honors Mother Earth. These experiences brought Janet's ritual of daily meditation by her sacred place to a deep metaphoric and unconscious experiential level.

For hunter and gatherer peoples, life itself naturally provided constant reminders of their connection to the Earth Mother. They lived this connection, and also celebrated it in rituals throughout the year. For we modern people, determining which daily ritual to maintain our connectedness is just a beginning. We must recognize the importance of maintaining our awareness of this connection throughout our daily lives if we wish to grow our sense of interdependence. Even if it is only a very simple ritual, the key is that we do it regularly.

EPILOGUE

RECLAIMING THE HUNTER-GATHERER WAYS

I'm the mad cosmic
Stones plants mountains
Greet me Bee rats
Lions and eagles
Stars twilights dawns
Rivers and jungles all ask me
What's new How you doing?
And while stars and waves have something to say
It's through my mouth they'll say it

VINCENTE HUIDOBRO

On the journey of writing this book I met many people, some who are very far from experiencing oneness with the Earth, and many who live and relate to her day in and day out. Most everyone has had experiences with this feeling of oneness as a child, but many have lost contact with that part of themselves, while others, like Gary Gripp, have never lost that sense of connection with the Earth. The inherent spirituality of this sense of oneness makes a person more open to the experiences of ecstatic trance. Though some beginners in my various trance groups at first exhibited distance or separation from our Earth Mother, it has not taken them long to regain the natural sense of oneness they experienced in childhood. Those who are already one with the Earth may seem not to need the transformative experience of ecstatic trance, though they can continue to grow closer to Earth with these experiences and deepen their connection. These ecstatic experiences are not rational, and thus they help people to move away from the restrictions of rational thinking, bringing them nearer to the instinctual rhythms of the Earth. I continue to be excited by the power of what Felicitas Goodman has offered the world in opening us to the power and possibilities of ecstatic trance.

Sue Birch, another instructor of ecstatic trance, once said that it is a sad commentary on modern life that the spirits are now known only as archetypes. Contacting the spirits, learning from the spirits, and being led by the spirits were and are central in the lives of hunter-gatherer peoples, and we too find these spirits alive and well in our nighttime dreams and ecstatic trance journeying. The postures were found in the ancient and contemporary art of the hunting and gathering peoples of the world, and it is from this artwork and from these peoples that we are led into the coming new age. The hunting and gathering peoples knew and know these spirits, and to discover their presence in our lives can bring us to an exhilarating sense of oneness with the Earth. These postures provide us with spirit guides from whom we have much to learn. They bring us to our center of harmony so that we are not a threat to animals, animals that come to us as they did back in the time of the Garden of Eden, or Garden of Idunn. These postures and the spirits they introduce us to assist us in journeying to discover the interdependence of all of life and to venerate the natural cycles—the seasons, the lunar cycle, and the cycle of night and day. They give us direction in moving toward spiritual maturity and elderhood. They bring alive within us our childhood experiences of oneness with the Earth. They teach us ways, ritualistic ways, to remind us how to keep on track in our growing experiences with the reality of interconnection.

In journeying with these experiences of ecstatic trance we are led spontaneously to experience oneness. But we can accomplish even more with intention, by asking the right questions of the diviners of antiquity and the spirits of the postures. Much of this book shows us how the method taught us by Felicitas Goodman spontaneously brings us into this new age, or New Dawn. Each component of this ritual—cleansing and calling the spirits of each direction; silently focusing on our breathing to quiet the mind; and the fifteen minutes of sitting, standing, or lying in the posture, accompanied by the beating of the drum or shaking of the rattle—each aspect brings us closer to experiencing our Great Mother, the Earth, in a very primal way.

Cleansing our bodies prepares our minds for calling of the spirits of the sacred directions, the spirits of the Earth, and the spirit of the posture, whether ancient or contemporary. As we focus for five minutes on our center of harmony, the spot just below the umbilicus that rises and falls as we breathe, we find that the spirits and the fauna of the Earth are attracted to us by the quieting of our minds, which brings us to a receptive state of consciousness. Then during the fifteen minutes of ecstatic journeying we find ourselves enmeshed in the experience of being one with the Earth.

Though we regularly and spontaneously have these experiences of oneness while in ecstatic trance, this feeling is facilitated even more directly when we ask the right question by going into the ecstatic experience with intent. We asked such questions as: "Show me what I need to do to be one with our Great Earth Mother," and "Lead me to relive, honor, and celebrate my childhood experiences of being one with the Earth," and "Teach me a ritual practice to keep my connection to our Great Earth Mother before me." There are many ways to frame a question or request depending on the person, the situation, and the issues of concern. The most logical posture to hold for this purpose would be a divination posture, asking for an answer to our question from the diviner. Other ways to frame a question might include "What spirit guide do I need to follow at this time?" or "Bring me a spirit guide to give me direction."

These are all just suggestions. Putting our thoughts into words is just a start, but we don't want to stay in the abstract place of the intellect. That is why integrating the experience within by using a death-rebirth or initiation posture as a follow-up can bring our initial question to a greater depth of consciousness, as we saw in Janet's experiences described in the previous chapter.

We are entering the time of the New Dawn, Nydagen, and with it the greedy ones who are ego-centered, who believe the Earth is to be exploited, will be left behind. In their panic of not understanding where the rest of the world is going they may strike out and try to stop what cannot be stopped by this incoming, unstoppable wave of higher consciousness. We are on the move, and though the future is not clear and we will undoubtedly make mistakes, our direction cannot be stopped, and hopefully this evolution will happen before we human beings destroy ourselves. This is an exciting time. Great beauty is to be found in rediscovering the spirits of the Earth and in following them. They have not deserted us. They are here. The spirits of the Earth and the spirits of the universe were alive for our ancestors, are alive among the hunter-gatherer people that exist today, were alive in our childhood, and are here to be rediscovered.

APPENDIX OF ECSTATIC POSTURES

Figure A.1. Bahia Metamorphosis Posture

Figure A.2. Calling the Spirits Posture

Figure A.3. Cernunnos Metamorphosis Posture

Figure A.4. Chalchihuitlique Metamorphosis Posture

Figure A.5. Chiltan Spirits Healing Posture

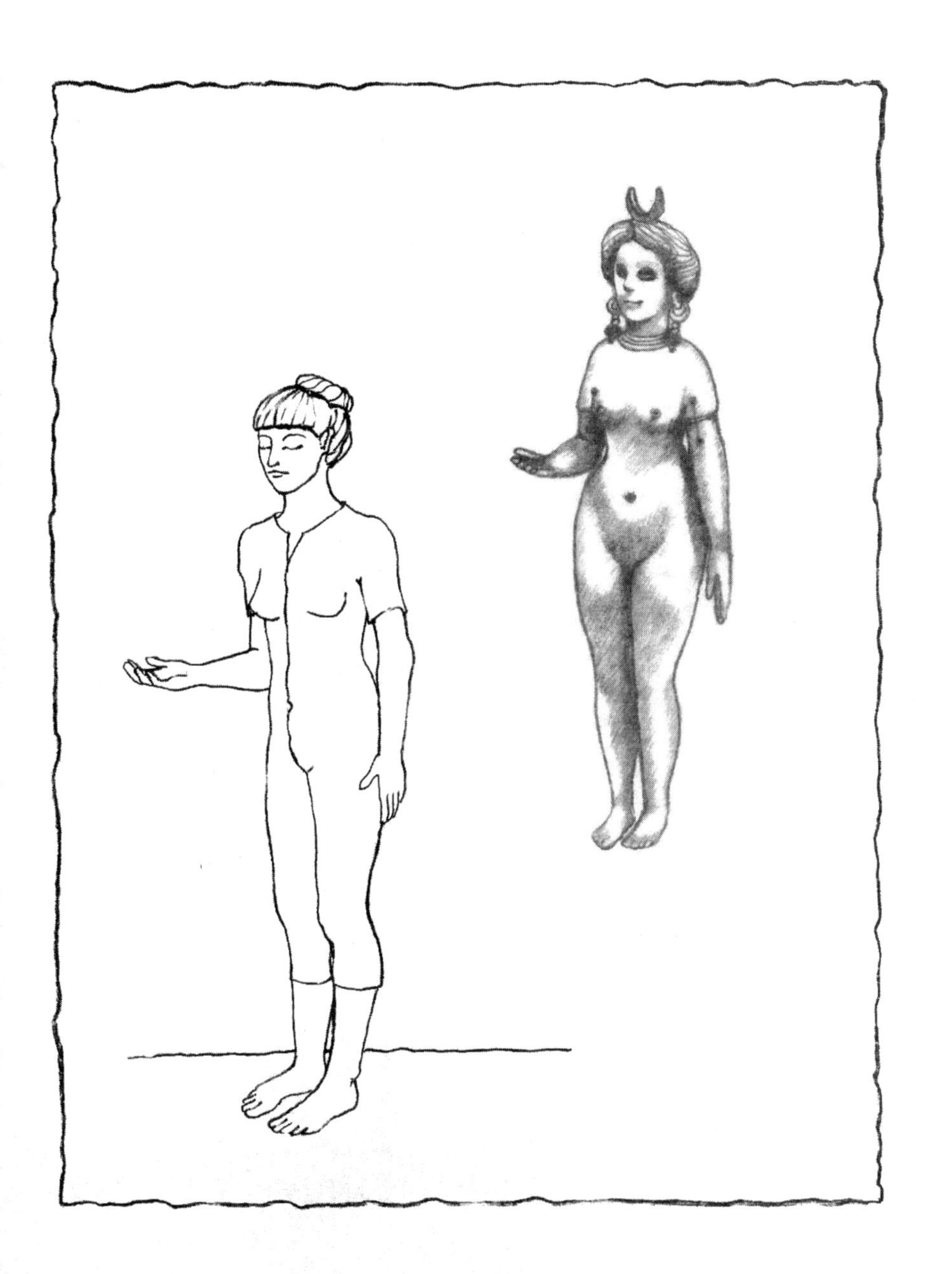

Figure A.6. Ishtar Initiation Posture

Figure A.7. Jama-Coaque Metamorphosis Posture

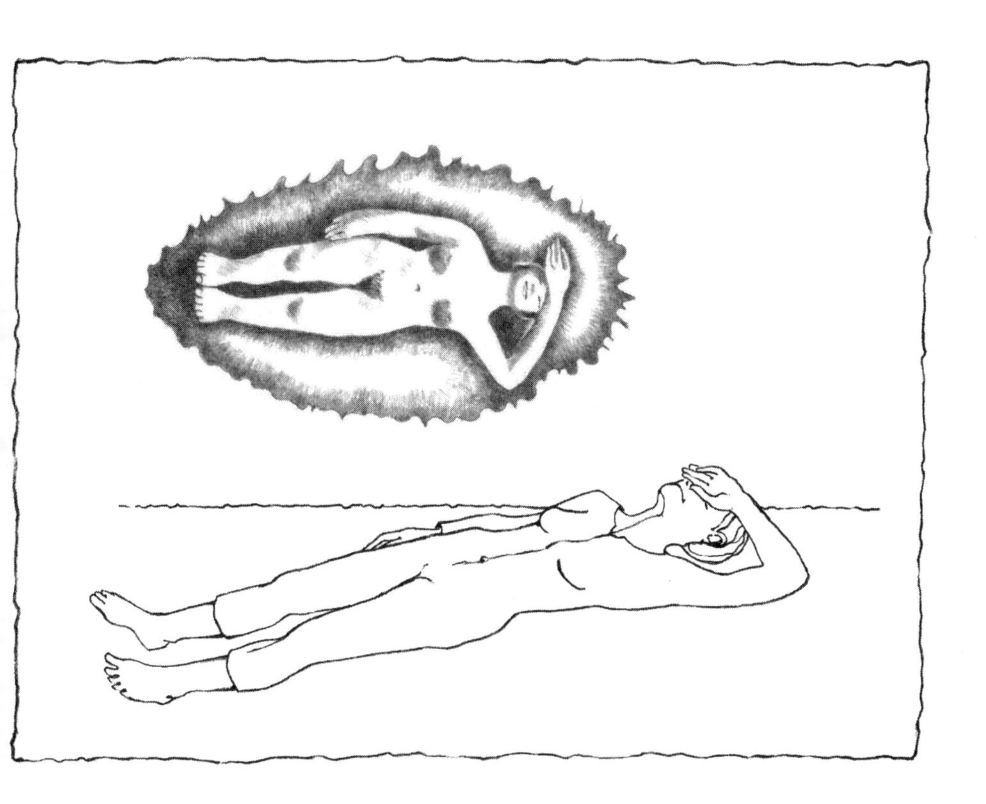

Figure A.8. Jivaro Underworld Posture

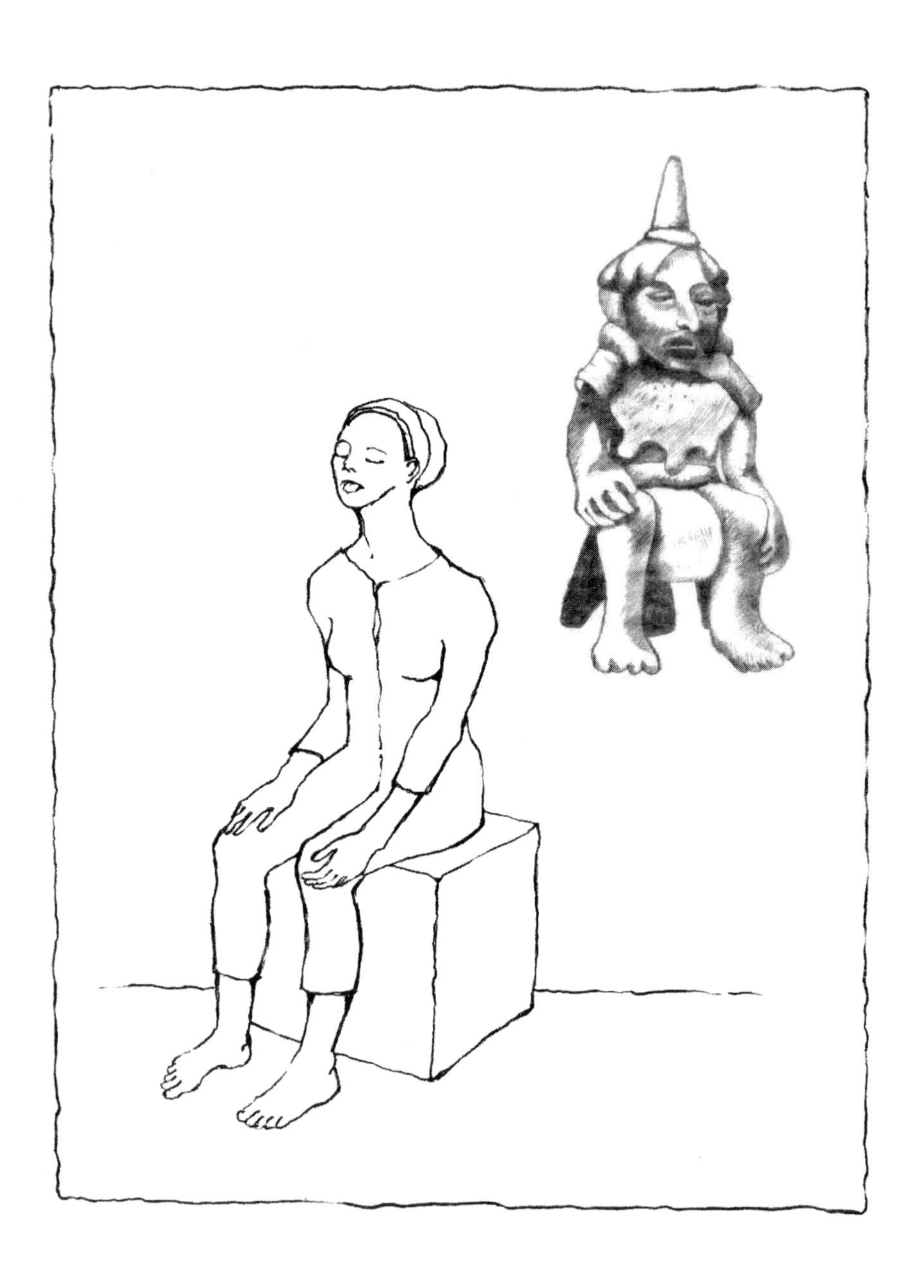

Figure A.9. Lady of Cholula Divination Posture

Figure A.10. Lady of Thessaly Initiation Posture

Figure A.11. Mayan Fish Woman Posture

Figure A.12. Mayan Oracle Divination Posture

Figure A.13. Nupe Mallam Divination Posture

Figure A.14. Olmec Diviner Posture

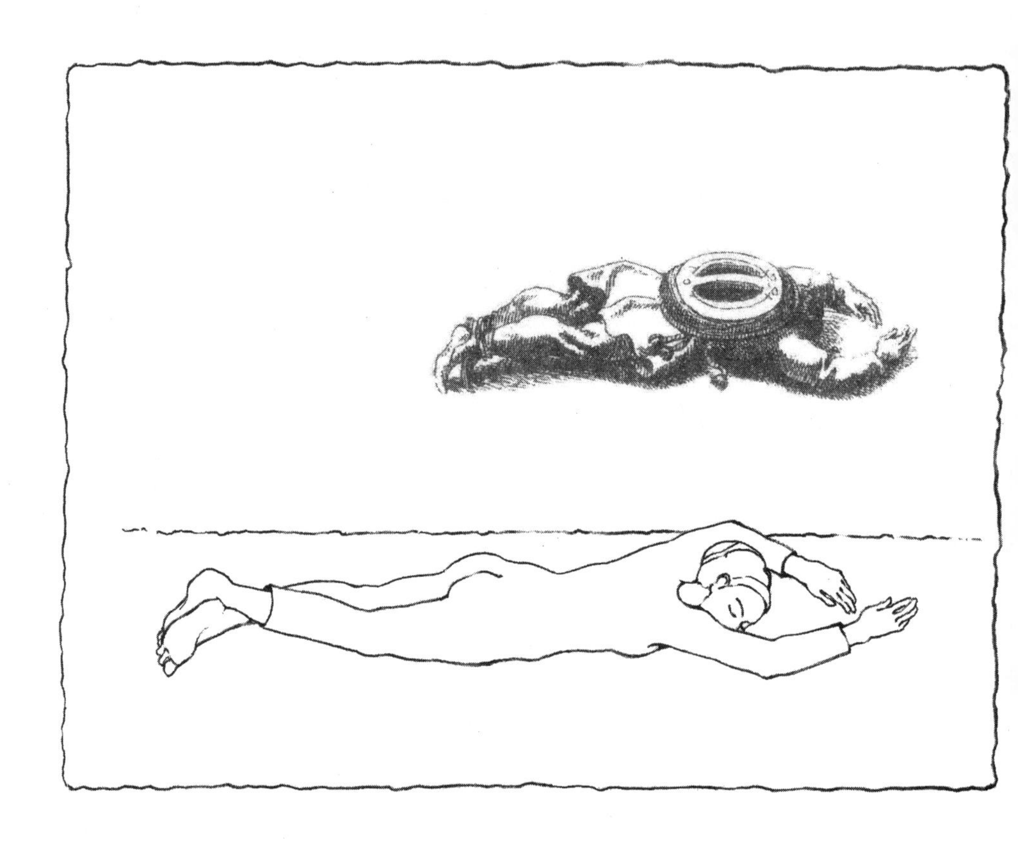

Figure A.15. Sami Underworld Posture

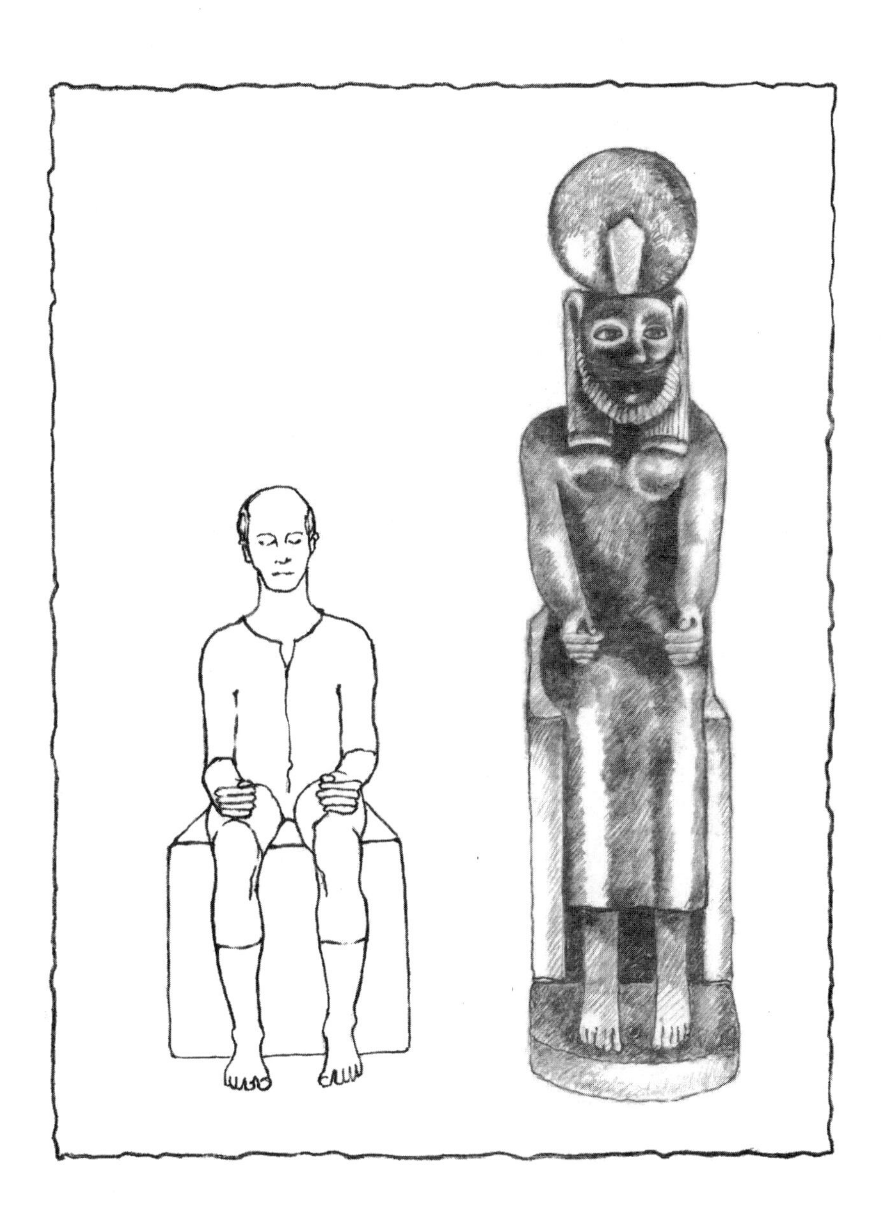

Figure A.16. Sekhmet Initiation Posture

Figure A.17. Shawabty Initiation Posture

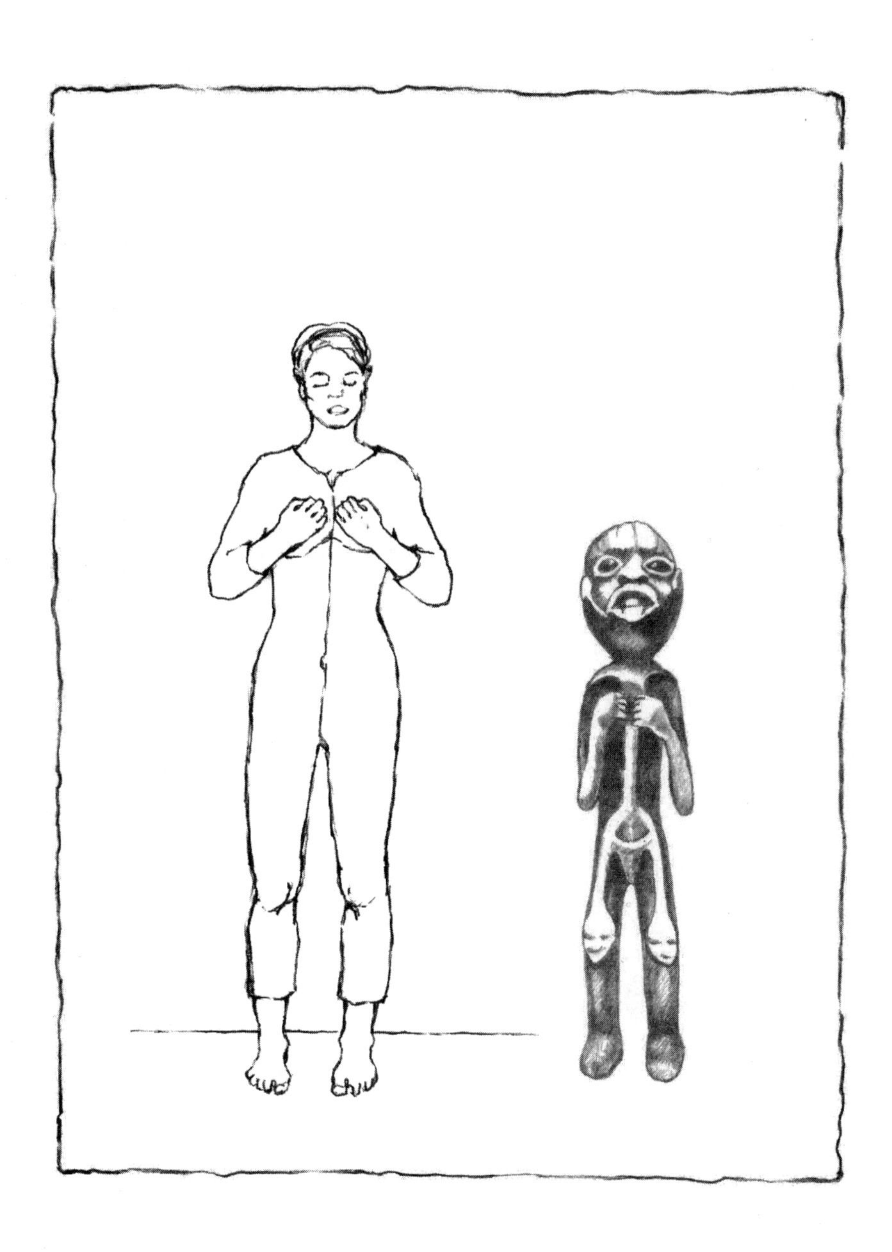

Figure A.18. Singing Shaman Posture

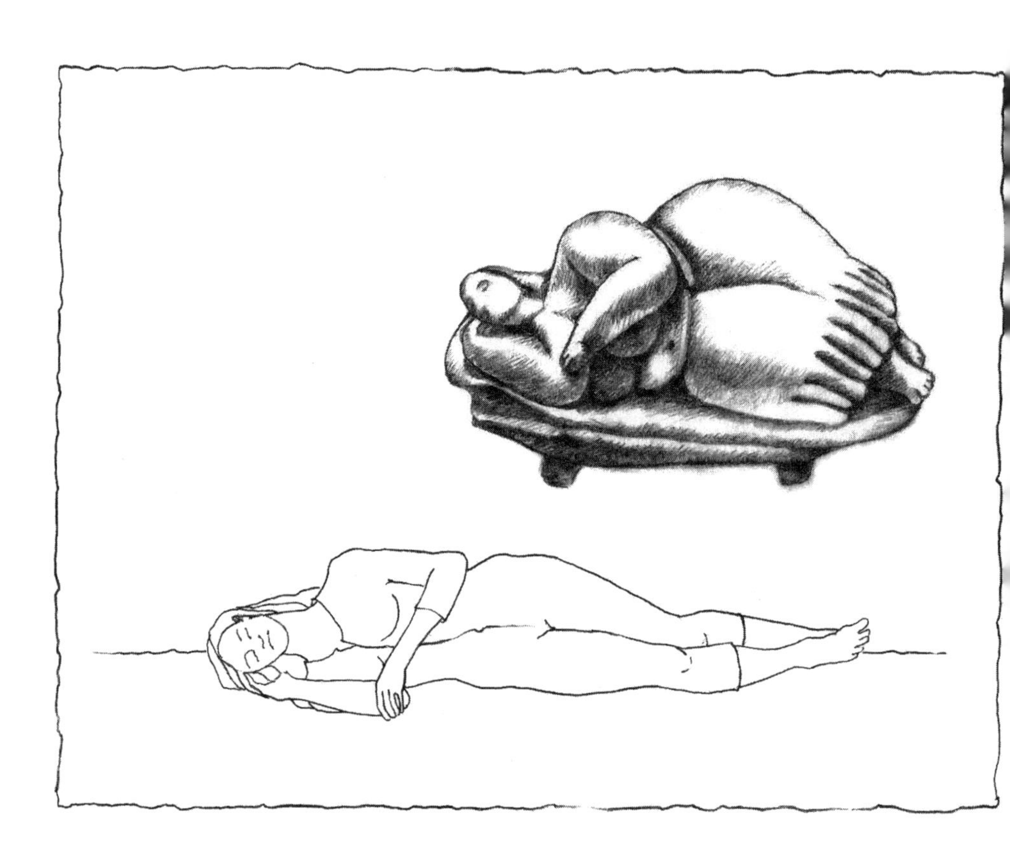

Figure A.19. Sleeping Lady of Malta Underworld Posture

Figure A.20. Tala Diviner Posture

Figure A.21. Tennessee Man Divination Posture

Figure A.22. Tlazolteotl Healing Posture

NOTES

With the exception of the Introduction, all epigraphs are from *Earth Prayers,* edited by Elizabeth Roberts and Elias Amidon.

INTRODUCTION. TO SAVE THE EARTH IS TO SAVE OURSELVES

1. Brian Swimme, quoted in De Quincey, *Radical Nature,* 5.
2. Mason, *Unnatural Order,* 26.
3. Cunliffe, *Europe between the Oceans,* 88–112.
4. Brink, *Baldr's Magic,* 258.
5. Mason, *Unnatural Order,* 27–28.
6. Goodman, *Ecstasy, Ritual, and Alternate Reality,* 17–18.
7. Shalins, *Stone Age Economics,* 1–39.
8. Berry, *Dream of the Earth,* 39.
9. Robert Bellah, quoted by Macy in Vaughan-Lee, *Spiritual Ecology,* 148
10. Berry, *Dream,* 37–38.
11. Macy, in Vaughan-Lee, *Spiritual Ecology,* 148.
12. Calleman, *Mayan Calendar,* 196.
13. Macy, in Vaughn-Lee, *Spiritual Ecology,* 155.
14. Kumar, in Vaughn-Lee, *Spiritual Ecology,* 134; author's italics.
15. Leopold, *Sand County Almanac,* 109.
16. Brink, *Baldr's Magic,* 142–46.
17. Quoted in Laszlo and Combs, *Thomas Berry,* 6.
18. De Quincey, *Radical Nature,* 101.

19. Geneen Marie Haugen, in Laszlo and Combs, *Thomas Berry,* 34.
20. Feuerstein, *Structures of Consciousness,* 51.
21. Curran, *Walking with the Green Man,* 153.
22. Lawer, personal communication.

CHAPTER 1. BECOMING ONE WITH THE GREAT MOTHER

1. Swimme and Tucker, *Journey of the Universe,* 29–30.
2. Gadon, *Once and Future Goddess,* 3.
3. Ibid, 110.
4. Ibid. 226.
5. Quoted in Gilligan, *In a Different Voice,* 167–68.
6. Mehl-Madrona, *Healing the Mind,* 12–14.
7. Combs, in Laszlo and Combs, *Thomas Berry,* 6.
8. Leopold, *Sand County Almanac,* 67.
9. Quoted in Vaughan-Lee, *Spiritual Ecology,* 85.
10. Fox, in Laszlo and Combs, *Thomas Berry,* 30.
11. Quoted in Laszlo and Combs, *Thomas Berry,* 71.

CHAPTER 2. STRENGTHENING OUR UNITY WITH THE EARTH

1. Berry, *Dream of the Earth,* 27.
2. De Quincey, *Radical Nature,* 101.
3. Lönnrot, *Kalevala,* viii–x.
4. Hollander, *Poetic Edda,* 14–41.

CHAPTER 3. THE ECSTATIC POSTURES

1. Gore, *Ecstatic Body Postures,* 6–7.
2. Feuerstein, *Structures of Consciousness,* 57.
3. Gebser, *Ever-Present Origin,* 29.

CHAPTER 5. SHAPE-SHIFTING

1. De Quincey, *Radical Nature,* 101.
2. Mastrangelo, "Animal Dreams," 2.

3. Ibid, 3.
4. Ibid, 4.
5. Swimme and Tucker, *Journey of the Universe,* 29–30.
6. Quoted in Mastrangelo, "Animal Dreams," 6.
7. Mastrangelo, "Animal Dreams," 15.
8. Ibid, 16.

CHAPTER 6. THE SEVEN DIRECTIONS

1. Swimme and Tucker, *Journey of the Universe,* 29–37.
2. Leopold, *Sand County Almanac,* 130–32.

CHAPTER 7. BECOMING AN ELDER

1. Korten, *Great Turning,* 54.

CHAPTER 8. GRIEVING FOR AND HEALING THE EARTH

1. Berry, *The Dream of the Earth,* 209.

BIBLIOGRAPHY

Auel, Jean M. *The Clan of the Cave Bear.* New York: Bantam Books, 1980.

Berry, Thomas. *The Dream of the Earth.* Berkeley, Ca.: Counterpoint, 2015.

Brink, Nicholas. *The Power of Ecstatic Trance: Practices for Healing, Spiritual Growth, and Accessing the Universal Mind.* Rochester, Vt.: Bear and Co., 2012.

———. *Baldr's Magic: The Power of Norse Shamanism and Ecstatic Trance.* Rochester, Vt.: Bear and Co., 2013.

Calleman, Carl Johan. *The Mayan Calendar and the Transformation of Consciousness.* Rochester, Vt.: Bear and Co., 2004.

Cunliffe, Barry. *Europe between the Oceans: 9000 BC–AD 1000.* New Haven, Conn.: Yale University Press, 2008.

Curran, Bob. *Walking with the Green Man.* Pompton Plains, N.J.: Career Press, 2007.

De Quincey, Christian. *Radical Nature: The Soul of Matter.* Rochester, Vt.: Park Street Press, 2002.

Eisler, Riane. *The Chalice and the Blade.* San Francisco, Ca.: Harper San Francisco, 1995.

Emerson, V. F. "Can Belief Systems Influence Behavior? Some Implications of Research on Meditation." *Newsletter Review.* R.M. Bucke Memorial Society, 5 (1972): 20–32.

Feuerstein, Georg. *Structures of Consciousness, the Genius of Jean Gebser: An Introduction and Critique.* Lower Lake, Ca.: Integral Publishing, 1987.

Gadon, Elinor. *The One & Future Goddess: A Sweeping Visual Chronicle of the Sacred Female and Her Reemergence in the Cultural Mythology of Our Time.* San Francisco, Ca.: Harper San Francisco, 1989.

Gebser, Jean. *The Ever-Present Origin.* Athens, Ohio: Ohio University Press, 1985.

Gilligan, Carol. *In a Different Voice.* Cambridge, Mass.: Harvard University Press, 1993.

Gimbutas, Marija. *The Goddesses and Gods of Old Europe: Myths and Cult Images.* Berkeley, Ca.: University of California Press, 1982.

———. *The Language of the Goddess.* New York: Thames & Hudson, 1989.

Goodman, Felicitas D. *Ecstasy, Ritual, and Alternate Reality: Religion in a Pluralistic World.* Bloomington, Ind.: Indiana University Press, 1988.

———. *Where the Spirits Ride the Wind: Trance Journeys and Other Ecstatic Experiences.* Bloomington, Ind.: Indiana University Press, 1990.

Gore, Belinda. *Ecstatic Body Postures: An Alternate Reality Workbook.* Rochester, Vt.: Bear and Co., 1995.

———. *The Ecstatic Experience: Healing Postures for Spirit Journeys.* Rochester, VT: Bear & Co., 2009.

Hollander, Lee, trans. *The Poetic Edda.* Austin, Tx.: University of Texas Press, 1962.

Korten, David. *The Great Turning: From Empire to Earth Community.* San Francisco, Ca.: Kumarian Press, 2006.

Laszlo, Ervin, and Allan Combs, eds. *Thomas Berry, Dreamer of the Earth: The Spiritual Ecology of the Father of Environmentalism.* Rochester, Vt.: Inner Traditions, 2011.

Leopold, Aldo. *A Sand County Almanac: And Sketches Here and There.* New York: Oxford University Press, 1949.

Lönnrot, Elias. *The Kalevala.* New York: Oxford University Press, 1989.

Lowenfels, Jeff, and Wayne Lewis. *Teaming with Microbes: The Organic Gardener's Guide to the Soil Food Web,* rev. ed. Portland, Ore.: Timber Press, 2010.

Mason, Jim. *An Unnatural Order: Roots of Our Destruction of Nature.* Herndon, Va.: Lantern Books, 2005.

Mastrangelo, Linda. Animal Dreams: A Wakeup Call from Forgotten Eden. Paper presented at the 2013 conference of the International Association for the Study of Dreams, Virginia Beach, Virginia, June 2013.

Mehl-Madrona, Lewis. *Healing the Mind Through the Power of Story: The Promise of Narrative Psychiatry.* Rochester, Vt.: Bear and Co., 2010.

Ray, Paul H. *The Cultural Creatives: How 50 Million People Are Changing the World.* New York: Broadway Books, 2001.

Roberts, Elizabeth and Elias Amidon, eds. *Earth Prayers: 365 Prayers, Poems, and Invocations from Around the World.* New York: Harper Collins, 1991.

Sahlins, Marshall. *Stone Age Economics.* New York: Routledge, 1972.

Storm, Hyemeyohsts. *Seven Arrows.* New York: Harper and Row, 1972.

Swimme, Brian, and M. E. Tucker. *Journey of the Universe.* New Haven, Conn.: Yale University Press, 2001.

Vaughan-Lee, Llewellyn, ed. *Spiritual Ecology: The Cry of the Earth.* The Golden Sufi Center, 2013.

INDEX